Linux System Programming Techniques

Become a proficient Linux system programmer using expert recipes and techniques

Jack-Benny Persson

BIRMINGHAM—MUMBAI

Linux System Programming Techniques

Group Product Manager: Wilson D'souza
Publishing Product Manager: Sankalp Khattri
Senior Editor: Shazeen Iqbal
Content Development Editor: Romy Dias
Technical Editor: Shruthi Shetty
Copy Editor: Safis Editing
Project Coordinator: Shagun Saini
Proofreader: Safis Editing
Indexer: Pratik Shirodkar
Production Designer: Shankar Kalbhor

First published: April 2021

Production reference: 2150621

Published by Packt Publishing Ltd.
Livery Place
35 Livery Street
Birmingham
B3 2PB, UK.

ISBN 978-1-78995-128-8

`www.packt.com`

Contributors

About the author

Jack-Benny Persson is a consultant and author based in Sweden. He has written several books about Linux and programming. His passion for Linux and other Unix-like systems started as a hobby more than 20 years ago. Since then, he has spent most of his spare time reading about Linux, tinkering with Linux servers, and writing about Linux administration. Today he has his own IT and media company in Sweden that focuses on Linux.

Jack-Benny holds an Advanced Higher Vocational Education Diploma as a Linux system specialist. He has also studied electronics, networking, and security.

I want to send a special thank you to the technical reviewer of this book—Ramon Fried. Without him, several coding errors would have slipped through. He has also pointed me toward more modern functions and system calls whenever I have leaned upon the old way of doing things. I also want to thank the team at Packt who has helped me with this book from start to finish: Sankalp Khattri, Shazeen Iqbal, Ronn Kurien, Romy Dias, and Neil D'mello.

About the reviewer

Ramon Fried holds a BSc. in computer science. He has worked with Linux for the past 15 years both as a system developer and as a kernel developer. His day-to-day job mostly revolves around embedded devices, device drivers, and bootloaders. He regularly contributes to the Linux kernel and is a network subsystem maintainer for the U-Boot project. Outside of work, he has an extensive list of hobbies that is forever growing. He is a musician, playing both the piano and guitar, a woodworker, and a welder.

I'd like to thank my wife, Hadas, and our three children, Uri, Anat, and Ayala, for their love and support.

Table of Contents

2
Making Your Programs Easy to Script

3
Diving Deep into C in Linux

4

Handling Errors in Your Programs

5

Working with File I/O and Filesystem Operations

6
Spawning Processes and Using Job Control

7

Using systemd to Handle Your Daemons

8

Creating Shared Libraries

9

Terminal I/O and Changing Terminal Behavior

10

Using Different Kinds of IPC

11
Using Threads in Your Programs

12
Debugging Your Programs

Other Books You May Enjoy

Index

Preface

Linux system programming is all about developing system programs for the Linux operating system. Linux is the world's most popular open-source operating system and runs on everything from big servers to small **Internet of Things** (**IoT**) devices. Knowing how to write system programs for Linux will enable you to extend the operating system and connect it with other programs and systems.

We'll start by learning how to make our programs easy to script and easy to interact with other programs. When we write system programs for Linux, we should always strive to make them small and do one thing only—and do it well. This is one of the key concepts in Linux: to create small programs that can exchange data with each other in simple ways.

As we move ahead, we'll take a deep dive into C and look at how the compiler works, what the linker does, how to write Makefiles, and much more.

Then, we'll learn all about forking and daemons. We'll also create our own daemon. We will then put our daemon under systemd's control. This will enable us to start, stop, and restart the daemon using built-in Linux tools.

We will also learn how to make our processes exchange information using different kinds of **Inter-Process Communication** (**IPC**). We'll also take a look at how to write threaded programs.

At the end of this book, we'll cover how to debug our programs using the **GNU Debugger** (**GDB**) and Valgrind.

By the end of this book, you'll be able to write a wide variety of system programs for Linux—everything from filters to daemons.

Who this book is for

This book is intended for anyone who wants to develop system programs for Linux and wants to have a deep understanding of the Linux system. Anyone facing any issues related to a particular part of Linux system programming and looking for some specific recipes or solutions can take advantage of this book.

What this book covers

Chapter 1, Getting the Necessary Tools and Writing Our First Linux Programs, shows you how to install the tools we need throughout this book. We also write our first program in this chapter.

Chapter 2, Making Your Programs Easy to Script, covers how—and why—we should make our programs easy to script and easy to be used by other programs on the system.

Chapter 3, Diving Deep into C in Linux, takes us on a journey into the inner workings of C programming in Linux. We learn how to use system calls, how the compiler works, how to use the Make tool, how to specify different C standards, and so on.

Chapter 4, Handling Errors in Your Programs, teaches us how to handle errors gracefully.

Chapter 5, Working with File I/O and Filesystem Operations, covers how to read and write to files, using both file descriptors and streams. This chapter also covers how to create and delete files and read file permissions using system calls.

Chapter 6, Spawning Processes and Using Job Control, covers how forking works, how to create a daemon, what parent processes are, and how to send jobs to the background and foreground.

Chapter 7, Using systemd to Handle Your Daemons, shows us how to put our daemon from the previous chapter under the control of systemd. This chapter also teaches us how to write logs to systemd's journal and how to read those logs.

Chapter 8, Creating Shared Libraries, teaches us what shared libraries are, why they're important, and how to make our own shared libraries.

Chapter 9, Terminal I/O and Changing Terminal Behavior, covers how to modify the terminal in different ways—for example, how to disable echoing for a password prompt.

Chapter 10, Using Different Kinds of IPC, is all about IPC—that is, how to make processes communicate with each other on the system. This chapter covers FIFO, Unix sockets, message queues, pipes, and shared memory.

Chapter 11, Using Threads in Your Programs, explains what threads are, how to write threaded programs, how to avoid race conditions, and how to optimize threaded programs.

Chapter 12, Debugging Your Programs, covers debugging using GDB and Valgrind.

To get the most out of this book

To get the most out of this book, you'll need a basic understanding of Linux, some basic commands, be familiar with moving around the filesystem, and installing new programs. It would help if you also have a basic understanding of programming, preferably the C language.

You will need a Linux computer with root access—either via su or sudo—to complete all the recipes. You'll also need to install the GCC compiler, the Make tool, GDB, Valgrind, and some other smaller tools. The particular Linux distribution doesn't matter that much. There are installation instructions in the book for these programs for Debian, Ubuntu, CentOS, Fedora, and Red Hat.

If you are using the digital version of this book, we advise you to type the code yourself or access the code via the GitHub repository (link available in the next section). Doing so will help you avoid any potential errors related to the copying and pasting of code.

Download the example code files

You can download the example code files for this book from GitHub at `https://github.com/PacktPublishing/Linux-System-Programming-Techniques`. In case there's an update to the code, it will be updated on the existing GitHub repository.

We also have other code bundles from our rich catalog of books and videos available at `https://github.com/PacktPublishing/`. Check them out!

Code in Action

Code in Action videos for this book can be viewed at `https://bit.ly/39ovGd6`.

Download the color images

We also provide a PDF file that has color images of the screenshots/diagrams used in this book. You can download it here: `http://www.packtpub.com/sites/default/files/downloads/9781789951288_ColorImages.pdf`.

Conventions used

There are a number of text conventions used throughout this book.

`Code in text`: Indicates code words in the text, directories, filenames, file extensions, pathnames, dummy URLs, user input, and so on. Here is an example: "Copy the `libprime.so.1` file to `/usr/local/lib`."

A block of code is set as follows:

```
#include <stdio.h>
int main(void)
{
    printf("Hello, world!\n");
    return 0;
}
```

When we wish to draw your attention to a particular part of a code block, the relevant lines or items are set in bold:

```
#include <stdio.h>
int main(void)
{
    printf("Hello, world!\n");
    return 0;
}
```

Any command-line input or output is written as follows:

```
$> mkdir cube
$> cd cube
```

In numbered listings, command-line input is set in bold. The `$>` characters indicate the prompt and aren't something you should write.

1. This is an example of a numbered listing:

   ```
   $> ./a.out
   Hello, world!
   ```

Long command lines that don't fit on a single line are broken up using the \ character. This is the same character as you use to break long lines in the Linux shell. The line under it has a > character to indicate that the line is a continuation of the previous line. The > character is *not* something you should write; the Linux shell will automatically put this character on a new line where the last line was broken up with a \ character. For example:

```
$> ./exist.sh /asdf &> /dev/null; \
> if [ $? -eq 3 ]; then echo "That doesn't exist"; fi
That doesn't exist
```

Key combinations are written in italics. Here is an example: "Press *Ctrl* + *C* to exit the program."

Bold: Indicates a new term, an important word, or words that you see onscreen.

> **Tips or important notes**
>
> Appear like this.

Sections

In this book, you will find several headings that appear frequently (*Getting ready*, *How to do it...*, *How it works...*, *There's more...*, and *See also*).

To give clear instructions on how to complete a recipe, use these sections as follows:

Getting ready

This section tells you what to expect in the recipe and describes how to set up any software or any preliminary settings required for the recipe.

How to do it...

This section contains the steps required to follow the recipe.

How it works...

This section usually consists of a detailed explanation of what happened in the previous section.

There's more...

This section consists of additional information about the recipe in order to make you more knowledgeable about the recipe.

See also

This section provides helpful links to other useful information for the recipe.

Get in touch

Feedback from our readers is always welcome.

General feedback: If you have questions about any aspect of this book, mention the book title in the subject of your message and email us at `customercare@packtpub.com`.

Errata: Although we have taken every care to ensure the accuracy of our content, mistakes do happen. If you have found a mistake in this book, we would be grateful if you would report this to us. Please visit `www.packtpub.com/support/errata`, selecting your book, clicking on the Errata Submission Form link, and entering the details.

Piracy: If you come across any illegal copies of our works in any form on the Internet, we would be grateful if you would provide us with the location address or website name. Please contact us at `copyright@packt.com` with a link to the material.

If you are interested in becoming an author: If there is a topic that you have expertise in and you are interested in either writing or contributing to a book, please visit `authors.packtpub.com`.

Reviews

Please leave a review. Once you have read and used this book, why not leave a review on the site that you purchased it from? Potential readers can then see and use your unbiased opinion to make purchase decisions, we at Packt can understand what you think about our products, and our authors can see your feedback on their book. Thank you!

For more information about Packt, please visit `packt.com`.

1 Getting the Necessary Tools and Writing Our First Linux Programs

In this chapter, we'll install the necessary tools on our Linux system, such as **GCC**, **GNU Make**, **GDB**, and **Valgrind**. We'll also try them out and see how they work. Knowing how to use these tools is the key to being a fast and efficient developer. We'll then write our first programs—Linux style. By understanding the different parts of a **C program**, you can easily interact with the rest of the system in a best practice manner. After that, we'll learn how to use the built-in manual pages (**man pages** for short) to look up **commands**, **libraries**, and **system calls**—a skill that we'll need a lot throughout this book. Knowing how to look up things in the relevant built-in manual page is often much faster—and more precise—than searching the internet for answers.

In this chapter, we are going to cover the following recipes:

- Installing GCC and GNU Make
- Installing GDB and Valgrind
- Writing a simple C program for Linux
- Writing a program that parses command-line options
- Looking up information in the built-in manual pages
- Searching the manual for information

Let's get started!

Technical requirements

For this chapter, you will need a computer with Linux already set up. It doesn't matter if it's a local machine or a remote machine. The particular distribution you use doesn't matter much either. We'll look at how to install the necessary programs in **Debian**-based distributions, as well as **Fedora**-based distributions. Most of the major Linux distributions are either Debian-based or Fedora-based.

You'll also be using a **text editor** a lot. Which one you choose is a matter of taste. The two most common are `vi` and `nano`, and they are available pretty much everywhere. We won't cover how to use a text editor in this book, though.

The C files for this chapter can be downloaded from `https://github.com/PacktPublishing/Linux-System-Programming-Techniques/tree/master/ch1`. The filenames on GitHub correspond to the filenames in this book.

You can also clone the entire repository to your computer. The files for this chapter are in the `ch1` Directory. You clone the repository with the following command:

```
$> git clone https://github.com/PacktPublishing/Linux-System-Programming-Techniques.git
```

If you don't have Git installed on your computer, you will need to follow some installation instructions, depending on your distribution.

Check out the following link to see the Code in Action video:
`https://bit.ly/3wdEoV6`

Installing Git to download the code repository

Installing Git is only necessary if you want to clone (download) the entire code repository for this book to your computer. The steps listed here assume that your user has `sudo` privileges. If this isn't the case, you can run `su` first to switch to the root user and skip `sudo` (assuming you know the root password).

Debian-based distributions

These instructions work for most Debian-based distributions, such as Ubuntu:

1. First, update the repository cache:

```
$> sudo apt update
```

2. Then, install Git using `apt`:

```
$> sudo apt install git
```

Fedora-based distributions

This instruction work for all newer Fedora-based distributions, such as CentOS and Red Hat (if you are using an old version, you might need to replace `dnf` with `yum`):

- Install the Git package using `dnf`:

```
$> sudo dnf install git
```

Installing GCC and GNU Make

In this section, we will install the essential tools that we'll need throughout this book; namely, GCC, the compiler. It's the **compiler** that turns the **C source code** into a **binary program** that we can run on the system. All the C code that we write will need to be compiled.

We'll also install GNU Make, a tool that we'll be using later on to automate how projects containing more than one source file are compiled.

Getting ready

Since we are installing software on the system, we'll need to be using either the **root user** or a user with `sudo` privileges. I will be using `sudo` in this recipe, but if you are on a system without `sudo`, you can switch to the root user with `su` before entering the commands (and then leave out `sudo`).

How to do it...

We will be installing what is called a meta-package or a group, a package that contains a collection of other packages. This meta-package includes both GCC, GNU Make, several manual pages, and other programs and libraries, which are nice to have when we're developing.

Debian-based systems

These steps work for all Debian-based systems, such as Debian, **Ubuntu**, and **Linux Mint**:

1. Update the repository cache to get the latest version in the next step:

```
$> sudo apt-get update
```

2. Install the `build-essential` package, and answer `y` when prompted:

```
$> sudo apt-get install build-essential
```

Fedora-based systems

This works for all Fedora-based systems, such as Fedora, **CentOS**, and **Red Hat**:

- Install a software group called *Development Tools*:

```
$> sudo dnf group install 'Development Tools'
```

Verify the installation (both Debian and Fedora)

These steps are the same for both Debian and Fedora:

1. Verify the installation by listing the versions installed. Note that the exact versions will differ from system to system; this is normal:

```
$> gcc --version
gcc (Debian 8.3.0-6) 8.3.0
Copyright (C) 2018 Free Software Foundation, Inc.
This is free software; see the source for copying
conditions.  There is NO
warranty; not even for MERCHANTABILITY or FITNESS FOR A
PARTICULAR PURPOSE.
$> make --version
GNU Make 4.2.1
Built for x86_64-pc-linux-gnu
Copyright (C) 1988-2016 Free Software Foundation, Inc.
License GPLv3+: GNU GPL version 3 or later http://gnu.
```

```
org/licenses/gpl.html
This is free software: you are free to change and
redistribute it. There is NO WARRANTY, to the extent
permitted by law.
```

2. Now, it's time to try out the GCC compiler by compiling a minimal C program. Please type the source code into an editor and save it as `first-example.c`. The program will print the text "Hello, world!" on the Terminal:

```
#include <stdio.h>
int main(void)
{
    printf("Hello, world!\n");
    return 0;
}
```

3. Now, compile it using GCC. This command produces a file called `a.out`:

```
$> gcc first-example.c
```

4. Now, let's try to run the program. To run a program in Linux that isn't in the usual directories for binaries (`/bin`, `/sbin`, `/usr/bin`, and so on), you need to type the special `./` sequence before the filename. This executes the program from the current path:

```
$> ./a.out
Hello, world!
```

5. Now, recompile the program. This time, we will specify a name for the program with the `-o` option (`-o` for *output*). This time, the program file will have the name `first-example`:

```
$> gcc first-example.c -o first-example
```

6. Let's rerun the program, this time with the new name, `first-example`:

```
$> ./first-example
Hello world!
```

7. Now, let's try to compile it using Make instead:

```
$> rm first-example
$> make first-example
cc     first-example.c   -o first-example
```

8. Finally, rerun the program:

```
$> ./first-example
Hello, world!
```

How it works...

Installing software on the system always requires root privileges, either via a regular root user or via `sudo`. Ubuntu, for example, uses `sudo` and has the regular root user disabled. Debian, on the other hand, doesn't use `sudo` at all in the default installation. To use it, you have to set it up yourself.

Debian and Ubuntu use the **apt** package manager to install software on the system. To get the latest version that is available in the repository, you need to update the cache. That's why we ran the `apt-get update` command before installing the packages.

Fedora-based systems use the **Red Hat Package Manager** (**RPM**) system to install the software. The program we use to install the package is `dnf` on newer versions. If you are using an older version, you might need to replace `dnf` with `yum`.

In both cases, we installed a group of packages that contain the utilities, manual pages, and compilers that we'll need throughout this book.

After the installation was complete, before trying to compile anything, we listed the GCC version and Make version.

Finally, we compiled a straightforward C program, first using GCC directly and then using Make. The first example with GCC produced a program with the name `a.out`, which stands for *assembler output*. That name has a long history and goes back to the first edition of Unix in 1971. Even though the file format, `a.out`, isn't used anymore, the name still lives on today.

Then, we specified a program name with the `-o` option, where `-o` stands for *output*. This produces a program with a name of our choosing. We gave the program the name `first-example`.

When we used Make, we didn't need to type in the filename of the source code. We only wrote the name we wanted for the binary program produced by the compiler. The Make program is smart enough to figure out that the source code has the same filename but that it ends with `.c`.

When we executed the program, we ran it as `./first-example`. The `./` sequence tells the shell that we want to run the program from the current directory. If we leave out `./`, it won't **execute**. By default, the shell only executes programs that are in the `$PATH` variable—usually `/bin`, `/usr/bin`, `/sbin`, and `/usr/sbin`.

Installing GDB and Valgrind

GDB and Valgrind are two useful **debugging** tools that we'll use later on in this book.

GDB is the GNU debugger, a tool that we can use to step through a program and see what's happening inside it. We can watch over variables, see how they change during runtime, set breakpoints where we want the program to pause, and even change variables. **Bugs** are inevitable, but with GDB, we can find these bugs.

Valgrind is also a tool we can use to find bugs, though it was made explicitly for finding **memory leaks**. Memory leaks can be challenging to find without a program such as Valgrind. Your program might work as expected for weeks, but then suddenly, things may start to go wrong. That's probably a memory leak.

Knowing how to use these tools will make you a better developer and your programs more secure.

Getting ready

Since we will be installing software here as well, we'll need to execute these commands with root privileges. If our system has a traditional root user, we can use that by switching to root with `su`. If we are on a system with `sudo`, and our regular user has administrative rights, you can use `sudo` to execute the commands instead. Here, I'll be using `sudo`.

How to do it...

If you are using Debian or Ubuntu, you'll need to use the `apt-get` tool. If you, on the other hand, are using a Fedora-based distribution, you'll need to use the `dnf` tool.

Debian-based systems

These steps are for Debian, Ubuntu, and Linux Mint:

1. Update the repository cache before installing the packages:

   ```
   $> sudo apt-get update
   ```

2. Install both GDB and Valgrind using `apt-get`. Answer `y` when prompted:

   ```
   $> sudo apt-get install gdb valgrind
   ```

Fedora-based systems

This step is for all Fedora-based systems, such as CentOS and Red Hat. If you are using an older system, you might need to replace `dnf` with `yum`:

- Install both GDB and Valgrind using `dnf`. Answer `y` when prompted:

```
$> sudo dnf install gdb valgrind
```

Verifying the installation

This step is the same for both Debian-based and Fedora-based systems:

- Verify the installation of GDB and Valgrind:

```
$> gdb --version
GNU gdb (Debian 8.2.1-2+b3) 8.2.1
Copyright (C) 2018 Free Software Foundation, Inc.
License GPLv3+: GNU GPL version 3 or later http://gnu.
org/licenses/gpl.html
This is free software: you are free to change and
redistribute it.
There is NO WARRANTY, to the extent permitted by law.
$> valgrind --version
valgrind-3.14.0
```

How it works...

GDB and Valgrind are two debugging tools that are not included in the group packages we installed in the previous recipe. That's why we need to install them as separate steps. The tool for installing software on Debian-based distributions is `apt-get`, while for Fedora, it's `dnf`. Since we are installing software on the system, we need to execute these commands with root privileges. That's why we needed to use `sudo`. Remember that if your user—or system—doesn't use `sudo`, you can use `su` to become root.

Finally, we verified the installations by listing the versions that were installed. The exact version can differ from system to system, though.

The reason why the versions differ is that every Linux distribution has its own software repository, and every Linux distribution maintains its own software versions as "latest". This means that the latest version of a program in a particular Linux distribution isn't necessarily the newest version of the program.

Writing a simple C program for Linux

In this recipe, we will be building a small **C program** that sums up the values that are passed to the program as **arguments**. The C program will contain some essential elements we need to know about when programming for Linux. These elements are **return values**, arguments, and **help texts**. As we progress through this book, these elements will show up, time and time again, along with some new ones that we'll learn about along the way.

Mastering these elements is the first step to writing great software for Linux.

Getting ready

The only thing you'll need for this recipe is the C source code, `sum.c`, and the GCC compiler. You can choose to type the code in yourself or download it from GitHub. Typing it in yourself gives you the benefit of learning how to write it.

How to do it...

Follow these steps to write your first program in Linux:

1. Open a text editor and type in the following code, naming the file `sum.c`. The program will sum up all the numbers that are entered as arguments into the program. The arguments to the program are contained in the `argv` array. To convert the arguments into integers, we can use the `atoi()` function:

```
#include <stdio.h>
#include <stdlib.h>
void printhelp(char progname[]);

int main(int argc, char *argv[])
{
    int i;
    int sum = 0;

    /* Simple sanity check */
    if (argc == 1)
    {
        printhelp(argv[0]);
        return 1;
    }

    for (i=1; i<argc; i++)
    {
```

```
            sum = sum + atoi(argv[i]);
        }
        printf("Total sum: %i\n", sum);
        return 0;
    }

    void printhelp(char progname[])
    {
        printf("%s integer ...\n", progname);
        printf("This program takes any number of "
            "integer values and sums them up\n");
    }
```

2. Now, it's time to compile the source code using GCC:

```
$> gcc sum.c -o sum
```

3. Run the program. Don't forget ./ before the filename:

```
$> ./sum
./sum integer …
This program takes any number of integer values and sums
them up
```

4. Now, let's check the **exit code** from the program before we do anything else:

```
$> echo $?
1
```

5. Let's rerun the program, this time with some **integers** that the program can sum up for us:

```
$> ./sum 45 55 12
Total sum: 112
```

6. Once again, we check the exit code from the program:

```
$> echo $?
0
```

How it works...

Let's begin by exploring the basics of the code so that we understand what the different parts do and why they matter.

The source code

First of all, we've included a **header file** called `stdio.h`. This file is needed for `printf()`. The name *stdio* stands for **standard input-output**. Since `printf()` prints characters on the screen, it's classed as a *stdio* function.

The other header file we included is `stdlib.h`, which stands for **standard library**. The standard library contains a long range of functions, including the `atoi()` function, which we can use to convert **strings** or **characters** into integers.

After that, we have a **function prototype** for our function called `printhelp()`. There is nothing particular to say about this; it's good C practice to keep the **function bodies** below `main()`, and the function prototypes at the very beginning. The function prototype tells the rest of the program which argument the function takes, as well as what type of value it returns.

Then, we declared the `main()` **function**. To be able to parse **arguments** to the program, which is common in Linux, we declare it as `int main(int argc, char *argv[])`.

The two variables, `argc` and `argv`, have special meanings. The first, `argc`, is an integer and contains the number of arguments that were passed to the program. It will always be at least 1, even if no arguments are passed to the program; the very first argument is the name of the program itself.

The next variable—or **array**, to be more precise—is `argv`, which contains all the arguments that were passed to the program at the **command line**. As we just mentioned, the very first argument, `argv[0]`, holds the name of the program—that is, the command line by which the program was executed. If the program was executed as `./sum`, then `argv[0]` contains the string `./sum`. If the program was executed as `/home/jack/sum`, then `argv[0]` contains the string `/home/jack/sum`.

It is this argument—or rather the program name—that we pass to the `printhelp()` function so that it prints the name of the program, along with the help text. It's good practice to do this is Linux and Unix environments.

After that, we performed a simple **sanity check**. This checks if the number of arguments given is precisely one; if it is, then the user hasn't typed any arguments into the program, which is considered an error here. Therefore, we print an error message to the screen using the `printhelp()` function that we built. Directly after that, we `return` from `main()` with the code 1, indicating to the **shell** and other programs that something went wrong. Anytime we return from `main()` using `return`, that code is sent to the shell and the program exits. These codes have special meanings, which we'll explore in more depth later in this book. Simply put, 0 indicates that everything is alright, while anything other than 0 is an error code. Using return values in Linux is a must; that's how other programs—and the shell—get notified of how the execution went.

A bit further down, we have the `for()` **loop**. Here, we used the number of arguments from `argc` to walk through the list of arguments. We started at 1 with `i=1`. We can't begin with 0 here, since index 0 in the `argv[]` array is the program name. Index 1 is the first argument; that is, the integer that we can pass to the program.

Inside the `for()` loop, we have `sum = sum + atoi(argv[i]);`. The important part we'll focus on here is `atoi(argv[i])`. All the arguments that we give to the program via the command line are passed on as strings. To be able to do calculations on them, we need to convert them into integers, which the `atoi()` function does for us. The name `atoi()` stands for *to integer*.

Once the result has been printed on the screen with `printf()`, we `return` from main with 0, indicating everything is okay. When we return from `main()`, we return from the entire process to the shell; in other words, the **parent process**.

Execution and return values

When we are executing programs outside the directories mentioned in the `$PATH` environment variable, we need to prepend the name of the file with `./`.

When the program finishes, it gives the return value to the shell, which, in turn, saves it to a variable called `?`. When another program ends, the variable is overwritten by the latest return value from that program. We print the value of the **environment variable** with `echo`, a small utility that prints text and variables on the screen directly from the shell. To print environment variables, we need to put a `$` sign in front of the variable name, such as `$?`.

There's more...

There are three other similar functions to `atoi()`, called `atol()`, `atoll()`, and `atof()`. The following are short descriptions for them:

- `atoi()` converts a string into an integer.
- `atol()` converts a string into a long integer.
- `atoll()` converts a string into a long long integer.
- `atof()` converts a string into a floating-point number (of type double).

If you want to explore the return values of other programs, you can execute programs such as `ls` with a directory that exists and print the variable with `echo $?`. Then, you can try to list a directory with `ls` that doesn't exist and print the value of `$?` again.

> **Tip**
>
> We've touched on the subject of the `$PATH` environment variable a couple of times in this chapter. If you want to know what that variable contains, you can print it with `echo $PATH`. If you want to add a new directory to the `$PATH` variable temporarily, let's say `/home/jack/bin`, you can execute the `PATH=${PATH}:/home/jack/bin` command.

Writing a program that parses command-line options

In this recipe, we will create a more advanced program—one that parses command-line **options**. In the previous recipe, we wrote a program that parsed arguments using `argc` and `argv`. We will use those variables here as well, but for options. Options are the hyphenated letters, such as `-a` or `-v`.

This program is similar to the previous one, with the difference that this program can both this; `-s` for "sum" and `-m` for "multiply."

Almost all programs in Linux take different options. Knowing how to parse options to the programs you create is a must; that is how the user changes the behavior of your program.

Getting ready

All you need is a text editor, the GCC compiler, and Make.

How to do it...

Since this source code will be a bit longer, it will be broken up into three pieces. The entire code goes into the same file, though. The complete program can be downloaded from GitHub at `https://github.com/PacktPublishing/Linux-System-Programming-Techniques/blob/master/ch1/new-sum.c`. Let's get started:

1. Open a text editor, type in the following code, and name it `new-sum.c`. This first bit is pretty similar to the previous recipe, except for some extra variables and a **macro** at the top:

```
#define _XOPEN_SOURCE 500
#include <stdio.h>
#include <stdlib.h>
#include <unistd.h>
void printhelp(char progname[]);

int main(int argc, char *argv[])
{
    int i, opt, sum;

    /* Simple sanity check */
    if (argc == 1)
    {
        printhelp(argv[0]);
        return 1;
    }
```

2. Now, continue typing in the same file. This part is for actually parsing the command-line options, the calculations, and printing the result. We parse the options using `getopt()` and a `switch` statement. Notice that this time, we can also multiply the numbers:

```
    /* Parse command-line options */
    while ((opt = getopt(argc, argv, "smh")) != -1)
    {
        switch (opt)
        {
           case 's': /* sum the integers */
               sum = 0;
               for (i=2; i<argc; i++)
                   sum = sum + atoi(argv[i]);
```

```
                break;
            case 'm': /* multiply the integers */
                sum = 1;
                for (i=2; i<argc; i++)
                    sum = sum * atoi(argv[i]);
                break;
            case 'h': /* -h for help */
                printhelp(argv[0]);
                return 0;
            default: /* in case of invalid options*/
                printhelp(argv[0]);
                return 1;
        }
    }
    printf("Total: %i\n", sum);
    return 0;
}
```

3. Finally, continuing in the same file, add the `printhelp()` function at the bottom. This function prints a help message, sometimes called a *usage* message. This message is displayed either when the user uses the `-h` option or some form of error occurs, for example, when no arguments are given:

```
void printhelp(char progname[])
{
    printf("%s [-s] [-m] integer ...\n", progname);
    printf("-s sums all the integers\n"
        "-m multiplies all the integers\n"
        "This program takes any number of integer "
        "values and either add or multiply them.\n"
        "For example: %s -m 5 5 5\n", progname);
}
```

4. Save and close the file.

5. Now, it's time to compile the program. This time, we'll try using Make instead:

```
$> make new-sum
cc     new-sum.c   -o new-sum
```

6. Test the program:

```
$> ./new-sum
./new-sum [-s] [-m] integer ...
```

```
-s sums all the integers
-m multiplies all the integers
This program takes any number of integer values and
either add or multiply them.
For example: ./new-sum -m 5 5 5
$> ./new-sum -s 5 5 5
Total: 15
$> ./new-sum -m 5 5 5
Total: 125
```

How it works...

The first bit is pretty similar to the previous recipe, except we have some more variables we **declare**. We also included another header file, `unistd.h`, which is required for the `getopt()` function, which we use to parse options to the program.

There is also another new weird-looking part; that is, the first line:

```
#define _XOPEN_SOURCE 500
```

We will cover this in great detail later on in this book. But for now, just know that it's a feature macro we use to adhere to the **XOPEN standard**. It isn't necessary to include this line; it will still work under Linux. But if we were to compile the program and display all warning messages (something we will learn how to do later on) and set a specific C standard, we would see a warning about the *implicit declaration of function getopt* if we didn't include it. It's good practice to include it, even if it works without it. And how do I know this, you might ask? It's in the manual page of `getopt()`, something we will cover in detail in the next recipe.

The getopt() function

The next step in this recipe—step two—is the exciting part. It is here that we parse the options using the `getopt()` function—which stands for *get options*.

The way to use `getopt()` is to loop through the arguments in a `while` loop and using a `switch` statement to catch the options. Let's take a closer look at the `while` loop and break it down into smaller pieces:

```
while ((opt = getopt(argc, argv, "smh")) != -1)
```

The `getopt()` function returns the actual letter of the option it parses. This means that the first bit, `opt = getopt`, saves the option to the `opt` variable, but only the actual letter. So, for example, `-h` is saved as `h`.

Then, we have the arguments that we must pass to the `getopt()` function, which is `argc` (the argument count), `argv` (the actual arguments), and, finally, the options that should be accepted (here `smh`, which is translated into `-s`, `-m`, and `-h`).

The last bit, `!= -1`, is for the `while` loop. When `getopt()` has no more options to return, it returns -1, indicating that it's done parsing options. That's when the `while` loop should end.

Inside the while loop

Inside the loop, we use a `switch` statement to perform specific actions for each option. Under each `case`, we perform the calculation and `break` out of that `case` when we're done. Just as in the previous recipe, we use `atoi()` to convert the argument strings into integers.

Under the `h` case (the `-h` option, for help), we print the help message and return with code 0. We asked for help, and hence it isn't an error. But below that, we have the default case, a case that is caught if no other option matches; that is, the user typed in an option that isn't accepted. This is indeed an error, so here, we return with code 1 instead, indicating an error.

The help message function

A help message should show the various options a program takes, its arguments, and a simple usage example.

With `printf()`, we can split long lines into multiple smaller lines in our code, just like we did here. The unique character sequence, `\n`, is a newline character. The line will break wherever this character is placed.

Compiling and running the program

In this recipe, we compiled the program using Make instead. The Make utility, in turn, uses `cc`, which is just a symbolic link to `gcc`. Later in this book, we'll learn how to change the behavior of Make by writing rules in Makefiles.

We then tried the program. First, we ran it without any options or arguments, causing the program to exit with the help text (and a return value of 1).

We then tried two options: `-s` to summarize all the integers and `-m` to multiply all the integers.

Looking up information in the built-in manual page

In this recipe, we will learn how to look up information in the built-in manual pages. We will learn how we can look up everything from commands, system calls, and **standard library functions**. The manual pages are mighty once you get used to using them. Instead of searching the internet for answers, it's often quicker—and more accurate—to take a look in the manual.

Getting ready

Some of the manual pages (library calls and system calls) are installed as part of the *build-essential* package for Debian and Ubuntu. In Fedora-based distributions such as CentOS, these are often already installed in the base system as part of a package called *man pages*. If you are missing some manual pages, make sure you have installed these packages. Take a look at the very first recipe in this chapter, on how to install packages, to learn more.

If you are on a minimal or slim installation, the `man` command might not be installed. If that is the case, you need to install two packages with the distribution package manager. The package names are *man-db* for the `man` command (same on nearly all distributions) and *manpages* (in Debian-based systems), or *man-pages* (in Fedora-based systems) for the actual manual pages. On Debian-based systems, you also need to install the *build-essential* package.

How to do it...

Let's explore the manual pages, step by step, as follows:

1. Type `man ls` into a console. You'll see the manual page for the `ls` command.
2. Scroll up and down the manual page, one line at a time, using either the *arrow* keys or the *Enter* key.
3. Scroll down a full page (window) at a time by pressing the *spacebar*.
4. Scroll up a full page by pressing the letter *b*. Keep pressing *b* until you reach the top.
5. Now, press / to open a search prompt.
6. Type `human-readable` into the search prompt and press *Enter*. The manual page is now automatically scrolled forward to the first occurrence of that word.
7. You can now press *n* to jump to the next occurrence of the word – if there is one.
8. Quit the manual by pressing *q*.

Investigating the different sections

Sometimes, there are multiple manual pages with the same name but in different sections. Here, we will investigate those sections and learn how to specify which section we are interested in:

1. Type `man printf` into the command prompt. What you will see is the manual page for the `printf` command, not the C function of the same name.
2. Quit the manual by pressing *q*.
3. Now, type `man 3 printf` into the console. This is the manual page of the `printf()` C function. `3` indicates section 3 of the manual. Look at the header of the manual page, and you'll see which section you are in right now. It should say **PRINTF(3)** at this very moment.
4. Let's list all the sections. Quit the manual page you are looking at and type `man man` into the console. Scroll down a bit until you find the table that lists all the sections. There, you will also find a short description of each section. As you can see, section 3 is for library calls, which is what `printf()` is.
5. Look up the manual for the `unlink()` system call by typing `man 2 unlink` into the console.
6. Quit the manual page and type `man unlink` into the console. This time, you will see the manual for the `unlink` command.

How it works...

The manual always starts at section 1 and opens the first manual it finds. That's why you are getting the `printf` and `unlink` commands, instead of the C function and system call when we leave out the section number. It's always a good idea to take a look at the header of the manual page that opens up to verify that you are reading the correct one.

There's more...

Remember from the previous recipe that I "just knew" that `getopt()` returns `-1` when there are no more options to parse? I didn't; it's all in the manual. Open up the manual for `getopt()` by typing in `man 3 getopt`. Scroll down to the *Return value* header. There, you can read all about what `getopt()` returns. Almost all manual pages that cover library functions and system calls have the following headings: Name, Synopsis, Description, Return value, Environment, Attributes, Conforming to, Notes, Example, and See also.

The Synopsis heading lists the header files we need to include for the particular function. This is really useful since we can't remember every function and its corresponding header file.

> **Tip**
> There is a lot of useful information in the manual about the manual itself – `man man` – so at least skim through it. We will be using the manual pages a lot to look up information about library functions and system calls in this book.

Searching the manual for information

If we don't know the exact name of a particular command, function, or system call, we can search all the manuals in the system for the correct one. In this recipe, we will learn how to use the `apropos` command to search the manual pages.

Getting ready

The same requirements apply here that applied for the previous recipe.

How to do it...

Let's search the manual for different words, narrowing our result for each step:

1. Type in `apropos directory`. A long list of manual pages will present itself. After each manual, there is a number inside parentheses. This number is the section that the manual page is located in.
2. To narrow the search down to only section 3 (library calls), type in `apropos -s 3 directory`.
3. Let's narrow down the search ever further. Type in `apropos -s 3 -a remove directory`. The `-a` option stands for *and*.

How it works...

The `apropos` command searches the manual pages descriptions and keywords. When we narrowed down the search with `apropos -s 3 -a remove directory`, the `-a` option stands for *and*, indicating that both *remove* and *directory* must be present. If we leave out the `-a` option, it searches for both keywords instead, regardless of whether one or both of them is present.

There is more information about how `apropos` works in the manual page for it (`man apropos`).

There's more...

If we just want to know what a particular command or function does, we can look up a short description of it using the `whatis` command, like so:

```
$> whatis getopt
getopt (1)           - parse command options (enhanced)
getopt (3)           - Parse command-line options
$> whatis creat
creat (2)            - open and possibly create a file
$> whatis opendir
opendir (3)          - open a directory
```

2
Making Your Programs Easy to Script

Linux and other **Unix** systems have strong **scripting** support. The whole idea of Unix, from the very beginning, was to make a system easy to develop on. One of these features is to take the output of one program and make it the input of another program—hence building new tools with existing programs. We should always keep this in mind when creating programs for Linux. The Unix philosophy is to make small programs that do one thing only—and do it well. By having many small programs that do only one thing, we can freely choose how to combine them. And by combining small programs, we can write shell scripts—a common task in Unix and Linux.

This chapter will teach us how to make programs that are easy to script and easy to interact with other programs. That way, other people will find them much more useful. It's even likely they will find new ways of using our programs that we haven't even thought of, making the programs more popular and easier to use.

In this chapter, we will cover the following recipes:

- Return values and how to read them
- Exiting a program with a relevant return value

- Redirecting stdin, stdout, and stderr
- Connecting programs using pipes
- Writing to stdout and stderr
- Reading from stdin
- Writing a pipe-friendly program
- Redirecting the result to file
- Reading environment variables

Let's get started!

Technical requirements

All you need for this chapter is a Linux computer with GCC and Make installed, preferably via one of the meta-packages or group installs mentioned in *Chapter 1, Getting the Necessary Tools and Writing Our First Linux Programs*. It's also preferable if you use the *Bash shell* for optimal compatibility. Most of the examples will work with other shells as well, but there's no guarantee that everything will work the same way on every possible shell out there. You can check which shell you are using by running `echo $SHELL` in your terminal. If you are using Bash, it will say `/bin/bash`.

You can download all the code for this chapter from `https://github.com/PacktPublishing/Linux-System-Programming-Techniques/tree/master/ch2`.

Check out the following link to see the Code in Action video: `https://bit.ly/3u5VItw`

Return values and how to read them

Return values are a big deal in Linux and other Unix and Unix-like systems. They are a big deal in C programming as well. Most functions in C return some value with `return`. It's that same `return` statement we use to return a value from `main()` to the shell. The original Unix operating system and the C programming language came around at the same time and from the same place. As soon as the C language was completed in the early 1970s, Unix was rewritten in C. Previously, it was written in assembler only. And hence, C and Unix fit together tightly.

The reason why return values are so crucial in Linux is that we can build shell scripts. Those shell scripts use other programs and, hopefully, our programs, as its parts. For the shell script to be able to check whether a program has succeeded or not, it reads the return value of that program.

In this recipe, we will write a program that tells the user if a file or directory exists or not.

Getting ready

It's recommended that you use Bash for this recipe. I can't guarantee compatibility with other shells.

How to do it...

In this recipe, we will write a small **shell script** that demonstrates the purpose of the return values, how to read them, and how to interpret them. Let's get started:

1. Before we write the code, we must investigate what return values the program uses that we will use in our script. Execute the following commands, and make a note of the return values we get. The `test` command is a small utility that tests certain conditions. In this example, we'll use it to determine if a file or directory exists. The `-e` option stands for *exists*. The `test` command doesn't give us any output; it just exits with a return value:

```
$> test -e /
$> echo $?
0
$> test -e /asdfasdf
$> echo $?
1
```

2. Now that we know what return values the `test` program gives us (0 when the file or directory exists, otherwise 1), we can move on and write our script. Write the following code in a file and save it as `exist.sh`. You can also download it from `https://github.com/PacktPublishing/Linux-System-Programming-Techniques/blob/master/ch2/exist.sh`. The shell script uses the `test` command to determine whether the specified file or directory exists:

```
#!/bin/bash

# Check if the user supplied exactly one argument
if [ "$#" -ne 1 ]; then
    echo "You must supply exactly one argument."
```

```
    echo "Example: $0 /etc"
    exit 1 # Return with value 1
fi

# Check if the file/directory exists
test -e "$1" # Perform the actual test
if [ "$?" -eq 0 ]; then
    echo "File or directory exists"
elif [ "$?" -eq 1 ]; then
    echo "File or directory does not exist"
    exit 3 # Return with a special code so other
           # programs can use the value to see if a
           # file dosen't exist
else
    echo "Unknown return value from test..."
    exit 1 # Unknown error occured, so exit with 1
fi
exit 0 # If the file or directory exists, we exit
       # with
```

3. Then, you need to make it *executable* with the following command:

```
$> chmod +x exist.sh
```

4. Now, it's time to try out our script. We try it with directories that do exist and with those that don't. We also check the exit code after each run:

```
$> ./exist.sh
You must supply exactly one argument.
Example: ./exist.sh /etc
$> echo $?
1
$> ./exist.sh /etc
File or directory exists
$> echo $?
0
$> ./exist.sh /asdfasdf
File or directory does not exist
$> echo $?
3
```

5. Now that we know that it's working and leaving the correct exit codes, we can write **one-liners** to use our script together with, for example, `echo` to print a text stating whether the file or directory exists:

```
$> ./exist.sh / && echo "Nice, that one exists"
File or directory exists
Nice, that one exists
$> ./exist.sh /asdf && echo "Nice, that one exists"
File or directory does not exist
```

6. We can also write a more complicated one-liner—one that takes advantage of the unique error code 3 we assigned to "file not found" in our script. Note that you shouldn't type > at the start of the second line. This character is automatically inserted by the shell when you end the first line with a backslash to indicate the continuation of a long line:

```
$> ./exist.sh /asdf &> /dev/null; \
> if [ $? -eq 3 ]; then echo "That doesn't exist"; fi
That doesn't exist
```

How it works...

The `test` program is a small utility designed to test files and directories, compare values, and so on. In our case, we used it to test if the specified file or directory exists (`-e` for exist).

The `test` program doesn't print anything; it just exits in silence. It does, however, leave a return value. It is that return value that we check with the `$?` variable. It's also the very same variable we check in the script's `if` statements.

There are some other special variables in the script that we used. The first one was `$#`, which contains the number of **arguments** passed to the script. It works like `argc` in C. At the very start of the script, we compared if `$#` is *not equal* to 1 (`-ne` stands for *not equal*). If `$#` is not equal to 1, an error message is printed and the script aborts with code 1.

The reason for putting `$#` inside quotes is just a safety mechanism. If, in some unforeseen event, `$#` were to contain spaces, we still want the content to be evaluated as a single value, not two. The same thing goes for the quotes around the other variables in the script.

The next special variable is `$0`. This variable contains argument 0, which is the name of the program, just as with `argv[0]` in C, as we saw *in Chapter 1, Getting the Necessary Tools and Writing Our First Linux Programs.*

The first argument to the program is stored in `$1`, as shown in the `test` case. The first argument in our case is the supplied filename or directory that we want to test.

Like our C programs, we want our scripts to exit with a relevant return value (or **exit code**, as it is also called). We use `exit` to leave the script and set a return value. In case the user doesn't supply precisely one argument, we exit with code 1, a general error code. And if the script is executed as it should, and the file or directory exists, we exit with code 0. If the script is executed as it should, but the file or directory doesn't exist, we exit with code 3, which isn't reserved for a particular use, but still indicates an error (all *non-zero* codes are error codes). This way, other scripts can fetch the return value of our script and act upon it.

In *Step 5*, we did just that—act upon the exit code from our script with the following command:

```
$> ./exist.sh / && echo "Nice, that one exists"
```

`&&` means "and". We can read the whole line as an `if` statement. If `exist.sh` is true—that is, exit code 0—then execute the `echo` command. If the `exit` code is anything other than 0, then the `echo` command is never executed.

In *Step 6*, we redirected all the output from the script to `/dev/null` and then used a complete `if` statement to check for error code 3. If error code 3 is encountered, we print a message with `echo`.

There's more...

There are a lot more tests and comparisons we can do with the `test` program. They are all listed in the manual; that is, `man 1 test`.

If you are unfamiliar with Bash and shell scripting, there is a lot of useful information in the manual page, `man 1 bash`.

The opposite of `&&` is `||` and is pronounced "or." So, the opposite of what we did in this recipe would be as follows:

```
$> ./exist.sh / || echo "That doesn't exist"
File or directory exists
$> ./exist.sh /asdf || echo "That doesn't exist"
File or directory does not exist
That doesn't exist
```

See also

If you want to dig deep into the world of Bash and shell scripting, there is an excellent guide at *The Linux Documentation Project*: `https://tldp.org/LDP/Bash-Beginners-Guide/html/index.html`.

Exiting a program with a relevant return value

In this recipe, we'll learn how to exit a C program with a relevant **return value**. We will look at two different ways to exit a program with a return value and how `return` fits together with the system from a broader perspective. We will also learn what some common return values mean.

Getting ready

For this recipe, we only need the GCC compiler and the Make tool.

How to do it…

We will write two different versions of a program here to show you two different methods of exiting. Let's get started:

1. We'll start by writing the first version using `return`, which we have seen previously. But this time, we will use it to return from **functions**, all the way back to `main()` and eventually the **parent process**, which is the shell. Save the following program in a file called `functions_ver1.c`. All the return statements are highlighted in the following code:

```
#include <stdio.h>
int func1(void);
int func2(void);

int main(int argc, char *argv[])
{
   printf("Inside main\n");
   printf("Calling function one\n");
   if (func1())
   {
      printf("Everything ok from function one\n");
      printf("Return with 0 from main - all ok\n");
      return 0;
   }
```

```
    else
    {
        printf("Caught an error from function one\n");
        printf("Return with 1 from main - error\n");
        return 1;
    }
    return 0; /* We shouldn't reach this, but
                 just in case */
}

int func1(void)
{
    printf("Inside function one\n");
    printf("Calling function two\n");
    if (func2())
    {
        printf("Everything ok from function two\n");
        return 1;
    }
    else
    {
        printf("Caught an error from function two\n");
        return 0;
    }
}

int func2(void)
{
    printf("Inside function two\n");
    printf("Returning with 0 (error) from "
        "function two\n");
    return 0;
}
```

2. Now, **compile** it:

```
$> gcc functions_ver1.c -o functions_ver1
```

3. Then, run it. Try to follow along and see which functions call and return to which other functions:

```
$> ./functions-ver1
Inside main
```

```
Calling function one
Inside function one
Calling function two
Inside function two
Returning with 0 (error) from function two
Caught an error from function two
Caught an error from function one
Return with 1 from main - error
```

4. Check the return value:

```
$> echo $?
1
```

5. Now, we rewrite the preceding program to use `exit()` inside the functions instead. What will happen then is that as soon as `exit()` is called, the program will **exit** with the specified value. If `exit()` is called inside another function, that function will not return to `main()` first. Save the following program in a new file as `functions_ver2.c`. All the `return` and `exit` statements are highlighted in the following code:

```
#include <stdio.h>
#include <stdlib.h>
int func1(void);
int func2(void);

int main(int argc, char *argv[])
{
   printf("Inside main\n");
   printf("Calling function one\n");
   if (func1())
   {
      printf("Everything ok from function one\n");
      printf("Return with 0 from main - all ok\n");
      return 0;
   }
   else
   {
      printf("Caught an error from funtcion one\n");
      printf("Return with 1 from main - error\n");
      return 1;
   }
   return 0; /* We shouldn't reach this, but just
```

```
                     in case */
}

int func1(void)
{
   printf("Inside function one\n");
   printf("Calling function two\n");
   if (func2())
   {
      printf("Everything ok from function two\n");
      exit(0);
   }
   else
   {
      printf("Caught an error from function two\n");
      exit(1);
   }
}
```

6. Now, compile this version:

```
$> gcc functions_ver2.c -o functions_ver2
```

7. Then, run it and see what happens (and compare the output from the previous program):

```
$> ./functions_ver2
Inside main
Calling function one
Inside function one
Calling function two
Inside function two
Returning with (error) from function two
```

8. Finally, check the return value:

```
$> echo $?
1
```

How it works...

Notice that in C, 0 is regarded as *false* or error, while anything else is considered to be *true* (or correct). This is the opposite of the return values to the shell. This can be a bit confusing at first. However, as far as the shell is concerned, 0 is "all ok," while anything else indicates an error.

The difference between the two versions is how the functions and the entire program returns. In the first version, each function returns to the calling function—in the order they were called. In the second version, each function exits with the `exit()` function. This means that the program will exit directly and return the specified value to the shell. The second version isn't good practice; it's much better to return to the calling function. If someone else were to use your function in another program, and it suddenly exits the entire program, that would be a big surprise. That's not usually how we do it. However, I wanted to demonstrate the difference between `exit()` and `return` here.

I also wanted to demonstrate another point. Just as a function returns to its calling function with `return`, a program returns to its parent process (usually the shell) in the same way. So, in a way, programs in Linux are treated as functions in a program.

The following diagram shows how Bash calls the program (the upper arrow), which then starts in `main()`, which then calls the next function (the arrows to the right), and so on. The arrows returning on the left show how each function returns to the calling function, and then finally to Bash:

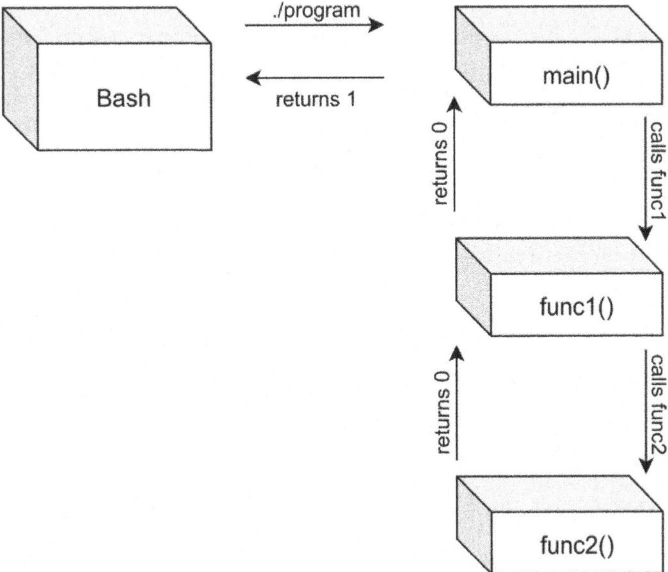

Figure 2.1 – Calling and returning

There's more...

There are a lot more return codes we can use. The most common ones are the ones we've seen here; `0` for *ok* and `1` for *error*. However, all other codes except `0` mean some form of error. Code `1` is a general error, while the other error codes are more specific. There isn't exactly a standard, but there are some commonly used codes. Some of the most common codes are as follows:

Code	Meaning
0	Ok
1	General error
2	Misuse of shell builtin
126	Can't execute the specified command
127	Command not found
128	Invalid argument to exit
128+n	Signal, 128 + signal number
130	Program caught an interrupt signal (128+2)
137	Program caught a kill signal (128+9)

Figure 2.2 – Common error codes in Linux and other UNIX-like systems

Except for these codes, there are some additional ones listed at the end of `/usr/include/sysexit.h`. The codes listed in that file range from `64` to `78` and address errors such as data format error, service unavailable, **I/O** errors, and more.

Redirecting stdin, stdout, and stderr

In this recipe, we will learn how to **redirect** *standard input*, *standard output*, and *standard error* to and from files. Redirecting data to and from files is one of the basic principles of Linux and other Unix systems.

stdin is the shorthand word for **standard input**. **stdout** and **stderr** are the shorthand words for **standard output** and **standard error**, respectively.

Getting ready

It's best if we use the Bash shell for this recipe for compatibility purposes.

How to do it...

To get the hang of redirections, we will be performing a bunch of experiments here. We are really going to twist and turn the redirections and see stdout, stderr, and stdin operate in all kinds of ways. Let's get started:

1. Let's start by saving a list of the files and directories in the top root directory. We can do this by redirecting standard output (stdout) from the `ls` command into a file:

```
$> cd
$> ls / > root-directory.txt
```

2. Now, take a look at the file with `cat`:

```
$> cat root-directory.txt
```

3. Now, let's try the `wc` command to count lines, words, and characters. Remember to press *Ctrl* + *D* when you have finished typing in the message:

```
$> wc
hello,
how are you?
Ctrl+D
      2       4      20
```

4. Now that we know how `wc` works, we can redirect its input to come from a file instead—the file we created with the file listing:

```
$> wc < root-directory.txt
29  29 177
```

5. What about standard error? Standard error is its own output stream, separated from standard output. If we redirect standard output and generate an error, we will still see the error message on the screen. Let's try it out:

```
$> ls /asdfasdf > non-existent.txt
ls: cannot access '/asdfasdf': No such file or directory
```

6. Just like standard output, we can redirect standard error. Notice that we don't get any error message here:

```
$> ls /asdfasdf 2> errors.txt
```

7. The error messages are saved in `errors.txt`:

```
$> cat errors.txt
ls: cannot access '/asdfasdf': No such file or directory
```

8. We can even redirect standard output and standard error at the same time, to different files:

```
$> ls /asdfasdf > root-directory.txt 2> errors.txt
```

9. We can also redirect standard output and error into the same file for convenience:

```
$> ls /asdfasdf &> all-output.txt
```

10. We can even redirect all three (stdin, stdout, and stderr) at the same time:

```
$> wc < all-output.txt > wc-output.txt 2> \
> wc-errors.txt
```

11. We can also write to standard error from the shell to write error messages of our own:

```
$> echo hello > /dev/stderr
hello
```

12. Another way of printing a message to stderr from Bash is like this:

```
$> echo hello 1>&2
hello
```

13. However, this doesn't prove that our hello message got printed to standard error. We can prove this by redirecting the standard output to a file. If we still see the error message, then it's printed on standard error. When we do this, we need to wrap the first statement in parenthesis to separate it from the last redirect:

```
$> (echo hello > /dev/stderr) > hello.txt
hello
$> (echo hello 1>&2) > hello.txt
hello
```

14. Stdin, stdout, and stderr are represented by files in the `/dev` directory. This means we can even redirect stdin from a file. This experiment doesn't do anything useful—we could have just typed `wc`, but it proves a point:

```
$> wc < /dev/stdin
hello, world!
```

```
Ctrl+D
      1       2      14
```

15. All of this means that we can even redirect a standard error message back to standard output:

```
$> (ls /asdfasdf 2> /dev/stdout) > \
> error-msg-from-stdout.txt
$> cat error-msg-from-stdout.txt
ls: cannot access '/asdfasdf': No such file or directory
```

How it works...

Standard output, or stdout, is where all the normal output from programs gets printed. Stdout is also referred to as **file descriptor** 1.

Standard error, or *stderr*, is where all error messages get printed. Stderr is also referred to as file descriptor 2. That is why we used `2>` when we redirected stderr to a file. If we wanted to, for clarity, we could have redirected *stdout* as `1>` instead of just >. But the default redirection with > is stdout, so there is no need to do this.

When we redirected both stdout and stderr in *Step 9*, we used an `&` sign. This reads as "stdout *and* stderr".

Standard input, or *stdin*, is where all input data is read from. Stdin is also referred to as file descriptor 0. Stdin redirects with a <, but just as with stdout and stderr, we can also write it as `0<`.

The reason for separating the two outputs, stdout and stderr, is so that when we redirect the output from a program to a file, we should still be able to see the error message on the screen. We also don't want the file to be cluttered with error messages.

Having separate outputs also makes it possible to have one file for the actual output, and another one as a log file for error messages. This is especially handy in scripts.

You might have heard the phrase "*Everything in Linux is either a file or a process*". That saying is true. There is no other *thing* in Linux, except for files or processes. Our experiments with `/dev/stdout`, `/dev/stderr`, and `/dev/stdin` proved this. Files represent even the input and output of programs.

In *Step 11*, we redirected the output to the `/dev/stderr` file, which is standard error. The message, therefore, got printed on standard error.

In *Step 12*, we pretty much did the same thing but without using the actual device file. The funny-looking `1>&2` redirection reads as "*send standard output to standard error*".

There's more...

Instead of using `/dev/stderr`, for example, we could have used `/dev/fd/2`, where **fd** stands for **file descriptor**. The same goes for stdout, which is `/dev/fd/1`, and stdin, which is `/dev/fd/0`. So, for example, the following will print the list to stderr:

```
$> ls / > /dev/fd/2
```

Just like we can send standard output to standard error with `1>&2`, we can do the opposite with `2>&1`, which means we can send standard error to standard output.

Connecting programs using pipes

In this recipe, we'll learn how to use **pipes** to connect programs. When we write our C programs, we always want to strive to make them easy to pipe together with other programs. That way, our programs will be much more useful. Sometimes, programs that are connected with pipes are called **filters**. The reason for this is that, often, when we connect programs with pipes, it is to filter or transform some data.

Getting ready

Just as in the previous recipe, it's recommended that we use the Bash shell.

How to do it...

Follow these steps to explore pipes in Linux:

1. We are already familiar with `wc` and `ls` from the previous recipe. Here, we will use them together with a pipe to count the number of files and directories in the root directory of the system. The pipe is the vertical line symbol:

   ```
   $> ls / | wc -l
   29
   ```

2. Let's make things a bit more interesting. This time, we want to list only **symbolic links** in the root directory (by using two programs with a pipe). The result will differ from system to system:

   ```
   $> ls -l / | grep lrwx
   lrwxrwxrwx   1 root root    31 okt 21 06:53 initrd.img -> boot/initrd.img-4.19.0-12-amd64
   lrwxrwxrwx   1 root root    31 okt 21 06:53 initrd.img.old -> boot/initrd.img-4.19.0-11-amd64
   lrwxrwxrwx   1 root root    28 okt 21 06:53 vmlinuz ->
   ```

```
boot/vmlinuz-4.19.0-12-amd64
lrwxrwxrwx   1 root root     28 okt 21 06:53 vmlinuz.old
-> boot/vmlinuz-4.19.0-11-amd64
```

3. Now, we only want the actual filenames, not the information about them. So, this time, we will add another program at the end called `awk`. In this example, we are telling `awk` to print the ninth field. One or more whitespaces separate each field:

```
$> ls -l / | grep lrwx | awk '{ print $9 }'
initrd.img
initrd.img.old
vmlinuz
vmlinuz.old
```

4. We can add another "**filter**", one that adds some text in front of every link. This can be accomplished using `sed` – `s` means *substitute*. Then, we can tell `sed` that we want to substitute the start of the line (^) with the text `This is a link:`:

```
$> ls -l / | grep lrwx | awk '{ print $9 }' \
> | sed 's/^/This is a link: /'
This is a link: initrd.img
This is a link: initrd.img.old
This is a link: vmlinuz
This is a link: vmlinuz.old
```

How it works...

A lot of things are going on here, but don't feel discouraged if you don't get it all. The importance of this recipe is to demonstrate how to use a *pipe* (the vertical line symbol, |).

In the very first step, we counted the number of files and directories in the root of the filesystem using `wc`. When we run `ls` interactively, we get a nice-looking list that spans the width of our terminal. The output is also most likely color-coded. But when we run `ls` by redirecting its output through a pipe, `ls` doesn't have a real terminal to output to, so it falls back to outputting the text one file or directory per line, without any colors. You can try this yourself if you like by running the following:

```
$> ls / | cat
```

Since `ls` it outputting one file or directory per line, we can count the number of lines with `wc` (the `-l` option).

In the next step (*Step 2*), we used `grep` to only list links from the output of `ls -l`. Links in the output from `ls -l` start with the letter `l` at the start of the line. After that is the access rights, which for links is `rwx` for everyone. This is what we search for with `lrwx` with `grep`.

Then, we only wanted the actual filenames, so we added a program called `awk`. The `awk` tool lets us single out a particular column or field in the output. We singled out the ninth column (`$9`), which is the filename.

By running the output from `ls` through two other tools, we created a list of only the links in the root directory.

In *Step 3*, we added another tool, or filter as it sometimes called. This tool is `sed`, a *stream editor*. With this program, we can make changes to the text. In this case, we added the text `This is a link:` in front of every link. The following is a short explanation of the line:

```
sed 's/^/This is a link: /'
```

`s` means "substitute"; that is, we wish to modify some text. Inside the two first slashes (`/`) is the text or expressions that should match what we want to modify. Here, we have the beginning of the line, `^`. Then, after the second slash, we have the text that we want to replace the matched text with, up until the final slash. Here, we have the text `This is a link:`.

There's more...

Beware of unnecessary piping; it's easy to get caught up in endless piping. One silly—but instructive—example is this:

```
$> ls / | cat | grep tmp
tmp
```

We could leave out `cat` and still get the same result:

```
$> ls / | grep tmp
tmp
```

The same goes for this one (which I am guilty of myself from time to time):

```
$> cat /etc/passwd | grep root
root:x:0:0:root:/root:/bin/bash
```

There is no reason to pipe the previous example at all. The `grep` utility can take a filename argument, like so:

```
$> grep root /etc/passwd
root:x:0:0:root:/root:/bin/bash
```

See also

For anyone interested in the history of Unix and how far back pipes go, there is an exciting video from 1982 on YouTube, uploaded by AT&T: `https://www.youtube.com/watch?v=tc4ROCJYbm0`.

Writing to stdout and stderr

In this recipe, we'll learn how to print text to both *stdout* and *stderr* in a C program. In the two previous recipes, we learned what stdout and stderr are, why they exist, and how to redirect them. Now, it's our turn to write correct programs that output error messages on standard error, and regular messages on standard output.

How to do it...

Follow these steps to learn how to write output to both stdout and stderr in a C program:

1. Write the following code in a file called `output.c` and save it. In this program, we will write output using three different functions: `printf()`, `fprintf()`, and `dprintf()`. With `fprintf()`, we can specify a file stream such as stdout or stderr, while with `dprintf()`, we can specify the file descriptor (1 for stdout and 2 for stderr, just as we have seen previously):

```
#define _POSIX_C_SOURCE 200809L
#include <stdio.h>

int main(void)
{
   printf("A regular message on stdout\n");

   /* Using streams with fprintf() */
   fprintf(stdout, "Also a regular message on "
      "stdout\n");
   fprintf(stderr, "An error message on stderr\n");

   /* Using file descriptors with dprintf().
```

```
     * This requires _POSIX_C_SOURCE 200809L
     * (man 3 dprintf)*/
    dprintf(1, "A regular message, printed to "
              "fd 1\n");
    dprintf(2, "An error message, printed to "
               "fd 2\n");
    return 0;
}
```

2. Compile the program:

```
$> gcc output.c -o output
```

3. Run the program like you usually would:

```
$> ./output
A regular message on stdout
Also a regular message on stdout
An error message on stderr
A regular message, printed to fd 1
An error message, printed to fd 2
```

4. To prove that the regular messages are printed to stdout, we can send the error messages to `/dev/null`, a black hole in the Linux system. Doing this will only display the messages printed to stdout:

```
$> ./output 2> /dev/null
A regular message on stdout
Also a regular message on stdout
A regular message, printed to fd 1
```

5. Now, we will do the reverse; we will send the messages printed to stdout to `/dev/null`, showing only the error messages that are printed to stderr:

```
$> ./output > /dev/null
An error message on stderr
An error message, printed to fd 2
```

6. Finally, let's send all messages, from both stdout and stderr, to `/dev/null`. This will display nothing:

```
$> ./output &> /dev/null
```

How it works...

The first example, where we used `printf()`, doesn't contain anything new or unique. All output printed with the regular `printf()` function is printed to stdout.

Then, we saw some new examples, including the two lines where we use `fprintf()`. That function, `fprintf()`, allows us to specify a **file stream** to print the text to. We will cover what a stream is later on in this book. But in short, a file stream is what we usually open when we want to read or write to a file in C using the standard library. And remember, everything is either a file or a process in Linux. When a program opens in Linux, three file streams are automatically opened—stdin, stdout, and stderr (assuming the program has included `stdio.h`).

Then, we looked at some examples of using `dprintf()`. This function allows us to specify a **file descriptor** to print to. We covered file descriptors in the previous recipes of this chapter, but we will discuss them in more depth later in this book. Three file descriptors are always open—0 (stdin), 1 (stdout), and 2 (stderr)—in every program we write on Linux. Here, we printed the regular message to file descriptor (*fd* for short) 1, and the error message to file descriptor 2.

To be correct in our code, we need to include the very first line (the `#define` line) for the sake of `dprintf()`. We can read all about it in the manual page (`man 3 dprintf`), under *Feature Test Macro Requirements*. The **macro** we define, `_POSIX_C_SOURCE`, is for **POSIX** standards and compatibility. We will cover this in more depth later in this book.

When we tested the program, we verified that the regular messages got printed to standard output by redirecting the error messages to a file called `/dev/null`, showing only the messages printed to standard output. Then, we did the reverse to verify that the error messages got printed to standard error.

The special file, `/dev/null`, acts as a black hole in Linux and other Unix systems. Everything we send to that file simply disappears. Try it out with `ls / &> /dev/null`, for example. No output will be displayed since everything is redirected to the black hole.

There's more...

I mentioned that three file streams are opened in a program, assuming it includes `stdio.h`, as well as three file descriptors. These three file descriptors are always opened, even if `stdio.h` is not included. If we were to include `unistd.h`, we could also use macro names for the three file descriptors.

The following table shows these file descriptors, their macro names, and file streams, which are handy for future reference:

Name	File descriptor number	File stream (stdio.h)	File desctiptor (unistd.h>
Standard input	0	stdin	STDIN_FILENO
Standard output	1	stdout	STDOUT_FILENO
Standard error	2	stderr	STDERR_FILENO

Figure 2.3 – File descriptors and file streams in Linux

Reading from stdin

In this recipe, we'll learn how to write a program in C that reads from standard input. Doing so enables your programs to take input from other programs via a *pipe*, making them easier to use as a filter, thus making them more useful in the long run.

Getting ready

You'll need the GCC compiler and preferably the Bash shell for this recipe, although it should work with any shell.

To fully understand the program that we are about to write, you should look at an ASCII table, an example of which can be found at the following URL: `https://github.com/PacktPublishing/Linux-System-Programming-Techniques/blob/master/ch2/ascii-table.md`.

How to do it...

In this recipe, we will write a program that takes single words as input, converts their cases (uppercase into lower and lowercase into upper), and prints the result to standard output. Let's get started:

1. Write the following code into a file and save it as `case-changer.c`. In this program, we use `fgets()` to read characters from stdin. We then use a `for` loop to loop over the input, character by character. Before we start the next loop with the next line of input, we must zero out the arrays using `memset()`:

```
#include <stdio.h>
#include <string.h>
```

```
int main(void)
{
    char c[20] = { 0 };
    char newcase[20] = { 0 };
    int i;
    while(fgets(c, sizeof(c), stdin) != NULL)
    {
        for(i=0; i<=sizeof(c); i++)
        {
            /* Upper case to lower case */
            if ( (c[i] >= 65) && (c[i] <= 90) )
            {
                newcase[i] = c[i] + 32;
            }
            /* Lower case to upper case */
            if ( (c[i] >= 97 && c[i] <= 122) )
            {
                newcase[i] = c[i] - 32;
            }
        }
        printf("%s\n", newcase);
        /* zero out the arrays so there are no
           left-overs in the next run */
        memset(c, 0, sizeof(c));
        memset(newcase, 0, sizeof(newcase));
    }
    return 0;
}
```

2. Compile the program:

```
$> gcc case-changer.c -o case-changer
```

3. Try it out by typing some words in it. Quit the program by pressing *Ctrl* + *D*:

```
$> ./case-changer
hello
HELLO
AbCdEf
aBcDeF
```

4. Now, try to *pipe* some input to it, for example, the first five lines from `ls`:

```
$> ls / | head -n 5 | ./case-changer
BIN
BOOT
DEV
ETC
HOME
```

5. Let's try to pipe some uppercase words into it from a manual page:

```
$> man ls | egrep '^[A-Z]+$' | ./case-changer
name
synopsis
description
author
copyrigh
```

How it works...

First, we created two character **arrays** of 20 bytes each and initialize them to 0.

Then, we used `fgets()`, wrapped in a `while` loop, to read characters from standard input. The `fgets()` function reads characters until it reaches a *newline* character or an **End Of File** (**EOF**). The characters that are read are stored in the `c` array, and also returned.

To read more input—that is, more than one word—we continue reading input with the help of the `while` loop. The `while` loop won't finish until we either press *Ctrl* + *D* or the input stream is empty.

The `fgets()` function returns the character read on success and `NULL` on error or when an EOF occurs while no characters have been read (that is, no more input). Let's break down the `fgets()` function so that we can understand it better:

```
fgets(c, sizeof(c), stdin)
```

The first argument, `c`, is where we store the data. In this case, it's our character array.

The second argument, `sizeof(c)`, is the maximum size we want to read. The `fgets()` function is safe here; it reads one less than the size we specify. In our case, it will only read 19 characters, leaving room for the **null character**.

The final and third argument, `stdin`, is the stream we want to read from—in our case, standard input.

Inside the `while` loop is where the case conversions are happening, character by character in the `for` loop. In the first `if` statement, we check if the current character is an uppercase one. If it is, then we add 32 to the character. For example, if the character is *A*, then it's represented by 65 in the **ASCII table**. When we add 32, we get 97, which is *a*. The same goes for the entire alphabet. It's always 32 characters apart between the uppercase and lowercase versions.

The next `if` statement does the reverse. If the character is a lowercase one, we subtract 32 and get the uppercase version.

Since we are only checking characters between 65 and 90, and 97 and 122, all other characters are ignored.

Once we printed the result on the screen, we reset the character arrays to all zeros with `memset()`. If we don't do this, we will have leftover characters in the next run.

Using the program

We tried the program by running it interactively and typing words into it. Each time we hit the *Enter* key, the word is transformed; the uppercase letters will become lowercase and vice versa.

Then, we piped data to it from the `ls` command. That output got converted into uppercase letters.

Then, we tried to pipe it uppercase words from the manual page (the headings). All the headings in a manual page are uppercase and start at the beginning of the line. This is what we "grep" for with `egrep`, and then pipe to our `case-changer` program.

There's more...

For more information about `fgets()`, see the manual page, `man 3 fgets`.

You can write a small program to print a minimum ASCII table for the letters *a-z* and *A-Z*. This small program also demonstrates that each character is represented by a number:

ascii-table.c

```
#include <stdio.h>

int main(void)
{
    char c;
    for (c = 65; c<=90; c++)
```

```
    {
        printf("%c = %d    ", c, c); /* upper case */
        printf("%c = %d\n", c+32, c+32); /* lower case */
    }
    return 0;
}
```

Writing a pipe-friendly program

In this recipe, we will learn how to write a program that is **pipe-friendly**. It will take input from standard input and output the result on standard output. Any error messages are going to be printed on standard error.

Getting ready

We'll need the GCC compiler, GNU Make, and preferably the **Bash** shell for this recipe.

How to do it...

In this recipe, we are going to write a program that converts miles per hour into kilometers per hour. As a test, we are going to *pipe* data to it from a text file that contains measurements from a car trial run with average speeds. The text file is in **miles per hour** (**mph**), but we want them in **kilometers per hour** (**kph**) instead. Let's get started:

1. Start by creating the following text file or download it from GitHub from `https://github.com/PacktPublishing/Linux-System-Programming-Techniques/blob/master/ch2/avg.txt`. If you are creating it yourself, name it `avg.txt`. This text will be used as the input for a program we will write. The text simulates measurement values from a car trial run:

```
10-minute average: 61 mph
30-minute average: 55 mph
45-minute average: 54 mph
60-minute average: 52 mph
90-minute average: 52 mph
99-minute average: nn mph
```

2. Now, create the actual program. Type in the following code and save it as `mph-to-kph.c`, or download it from GitHub from `https://github.com/PacktPublishing/Linux-System-Programming-Techniques/blob/master/ch2/mph-to-kph.c`. This program will convert miles per hour into kilometers per hour. This conversion is performed in the `printf()` statement:

```
#include <stdio.h>
#include <stdlib.h>
#include <string.h>

int main(void)
{
    char mph[10] = { 0 };

    while(fgets(mph, sizeof(mph), stdin) != NULL)
    {
        /* Check if mph is numeric
         * (and do conversion) */
        if( strspn(mph, "0123456789.-\n") ==
            strlen(mph) )
        {
            printf("%.1f\n", (atof(mph)*1.60934) );
        }
        /* If mph is NOT numeric, print error
         * and return */
        else
        {
            fprintf(stderr, "Found non-numeric"
                " value\n");
            return 1;
        }
    }
    return 0;
}
```

3. Compile the program:

```
$> gcc mph-to-kph.c -o mph-to-kph
```

4. Test the program by running it interactively. Type in some miles per hour values and hit *Enter* after each value. The program will print out the corresponding value in kilometers per hour:

```
$> ./mph-to-kph
50
80.5
60
96.6
100
160.9
hello
Found non-numeric value
$> echo $?
1
$> ./mph-to-kph
50
80.5
Ctrl+D
$> echo $?
0
```

5. Now, it's time to use our program as a filter to transform the table containing miles per hour into kilometers per hour. But first, we must filter out only the mph values. We can do this with `awk`:

```
$> cat avg.txt | awk '{ print $3 }'
61
55
54
52
52
nn
```

6. Now that we have a list of the numbers only, we can add our `mph-to-kph` program at the end to convert the values:

```
$> cat avg.txt | awk '{ print $3 }' | ./mph-to-kph
98.2
88.5
86.9
83.7
```

```
83.7
Found non-numeric value
```

7. Since the last value is `nn`, a non-numeric value, which is an error in the measurement, we don't want to show the error message in the output. Therefore, we redirect stderr to `/dev/null`. Note the parenthesis around the expression, before the redirect:

```
$> (cat avg.txt | awk '{ print $3 }' | \
> ./mph-to-kph) 2> /dev/null
98.2
88.5
86.9
83.7
83.7
```

8. This is much prettier! However, we also want to add *km/h* at the end of every line to know what the value is. We can use `sed` to accomplish this:

```
$> (cat avg.txt | awk '{ print $3 }' | \
> ./mph-to-kph) 2> /dev/null | sed 's/$/ km\/h/'
98.2 km/h
88.5 km/h
86.9 km/h
83.7 km/h
83.7 km/h
```

How it works...

This program is similar to the one from the previous recipe. The features we added here check if the input data is numeric or not, and if it isn't, the program aborts with an error message that is printed to stderr. The regular output is still printed to stdout, as far as it goes without an error.

The program is only printing the numeric values, no other information. This makes it better as a filter, since the *km/h* text can be added by the user with other programs. That way, the program can be useful for many more scenarios that we haven't thought about.

The line where we check for numeric input might require some explanation:

```
if( strspn(mph, "0123456789.-\n") == strlen(mph) )
```

The `strspn()` function only reads the characters that we specified in the second argument to the function and then returns the number of read characters. We can then compare the number of characters read by `strspn()` with the entire length of the string, which we get with `strlen()`. If those match, we know that every character is either numeric, a dot, a minus, or a newline. If they don't match, this means an illegal character was found in the string.

For `strspn()` and `strlen()` to work, we included `string.h`. For `atof()` to work, we included `stdlib.h`.

Piping data to the program

In *Step 5*, we selected only the third field—the mph value—using the `awk` program. The awk `$3` variable means field number 3. Each field is a new word, separated by a space.

In *Step 6*, we redirected the output from the `awk` program—the mph values—into our `mph-to-kph` program. As a result, our program printed the km/h values on the screen.

In *Step 7*, we redirected the error messages to `/dev/null` so that the output from the program is clean.

Finally, in *Step 8*, we added the text *km/h* after the kph values in the output. We did this by using the `sed` program. The `sed` program can look a bit cryptic, so let's break it down:

```
sed 's/$/ km\/h/'
```

This `sed` script is similar to the previous ones we have seen. But this time, we substituted the end of the line with a `$` sign instead of the beginning with `^`. So, what we did here is substitute the end of the line with the text "km/h". Note, though, that we needed to *escape* the slash in "km/h" with a backslash.

There's more...

There's a lot of useful information about `strlen()` and `strspn()` in the respective manual pages. You can read them with `man 3 strlen` and `man 3 strspn`.

Redirecting the result to a file

In this recipe, we will learn how to redirect the output of a program to two different files. We are also going to learn some best practices when writing a **filter**, a program specifically made to be connected with other programs with a pipe.

The program we will build in this recipe is a new version of the program from the previous recipe. The `mph-to-kph` program in the previous recipe had one drawback: it always stopped when it found a non-numeric character. Often, when we run filters on long input data, we want the program to continue running, even if it has detected some erroneous data. This is what we are going to fix in this version.

We will keep the default behavior just as it was previously; that is, it will abort the program when it encounters a non-numeric value. However, we will add an option (`-c`) so that it can continue running the program even if a non-numeric value was detected. Then, it's up to the end user to decide how he or she wants to run it.

Getting ready

All the requirements listed in the *Technical requirements* section of this chapter apply here (the GCC compiler, the Make tool, and the Bash shell).

How to do it...

This program will be a bit longer, but if you like, you can download it from GitHub at `https://github.com/PacktPublishing/Linux-System-Programming-Techniques/blob/master/ch2/mph-to-kph_v2.c`. Since the code is a bit longer, I will be splitting it up into several steps. However, all of the code still goes into a single file called `mph-to-kph_v2.c`. Let's get started:

1. Let's start with the feature macro and the required header files. Since we are going to use `getopt()`, we need the `_XOPEN_SOURCE` macro, as well as the `unistd.h` header file:

```
#define _XOPEN_SOURCE 500
#include <stdio.h>
#include <stdlib.h>
#include <string.h>
#include <unistd.h
```

2. Next, we will add the function prototype for the help function. We will also start writing the `main()` function body:

```
void printHelp(FILE *stream, char progname[]);

int main(int argc, char *argv[])
{
   char mph[10] = { 0 };
```

```
    int opt;
    int cont = 0;
```

3. Then, we will add the `getopt()` function inside a `while` loop. This is similar to the *Writing a program that parses command-line options recipe* from *Chapter 1, Getting the Necessary Tools and Writing Our First Linux Programs*:

```
/* Parse command-line options */
    while ((opt = getopt(argc, argv, "ch")) != -1)
    {
        switch(opt)
        {
            case 'h':
                printHelp(stdout, argv[0]);
                return 0;
            case 'c':
                cont = 1;
                break;
            default:
                printHelp(stderr, argv[0]);
                return 1;
        }
    }
```

4. Then, we must create another `while` loop, where we will fetch data from stdin with `fgets()`:

```
while(fgets(mph, sizeof(mph), stdin) != NULL)
    {
        /* Check if mph is numeric
         * (and do conversion) */
        if( strspn(mph, "0123456789.-\n") ==
                strlen(mph) )
        {
            printf("%.1f\n", (atof(mph)*1.60934) );
        }
        /* If mph is NOT numeric, print error
         * and return */
        else
        {
            fprintf(stderr, "Found non-numeric "
                "value\n");
            if (cont == 1) /* Check if -c is set */
```

```
            {
                continue; /* Skip and continue if
                               * -c is set */
            }
            else
            {
                return 1; /* Abort if -c is not set */
            }
        }
    }
    return 0;
}
```

5. Finally, we must write the function body for the `help` function:

```
void printHelp(FILE *stream, char progname[])
{
    fprintf(stream, "%s [-c] [-h]\n", progname);
    fprintf(stream, " -c continues even though a non"
        "-numeric value was detected in the input\n"
        " -h print help\n");
}
```

6. Compile the program using Make:

```
$> make mph-to-kph_v2
cc     mph-to-kph_v2.c    -o mph-to-kph_v2
```

7. Let's try it out, without any options, by giving it some numeric values and a non-numeric value. The result should be the same as what we received previously:

```
$> ./mph-to-kph_v2
60
96.6
40
64.4
hello
Found non-numeric value
```

8. Now, let's try it out using the `-c` option so that we can continue running the program even though a non-numeric value has been detected. Type some numeric and non-numeric values into the program:

```
$> ./mph-to-kph_v2 -c
50
80.5
90
144.8
hello
Found non-numeric value
10
16.1
20
32.2
```

9. That worked just fine! Now, let's add some more data to the `avg.txt` file and save it as `avg-with-garbage.txt`. This time, there will be more lines with non-numeric values. You can also download the file from `https://github.com/PacktPublishing/Linux-System-Programming-Techniques/blob/master/ch2/avg-with-garbage.txt`:

```
10-minute average: 61 mph
30-minute average: 55 mph
45-minute average: 54 mph
60-minute average: 52 mph
90-minute average: 52 mph
99-minute average: nn mph
120-minute average: 49 mph
160-minute average: 47 mph
180-minute average: nn mph
error reading data from interface
200-minute average: 43 mph
```

10. Now, let's run `awk` on that file again to see only the values:

```
$> cat avg-with-garbage.txt | awk '{ print $3 }'
61
55
54
52
52
nn
```

```
49
47
nn
data
43
```

11. Now comes the moment of truth. Let's add the `mph-to-kph_v2` program at the end with the `-c` option. This should convert all the mph values into kph values and continue running, even though non-numeric values will be found:

```
$> cat avg-with-garbage.txt | awk '{ print $3 }' \
> | ./mph-to-kph_v2 -c
98.2
88.5
86.9
83.7
83.7
Found non-numeric value
78.9
75.6
Found non-numeric value
Found non-numeric value
69.2
```

12. That worked! The program continued, even though there were non-numeric values. Since the error messages are printed to stderr and the values are printed to stdout, we can redirect the output to two different files. That leaves us with a clean output file and a separate error file:

```
$> (cat avg-with-garbage.txt | awk '{ print $3 }' \
> | ./mph-to-kph_v2 -c) 2> errors.txt 1> output.txt
```

13. Let's take a look at the two files:

```
$> cat output.txt
98.2
88.5
86.9
83.7
83.7
78.9
75.6
69.2
```

```
$> cat errors.txt
Found non-numeric value
Found non-numeric value
Found non-numeric value
```

How it works...

The code itself is similar to what we had in the previous recipe, except for the added `getopt()` and the help function. We covered `getopt()` in detail in *Chapter 1, Getting the Necessary Tools and Writing Our First Linux Programs*, so there's no need to cover it again here.

To continue reading data from stdin when a non-numeric value is found (while using the `-c` option), we use `continue` to skip one iteration of the loop. Instead of aborting the program, we print an error message to stderr and then move on to the next iteration, leaving the program running.

Also, note that we passed two arguments to the `printHelp()` function. The first argument is a `FILE` *pointer*. We use this to pass *stderr* or *stdout* to the function. Stdout and stderr are *streams*, which can be reached via their `FILE` pointer. This way, we can choose if the help message should be printed to stdout (in case the user asked for the help) or to stderr (in case there was an error).

The second argument is the name of the program, as we have seen already.

We then compiled and tested the program. Without the `-c` option, it works just as it did previously.

After that, we tried the program with data from a file that contains some garbage. That's usually how data looks; it's often not "perfect". That's why we added the option to continue, even though non-numeric values were found.

Just like in the previous recipe, we used `awk` to select only the third field (`print $3`) from the file.

The exciting part is *Step 12*, where we redirected both *stderr* and *stdout*. We separated the two outputs into two different files. That way, we have a clean output file with only the km/h values. We can then use that file for further processing since it doesn't contain any error messages.

We could have written the program to do all the steps for us, such as filter out the values from the text file, do the conversions, and then write the result to a new file. But that's an **anti-pattern** in Linux and Unix. Instead, we want to write small tools that do one thing only—and do it well. That way, the program can be used on other files with a different structure, or for a completely different purpose. We could even grab the data straight from a device or modem if we wanted to and pipe it into our program. The tools for extracting the correct fields from the file (or device) have already been created; there's no need to reinvent the wheel.

Notice that we needed to enclose the entire command, with pipes and all, before redirecting the output and error messages.

There's more...

Eric S. Raymond has written some excellent rules to stick to when developing software for Linux and Unix. They can all be found in his book, *The Art of Unix Programming*. Two of the rules that apply to us in this recipe include the *Rule of Modularity*, which says that we should write simple parts that are connected with clean interfaces. The other rule that applies to us is the *Rule of Composition*, which says to write programs that will be connected to other programs.

His book is available for free online at `http://www.catb.org/~esr/writings/taoup/html/`.

Reading environment variables

Another way to communicate with the shell—and to configure a program—is via **environment variables**. By default, there are a lot of environment variables already set. These variables contain information on just about anything regarding your user and your settings. Some examples include the username, which type of terminal you are using, the path variable we discussed in previous recipes, your preferred editor, your preferred locale and language, and more.

Knowing how to read these variables will make it much easier for you to adapt your programs to the user's environment.

In this recipe, we will write a program that reads environment variables, adapts its output, and prints some information about the user and the session.

Getting ready

For this recipe, we can use just about any shell. Other than a shell, we'll need the GCC compiler.

How to do it...

Follow these steps to write a program that reads environment variables:

1. Save the following code into a file called `env-var.c`. You can also download the whole program from `https://github.com/PacktPublishing/Linux-System-Programming-Techniques/blob/master/ch2/env-var.c`. This program will read some common environment variables from your shell using the `getenv()` function. The strange-looking number sequences (`\033[0;31`) are used to color the output:

```
#include <stdio.h>
#include <stdlib.h>
#include <string.h>

int main(void)
{
   /* Using getenv() to fetch env. variables */
   printf("Your username is %s\n", getenv("USER"));
   printf("Your home directory is %s\n",
      getenv("HOME"));
   printf("Your preferred editor is %s\n",
      getenv("EDITOR"));
   printf("Your shell is %s\n", getenv("SHELL"));

   /* Check if the current terminal support colors*/
   if ( strstr(getenv("TERM"), "256color")  )
   {
      /* Color the output with \033 + colorcode */
      printf("\033[0;31mYour \033[0;32mterminal "
         "\033[0;35msupport "
         "\033[0;33mcolors\033[0m\n");
   }
   else
   {
      printf("Your terminal doesn't support"
         " colors\n");
   }
```

```
    return 0;
}
```

2. Compile the program using GCC:

```
$> gcc env-var.c -o env-var
```

3. Run the program. The information that will be printed for you will differ from mine. The last line will also be in color if your terminal supports it. If it doesn't, it will tell you that your terminal doesn't support colors:

```
$> ./env-var
Your username is jake
Your home directory is /home/jake
Your preferred editor is vim
Your shell is /bin/bash
Your terminal support colors
```

4. Let's investigate the environment variables we used by using `echo`. Make a note of the `$TERM` variable. The dollar sign (`$`) tells the shell that we want to print the `TERM` variable, not the word *TERM*:

```
$> echo $USER
jake
$> echo $HOME
/home/jake
$> echo $EDITOR
vim
$> echo $SHELL
/bin/bash
$> echo $TERM
screen-256color
```

5. If we were to change the `$TERM` variable to a regular `xterm`, without color support, we would get a different output from the program:

```
$> export TERM=xterm
$> ./env-var
Your username is jake
Your home directory is /home/jake
Your preferred editor is vim
Your shell is /bin/bash
Your terminal doesn't support colors
```

6. Before moving on, we should reset our terminal to the value it was before we changed it. This will probably be something else on your computer:

```
$> export TERM=screen-256color
```

7. It's also possible to set an environment variable temporarily for the duration of the program. We can do this by setting the variable and executing the program on the same line. Notice that when the program ends, the variable is still the same as it was previously. We just override the variable when the program executes:

```
$> echo $TERM
xterm-256color
$> TERM=xterm ./env-var
Your username is jake
Your home directory is /home/jake
Your preferred editor is vim
Your shell is /bin/bash
Your terminal doesn't support colors
$> echo $TERM
xterm-256colo
```

8. We can also print a complete list of all the environment variables using the `env` command. The list will probably be several pages long. All of these variables can be accessed using the `getenv()` C function:

```
$> env
```

How it works...

We use the `getenv()` function to get the values from the shell's environment variables. We print these variables to the screen.

Then, at the end of the program, we check if the current terminal has color support. This is usually denoted by something such as `xterm-256color`, `screen-256color`, and so on. We then use the `strstr()` function (from `string.h`) to check if the `$TERM` variable contains the `256color` substring. If it does, the terminal has color support, and we print a colorized message on the screen. If it doesn't, however, we print that the terminal doesn't have color support, without using any colors.

All of these variables are the shell's *environment variables* and can be printed with the `echo` command; for example, `echo $TERM`. We can also set our own environment variables in the shell; for instance, `export FULLNAME=Jack-Benny`. Likewise, we can change existing ones by overwriting them, just as we did with the `$TERM` variable. We can also override them by setting them at runtime, like we did with `TERM=xterm ./env-var`.

Regular variables set with the `FULLNAME=Jack-Benny` syntax are only available to the current shell and are hence called **local variables**. When we set variables using the `export` command, they become **global variables** or *environment variables*, a more common name, available to both **subshells** and child processes.

There's more...

We can also change environment variables and create new ones in a C program by using the `setenv()` function. However, when we do so, those variables won't be available in the shell that started the program. The program we run is a **child process** of the shell, and hence it can't change the shell's variable; that is, its **parent process**. But any other programs started from inside our own program will be able to see those variables. We will discuss parent and child processes in more depth later in this book.

Here is a short example of how to use `setenv()`. The `1` in the third argument to `setenv()` means that we want to overwrite the variable if it already exists. If we change it to a `0`, it prevents overwriting:

env-var-set.c

```
#define _POSIX_C_SOURCE 200112L
#include <stdio.h>
#include <stdlib.h>

int main(void)
{
    setenv("FULLNAME", "Jack-Benny", 1);
    printf("Your full name is %s\n", getenv("FULLNAME"));
    return 0;
}
```

If we compile and run the program and then try to read `$FULLNAME` from the shell, we'll notice that it doesn't exist:

```
$> gcc env-var-set.c -o env-var-set
$> ./env-var-set
Your full name is Jack-Benny
$> echo $FULLNAME
```

3
Diving Deep into C in Linux

It's time to take an in-depth look at C programming in Linux. Here, we will learn more about the **compiler**, the four stages from source code to **binary program**, how to use the **Make** tool, and differences between system calls and standard library functions. We will also take a look at some essential header files when it comes to Linux, and look at some **C** and **Portable Operating System Interface** (**POSIX**) **standards**. C is tightly integrated with Linux, and mastering C will help you understand Linux.

In this chapter, we will develop both programs and libraries for Linux. We will also write both a generic **Makefile** and more advanced ones for more significant projects. While doing this, we will also learn about the different **C standards**, why they matter, and how they affect your programs.

This chapter will cover the following recipes:

- Linking against libraries using the **GNU Compiler Collection** (**GCC**)
- Changing C standards
- Using system calls
- sand when not to use them

- Getting information about Linux- and Unix-specific header files
- Defining feature test macros
- Looking at the four stages of compilation
- Compiling with Make
- Writing a generic Makefile with GCC options
- Writing a simple Makefile
- Writing a more advanced Makefile

Technical requirements

In this chapter, you will need the Make tool and the GCC compiler, preferably installed via the meta-package or group install mentioned in *Chapter 1, Getting the Necessary Tools and Writing Our First Linux Programs.*

All source code for this chapter is available at `https://github.com/PacktPublishing/Linux-System-Programming-Techniques/tree/master/ch3`.

Check out the following link to see the Code in Action video:
`https://bit.ly/3zrbi6s`

Linking against libraries using GCC

In this recipe, we will learn how to link a program to an external **library**, both one that's installed system-wide and one that resides in our home directory. Before we can link to a library, however, we need to create it. This is also something that we are going to cover in this recipe. Knowing how to link against libraries will enable you to make use of a wide variety of ready-to-use functions. Instead of writing everything by yourself, you can use libraries that are already available. Often, there is no need to reinvent the wheel, thus saving you a lot of time.

Getting ready

For this recipe, you'll only need what's listed under the *Technical requirements* section of this chapter.

How to do it...

Here, we will learn how to link against both a **shared library** installed on your system and a library from your home directory. We will begin with a library already on your system: the **math library**.

Linking against the math library

Here, we will make a small program that calculates the compound interest on a bank account. For this, we need the `pow()` function, which is included in the math library.

1. Write the following code and save it in a file called `interest.c`. Note that we include `math.h` at the top. The `pow()` function's first argument is the base; the second argument is the exponent:

```
#include <stdio.h>
#include <math.h>

int main(void)
{
    int years = 15; /* The number of years you will
                     * keep the money in the bank
                     * account */
    int savings = 99000; /* The inital amount */
    float interest = 1.5; /* The interest in % */

    printf("The total savings after %d years "
        "is %.2f\n", years,
        savings * pow(1+(interest/100), years));
    return 0;
}
```

2. Now, compile and **link** the program. The option to link against a library is `-l`, and the name of the library is `m` (see the `man 3 pow` manual page for more information):

```
$> gcc interest.c -o interest -lm
```

3. And finally, let's try the program:

```
$> ./interest
The total savings after 15 years is 123772.95
```

Creating our own library

Here, we'll create our very own shared library. In the next section of this recipe, we'll link a program to this library. The library we are creating here is used to find out if a number is a prime number or not.

1. Let's start with creating a simple header file. This file will only contain a single line—the function prototype. Write the following content in a file and name it `prime.h`:

```
int isprime(long int number);
```

2. Now, it's time to write the actual function that will be included in the library. Write the following code in a file and save it as `primc.c`:

```
int isprime(long int number)
{
    long int j;
    int prime = 1;

    /* Test if the number is divisible, starting
     * from 2 */
    for(j=2; j<number; j++)
    {
        /* Use the modulo operator to test if the
         * number is evenly divisible, i.e., a
         * prime number */
        if(number%j == 0)
        {
            prime = 0;
        }
    }
    if(prime == 1)
    {
        return 1;
    }
    else
    {
        return 0;
    }
}
```

3. We need to convert this to a library somehow. The first step is to compile it into something that's called an object file. We also need to parse some extra arguments to the compiler to make it work in a library. More specifically, we need to make it **Position-Independent Code**, or **PIC** for short. The following compiler command produces a file called `prime.o`, which we'll see with the `ls -l` command. We'll learn more about object files later in this chapter:

```
$> gcc -Wall -Wextra -pedantic -fPIC -c prime.c
$> ls -l prime.o
-rw-r--r-- 1 jake jake 1296 nov 28 19:18 prime.o
```

4. Now, we must package the object file as a library. In the following command, the `-shared` option is just what it sounds like: it creates a **shared library**. The `-Wl,-soname,libprime.so` options are for the linker. This tells the linker that the shared library name (`soname`) will be `libprime.so`. The `-o` option specifies the output filename, which is `libprime.so`. This is a standard naming convention for **dynamically linked libraries**. The `so` ending stands for *shared object*. When the library is to be used system-wide, a number is often added to indicate the version. At the very end of the command, we have the `prime.o` object file that is included in this library:

```
$> gcc -shared -Wl,-soname,libprime.so -o \
> libprime.so prime.o
```

Linking against a library in your home directory

Sometimes, you have a shared library you want to link against in your home directory (or some other directory). Maybe it's a library you downloaded from the internet or a library you have built yourself, as in this case. We will learn more about making our own libraries in a later chapter of this book. Here, we use the small sample library we've just made, called `libprime.so`.

1. Write the following source code in a file and name it `is-it-a-prime.c`. This program will use the library we just downloaded. We must also include the header file we created, `prime.h`. Note the different syntax for including a local header file (not a system-wide header file):

```
#include <stdio.h>
#include <stdlib.h>
#include <string.h>
#include "prime.h"
```

```
int main(int argc, char *argv[])
{
   long int num;
   /* Only one argument is accepted */
   if (argc != 2)
   {
      fprintf(stderr, "Usage: %s number\n",
         argv[0]);
      return 1;
   }
   /* Only numbers 0-9 are accepted */
   if ( strspn(argv[1], "0123456789") !=
      strlen(argv[1]) )
   {
      fprintf(stderr, "Only numeric values are "
         "accepted\n");
      return 1;
   }
   num = atol(argv[1]); /* String to long */
   if (isprime(num)) /* Check if num is a prime */
   {
      printf("%ld is a prime\n", num);
   }
   else
   {
      printf("%ld is not a prime\n", num);
   }

   return 0;
}
```

2. Now, compile it and link it to `libprime.so`. Since the library resides in our home directory, we need to specify the path to it:

```
$> gcc -L${PWD} is-it-a-prime.c \
> -o is-it-a-prime -lprime
```

3. We need to set the `$LD_LIBRARY_PATH` **environment variable** to our current directory (where the library resides) before we can run the program. The reason for this is that the library is dynamically linked and is not on the usual system path for libraries:

```
$> export LD_LIBRARY_PATH=${PWD}:${LD_LIBRARY_PATH}
```

4. And now, we can finally run the program. Test it with some different numbers to find out if they are prime numbers or not:

```
$> ./is-it-a-prime 11
11 is a prime
$> ./is-it-a-prime 13
13 is a prime
$> ./is-it-a-prime 15
15 is not a prime
$> ./is-it-a-prime 1000024073
1000024073 is a prime
$> ./is-it-a-prime 1000024075
1000024075 is not a prime
```

We can see which libraries a program is depending upon with the `ldd` program. If we examine the `is-it-a-prime` program, we'll see that it depends upon our `libprime.so` library. There are also other dependencies, such as `libc.so.6`, which is the standard C library:

```
$> ldd is-it-a-prime
    linux-vdso.so.1 (0x00007ffc3c9f2000)
    libprime.so => /home/jake/libprime.so
(0x00007fd8b1e48000)
    libc.so.6 => /lib/x86_64-linux-gnu/libc.so.6
(0x00007fd8b1c4c000)
    /lib64/ld-linux-x86-64.so.2 (0x00007fd8b1e54000)
```

How it works…

The pow() function we used in the *Linking against the math library* section requires us to link against the math library, libm.so. You can find this file in one of the system's library locations, often in /usr/lib or /usr/lib64. On Debian and Ubuntu, it's often /usr/lib/x86_64-linux-gnu (for 64-bit systems). Since the file is in the system's default library location, we can include it using only the -l option. The full name of the library file is libm.so, but when we specify the library to link against, we only specify the m part (that is, we remove the lib part and the .so extension). There shouldn't be any space between -l and the m part, so to link against it, we type -lm.

The reason we need to link against the library to use the pow() function is that the math library is separate from the standard C library, libc.so. All the functions we have used previously have been part of the *standard library*, which is the libc.so file. This library is linked by default, so there's no need to specify it. If we really wanted to specify the linkage to libc.so when compiling, we could do so with gcc some-program.c -o some-program -lc.

The pow() function takes two arguments, *x*, and *y*, such as pow(x,y). The function then returns the value of *x* raised to the power of *y*. For example, pow(2,8) will return 256. The returned value is a **double float**, and both *x* and *y* are double floats.

The formula for calculating compound interest is shown here:

$$P \times \left(1 + \frac{r}{100}\right)^{y}$$

Here, *P* is the starting capital you put in the account, *r* is the interest rate in percent, and *y* is the number of years that the money should stay untouched in the account.

Linking against a library in your home directory

In the is-it-a-prime.c C program, we needed to include the prime.h header file. The header file only contains one line: the function prototype for the isprime() function. The actual isprime() function is included in the libprime.so library we created from prime.o, which we created from prime.c. A .so file is a **shared library** or **shared object file**. A shared library contains compiled object files for functions. We will cover what object files are later in this chapter.

When we want to link against a library that we have downloaded or created ourselves, and that is not installed in the system's default location for libraries, things get a bit more complicated.

First, we need to specify the library's name and the path where the library is located. The path is specified with the `-L` option. Here, we set the path to the current directory where we created the library. `${PWD}` is a shell environment variable that contains the full path to the current directory. You can try it with `echo ${PWD}`.

But then, to be able to run the program, we need to set an environment variable called `$LD_LIBRARY_PATH` to our current directory (and whatever it already contains). The reason for this is that the program is **dynamically linked** against the library, meaning that the library isn't included within the program; it's outside the program. For the program to find the library, we need to tell it where to look, and this is what we do with `$LD_LIBRARY_PATH`. We also don't want to overwrite what's already in the `$LD_LIBRARY_PATH` variable; that's why we also include the variable's content. If we hadn't set that environment variable, we would get an error message when executing the program, saying "*error while loading shared libraries: libprime.so*". When we listed the dependencies with `ldd`, we saw that `libprime.so` is located in a home directory, not in the system's library locations.

There's more...

If you are interested in reading more about the standard C library, you can read `man libc`. To read more about the `pow()` function, you can read `man 3 pow`.

I also encourage you to read the manual page for `ldd` with `man ldd`. Also, check out some program's dependencies with `ldd`—for example, the `interest` program we wrote in this recipe. While doing so, you'll see `libm.so` and its location in the system. You can also try `ldd` on system binaries, such as `/bin/ls`.

Changing C standards

In this recipe, we will be learning and exploring different **C standards**, what they are, why they matter, and how they affect our programs. We will also learn how to set the C standard at **compile** time.

The most commonly used C standards today are **C89**, **C99**, and **C11** (C89 for 1989, C11 for 2011, and so on). Many compilers still default to using C89 because it's the most compatible, widespread, and complete implementation. However, C99 is a more flexible and modern implementation. Often, under newer versions of Linux, the default is **C18**, together with some POSIX standards.

We will write two programs and compile them with both C89 and C99, and see their differences.

Getting ready

All you need for this recipe is a Linux computer with GCC installed, preferably via the meta-package or package group described in *Chapter 1, Getting the Necessary Tools and Writing our First Linux Programs.*

How to do it...

Follow along to explore the differences between the C standards.

1. Write the small C program shown here and save it as `no-return.c`. Note the missing `return` statement:

```
#include <stdio.h>

int main(void)
{
    printf("Hello, world\n");
}
```

2. Now, compile it using the C89 standard:

```
$> gcc -std=c89 no-return.c -o no-return
```

3. Run the program and check the exit code:

```
$> ./no-return
Hello, world
$> echo $?
13
```

4. Now, recompile the program with the same C standard, but enable *all warnings*, *extra warnings*, and *pedantic* checking (`-W` is the option for warnings, and `all` is which warnings, hence `-Wall`). Note the error message we get from GCC:

```
$> gcc -Wall -Wextra -pedantic -std=c89 \
> no-return.c -o no-return
no-return.c: In function 'main':
no-return.c:6:1: warning: control reaches end of non-void
function [-Wreturn-type]
 }
 ^
```

5. Now, recompile the program using the C99 standard instead and enable all warnings and pedantic checking. No errors should be displayed this time:

```
$> gcc -Wall -Wextra -pedantic -std=c99 \
> no-return.c -o no-return
```

6. Rerun the program and check the exit code. Note the difference:

```
$> ./no-return
Hello, world
$> echo $?
0
```

7. Write the following program and name it `for-test.c`. This program creates an `i` integer variable inside the `for` loop. This is only allowed in C99:

```
#include <stdio.h>

int main(void)
{
    for (int i = 10; i>0; i--)
    {
        printf("%d\n", i);
    }
    return 0;
}
```

8. Compile it using the C99 standard:

```
$> gcc -std=c99 for-test.c -o for-test
```

9. Then, run it. Everything should work just fine:

```
$> ./for-test
10
9
8
7
6
5
4
3
2
1
```

10. Now, instead, try to compile it with the C89 standard. Note that the error message clearly explains that this only works in C99 or higher. The error messages from GCC are useful, so always make sure to read them. They can save you a lot of time:

```
$> gcc -std=c89 for-test.c -o for-test
for-test.c: In function 'main':
for-test.c:5:5: error: 'for' loop initial declarations are only allowed in C99 or C11 mode
     for (int i = 10; i>0; i--)
     ^~~
```

11. Now, write the following small program and name it `comments.c`. In this program, we use C99 comments (also called C++ comments):

```
#include <stdio.h>

int main(void)
{
    // A C99 comment
    printf("hello, world\n");
    return 0;
}
```

12. Compile it using C99:

```
$> gcc -std=c99 comments.c -o comments
```

13. And now, try to compile it using C89. Note that this error message is also helpful:

```
$> gcc -std=c89 comments.c -o comments
comments.c: In function 'main':
comments.c:5:5: error: C++ style comments are not allowed in ISO C90
     // A C99 comment
     ^
comments.c:5:5: error: (this will be reported only once per input file)
```

How it works...

These are some of the more common differences between C89 and C99. There are other differences that aren't apparent in Linux using GCC. We will discuss some of those invisible differences in the *There's more...* section of this recipe.

We change the C standard with the `-std` option to GCC. In this recipe, we try the two standards, C89 and C99.

In *Steps 1-6*, we saw the difference in what happens when we forget the return value. In C99, a return value of 0 is assumed since no other value was specified. In C89, on the other hand, it's not okay to forget the return value. The program will still compile, but the program will return the value 13 (an error code), which is wrong since no error occurred in our program. The actual code returned could differ, though, but it will always be greater than 0. When we enabled *all warnings*, *extra warnings*, and *pedantic* checking of the code (`-Wall -Wextra -pedantic`), we also saw that the compiler issued a warning message, meaning it isn't legal to forget the return value. So, always return a value with `return` in C89.

Then, in *Steps 7-10*, we saw that in C99 it's okay to declare a new variable inside a `for` loop, something that is not okay in C89.

In *Steps 11-13*, we saw a new way of using comments, two slashes `//`. This isn't legal in C89.

There's more...

There are more C standards and dialects than just C89 and C99. Just to mention a few more, there are *C11*, *GNU99* (GNU's dialect of C99), *GNU11* (GNU's dialect of C11), and some others, but the most commonly used today are C89, C99, and C11. C18 is starting to appear as default for some compilers and distributions.

There are actually more differences between C89 and C99 than what we've seen here. Some of these differences can't be demonstrated in Linux with GCC, since GCC has implemented workarounds for the differences. The same goes for some other compilers out there. But in C89, for example, the `long long int` type isn't specified; it was specified in C99. But despite that, some compilers (including GCC) support `long long int` in C89, but we should be careful with using it in C89 since not all compilers support it. If you want to use `long long int`, it's safer to use C99, C11, or C18.

I recommend that you always compile your programs with the `-Wall`, `-Wextra`, and `-pedantic` options. These will warn you about all sorts of things that would otherwise go unnoticed.

Using system calls - and when not to use them

System calls are an exciting topic in any conversation about Unix and Linux. They are one of the lowest parts when it comes to system programming in Linux. If we were to look at this from a top-down approach, the shell and the binaries we run would be at the top. Just below that, we have the standard C library functions, such as `printf()`, `fgets()`, `putc()`, and so on. Below them, at the lowest levels, we have the system calls, such as `creat()`, `write()`, and so on:

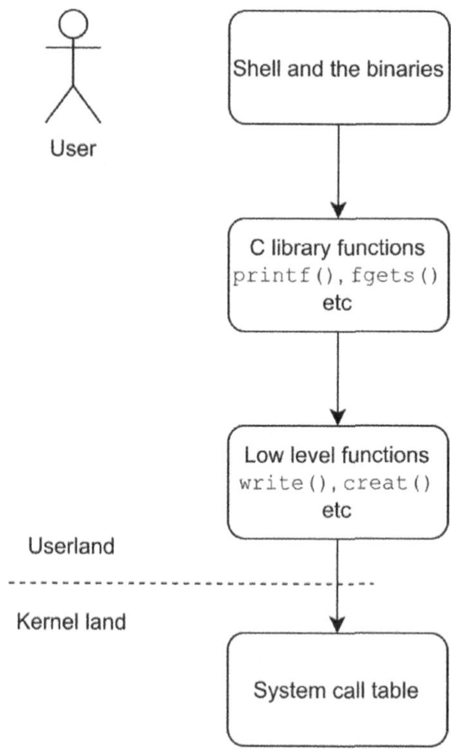

Figure 3.1 – High-level functions and low-level functions

When I talk about system calls here in this book, I mean system calls as C functions provided by the kernel, not the actual system call table. The system call functions we use here reside in **user space**, but the functions themselves execute in **kernel space**.

Many of the standard C library functions, such as `putc()`, use one or more system call functions behind the curtains. The `putc()` function is an excellent example; this uses `write()` to print a character on the screen (which is a system call). There are also standard C library functions that don't use any system calls at all, such as `atoi()`, which resides entirely in user space. There is no need to involve the kernel to convert a string into a number.

Generally speaking, if there is a standard C library function available, we should use that instead of a system call. System calls are often harder to work with and more primitive. Think of system calls as *low-level* operations, and standard C functions as *high-level* operations.

There are cases, though, when we need to use system calls, or when they are easier to use or more beneficial. Learning when and why to use system calls will make you a better system programmer altogether. For example, there are many filesystem operations we can perform on Linux via system calls that aren't available elsewhere. Another example when we need to use a system call is when we want to `fork()` a process, something we will discuss in more detail later on. In other words, we need to use system calls when we need to perform some form of *system operation*.

Getting ready

In this recipe, we will be using a Linux-specific system call, so you'll need a Linux computer (which you most probably already have since you're reading this book). But do notice that the `sysinfo()` system call won't work under FreeBSD or macOS.

How to do it...

There isn't actually much difference between using a function from the standard C library versus using a system call function. System calls in Linux are declared in `unistd.h`, so we need to include this file when using system calls.

1. Write the following small program and name it `sys-write.c`. It uses the `write()` system call. Notice that we don't include `stdio.h` here. Since we aren't using any `printf()` function or any of the stdin, stdout, or stderr file streams, we don't need `stdio.h` here. We print directly to file descriptor 1, which is standard output. The three standard file descriptors are always opened:

```
#include <unistd.h>

int main(void)
{
    write(1, "hello, world\n", 13);
    return 0;
}
```

2. Compile it. From now on, we will always include `-Wall`, `-Wextra`, and `-pedantic` to write cleaner and better code:

```
$> gcc -Wall -Wextra -pedantic -std=c99 \
> sys-write.c -o sys-write
```

3. Run the program:

```
$> ./sys-write
hello, world
```

4. Now, write the same program but with the `fputs()` function instead—a higher-level function. Notice that we include `stdio.h` here, instead of `unistd.h`. Name the program `write-chars.c`:

```
#include <stdio.h>

int main(void)
{
    fputs("hello, world\n", stdout);
    return 0;
}
```

5. Compile it:

```
$> gcc -Wall -Wextra -pedantic -std=c99 \
> write-chars.c -o write-chars
```

6. Then, run it:

```
$> ./write-chars
hello, world
```

7. Now, it's time to write a program that reads some user and system information. Save the program as `my-sys.c`. All the system calls in the program are highlighted. This program fetches your user's ID, current working directory, the machine's total and free **random-access memory** (**RAM**), and current **process ID** (**PID**):

```
#include <stdio.h>
#include <unistd.h>
#include <sys/types.h>
#include <sys/sysinfo.h>

int main(void)
{
```

```
    char cwd[100] = { 0 }; /* for current dir */
    struct sysinfo si; /* for system information */

    getcwd(cwd, 100); /* get current working dir */
    sysinfo(&si); /* get system information
                   * (linux only) */

    printf("Your user ID is %d\n", getuid());
    printf("Your effective user ID is %d\n",
       geteuid());
    printf("Your current working directory is %s\n",
       cwd);
    printf("Your machine has %ld megabytes of "
       "total RAM\n", si.totalram / 1024  / 1024);
    printf("Your machine has %ld megabytes of "
       "free RAM\n", si.freeram / 1024 / 1024);
    printf("Currently, there are %d processes "
       "running\n", si.procs);
    printf("This process ID is %d\n", getpid());
    printf("The parent process ID is %d\n",
       getppid());
    return 0;
}
```

8. Compile the program:

```
$> gcc -Wall -Wextra -pedantic -std=c99 my-sys.c -o \
> my-sys
```

9. Then, run the program. You should now see some information about your user and the machine you are using:

```
$> ./my-sys
Your user ID is 1000
Your effective user ID is 1000
Your current working directory is /mnt/localnas_disk2/
linux-sys/ch3/code
Your machine has 31033 megabytes of total RAM
Your machine has 6117 megabytes of free RAM
Currently, there are 2496 processes running
This process ID is 30421
The parent process ID is 11101
```

How it works...

In *Steps 1-6*, we explored the difference between `write()` and `fputs()`. The difference might not be that obvious but `write()`, the system call, uses **file descriptors** instead of **file streams**. This goes for almost all system calls. File descriptors are more primitive than file streams. The same top-to-bottom approach goes for file descriptors versus file streams. File streams are layered on top of file descriptors and provide a higher-level interface. Sometimes, though, we need to use file descriptors instead, as these offer more control. File streams, on the other hand, offer a more powerful and richer input and output, with formatted output—for example, such as `printf()`.

In *Steps 7-9*, we wrote a program that fetches some system and user information. Here, we included three system call-specific header files: `unistd.h`, `sys/types.h`, and `sys/sysinfo.h`.

We have already seen `unistd.h`, a common header file for system calls in Unix and Linux systems. The `sys/types.h` header file is another common header file for system calls, especially when it comes to getting values from the system. This header file contains special variable types; for example, `uid_t` and `gid_t` for **user ID** (**UID**) and **group ID** (**GID**). These are usually an `int`. Others are `ino_t` for **inode** numbers, `pid_t` for PIDs, and so on.

The `sys/sysinfo.h` header file is specifically for the `sysinfo()` function, which is a system call specifically for Linux, and hence this won't work under other Unix systems such as macOS, Solaris, or FreeBSD/OpenBSD/NetBSD. This header file declares the `sysinfo` struct, which we populate with information by calling the `sysinfo()` function.

The first system call we use in the program is `getcwd()`, to get the current working directory. The function takes two arguments: a buffer where it should save the path, and the length of that buffer.

The next system call is the Linux-specific `sysinfo()` function. This one gives us a lot of information. When the function executes, all data is saved to the struct `sysinfo`. This information includes the **uptime** of the system; **load average**; total amount of memory; available and used memory; total and available **swap space**; and the total number of processes running. In `man 2 sysinfo`, you can find information on the variables in the struct `sysinfo` and their data types. Further down in the code, we print some of these values using `printf()`—for example, `si.totalram`, which contains the size of the system's memory.

The rest of the system calls are called directly from `printf()` and returns integer values.

There's more...

There is a lot of detailed information about Linux system calls in the manual. A good starting point is `man 2 intro` and `man 2 syscalls`.

> Tip
>
> Most system calls will return -1 if an error occurs. It's generally a good idea to check for this value to detect errors.

Getting information about Linux- and Unix-specific header files

There are a lot of specific functions and **header files** for Linux and other Unix systems. Generally speaking these are **POSIX** functions, even though some are Linux-specific, such as `sysinfo()`. We have already seen two of the POSIX files in the previous recipe: `unistd.h` and `sys/types.h`. Since they're POSIX files, they're available in all Unix-like systems such as Linux, FreeBSD, OpenBSD, macOS, and Solaris.

In this recipe, we will learn more about these POSIX header files, what they do, and when and how you can use them. We will also learn how to look up information about these files in the manual page.

Getting ready

In this recipe, we will look up header files in the manual. If you are using a Fedora-based system, such as **CentOS**, **Fedora**, or **Red Hat**, these manual pages are already installed on your system. If for some reason they are missing, you can install them with `dnf install man-pages` as root, or with `sudo`.

If, on the other hand, you are using a Debian-based system such as **Ubuntu** or **Debian**, you will need to install those manual pages first. Follow the instructions here to install the manual pages required for this recipe.

Debian

Debian is more strict about not including non-free software, so there are a few extra steps we need to take.

1. Open up `/etc/apt/sources.list` in an editor as root.
2. Add the word `non-free` after the lines that say `main` at the end of them (with a space between `main` and `non-free`).

3. Save the file.
4. Run `apt update` as root.
5. Install the manual pages by running `apt install manpages-posix-dev` as root.

Ubuntu

Ubuntu and other distributions based on Ubuntu aren't as strict about non-free software, so here we can install the correct package right away.

Simply run `sudo apt install manpages-posix-dev`.

How to do it...

There are many header files to cover, so what's more important is learning how to know which header files we should use and how to find information about them, reading their manual pages, and knowing how to list them all. We will cover all of this here.

In the previous recipe, we used the `sysinfo()` and `getpid()` functions. Here, we will learn how to find every possible piece of information related to those system calls and the required header files.

1. First of all, we start by reading the manual page for `sysinfo()`:

   ```
   $> man 2 sysinfo
   ```

   Under the **SYNOPSIS** heading, we find the following two lines:

   ```
   #include <sys/sysinfo.h>
   int sysinfo(struct sysinfo *info);
   ```

2. This information means that we need to include `sys/sysinfo.h` to use `sysinfo()`. It also shows that the function takes a struct called `sysinfo` as an argument. Under **DESCRIPTION**, we see what the `sysinfo` struct looks like.
3. Now, let's look up `getpid()`. It's a POSIX function, and hence there is more information available:

   ```
   $> man 2 getpid
   ```

   Here, under **SYNOPSIS**, we that we need to include two header files: `sys/types.h` and `unistd.h`. We also see that the function returns a value of type `pid_t`.

4. Let's continue investigating. Open up the manual page for `sys/types.h`:

```
$> man sys_types.h
```

Under **NAME**, we see that the file contains data types. Under **DESCRIPTION**, we find that a `pid_t` data type is used for *process IDs* and *process group IDs*, but that doesn't tell us what kind of data type it actually is. So, let's continue to scroll down until we find a subheading saying **Additionally**. Here, we see a sentence that says: "`blksize_t`, `pid_t`, and `ssize_t` shall be signed integer types." Mission accomplished—now, we know that it's a signed integer type and that we can use the `%d` formatting operator to print it.

5. But let's investigate further. Let's read the manual page for `unistd.h`:

```
$> man unistd.h
```

6. Now, search this manual page for the word `pid_t`, and we'll find even more information about it.

Type a / character and then type `pid_t`, and press *Enter* to search. Press the letter *n* on your keyboard to search for the next occurrence of the word. You'll find that other functions also return a `pid_t` type—for example, `fork()`, `getpgrp()`, and `getsid()`, to mention a few.

7. While you are reading the manual page for `unistd.h`, you can also see all functions that are declared in this header file. If you can't find it, search for `Declarations`. Press /, type `Declarations`, and press *Enter*.

How it works...

The manual pages in the *7posix* or *0p* special section, depending on your Linux distribution, are from something called *POSIX Programmer's Manual*. If you open, for example, `man unistd.h`, you can see the text *POSIX Programmer's Manual*, as opposed to `man 2 write`, which says *Linux Programmer's Manual*. *POSIX Programmer's Manual* is from the **Institute of Electrical and Electronics Engineers** (**IEEE**) and **The Open Group**, not from the **GNU Project** or the Linux community.

Since *POSIX Programmer's Manual* isn't free (as in open source), Debian has chosen not to include it in their main repository. That's why we need to add the non-free repository to Debian.

POSIX is a set of standards specified by IEEE. The purpose of the standard is to have a common programming interface among all POSIX operating systems (most Unix and Unix-like systems). If you only use POSIX functions and POSIX header files in your program, it will be compatible with all other Unix and Unix-like systems out there. The actual implementation can differ from system to system, but the overall functions should be the same.

Sometimes, when we need some specific information (such as which type `pid_t` is), we need to read more than one manual page, as we did in this recipe.

The main takeaway here is to use the manual page for the function to find the corresponding header file, and then to use the manual page for the header file to find more specific information.

There's more...

The manual pages for POSIX header files are in a special section of the manual page, not listed in `man man`. Under Fedora and CentOS, the section is called *0p*, and under Debian and Ubuntu, it's called *7posix*.

> **Tip**
>
> You can list all of the manual pages available in a given section using the `apropos` command with a dot (a dot means to match all).
>
> For example, to list all of the manual pages in *Section 2*, type `apropos -s 2 .` (include the dot—it's part of the command). To list all of the manual pages in the *7posix* special section under Ubuntu, type `apropos -s 7posix .`

Defining feature test macros

In this recipe, we'll learn what some common POSIX standards are, how and why to use them, and how we specify them using **feature test macros**.

We have already seen several examples of when we have included either a POSIX standard or some specific C standard. For example, when we used `getopt()`, we defined `_XOPEN_SOURCE 500` at the very top of the source code file (`mph-to-kph_v2.c` from *Chapter 2, Making Your Programs Easy to Script*).

A feature test macro controls the definitions that are exposed by system header files. We can leverage this in two ways. Either we can use it to create portable applications by using a feature test macro that prevents us from using non-standard definitions or we can use it the other way around, allowing us to use non-standard definitions.

Getting ready

We will write two small programs in this recipe, `str-posix.c` and `which-c.c`. You can either download them from `https://github.com/PacktPublishing/Linux-System-Programming-Techniques/tree/master/ch3` or follow along and write them. You'll also need the GCC compiler we installed in *Chapter 1, Getting the Necessary Tools and Writing Our First Linux Programs*. It's also a good idea to have access to all the manual pages, including the ones from *POSIX Programmer's Manual* covered in the previous recipe.

How to do it...

Here, we will explore the dark corners of the inner workings of feature test macros, POSIX and C standards, and other related things.

1. Write the following code and save it in a file called `str-posix.c`. This program will simply copy a string using `strdup()` and then print it. Note that we include `string.h` here:

```
#include <string.h>
#include <stdio.h>

int main(void)
{
    char a[] = "Hello";
    char *b;
    b = strdup(a);
    printf("b = %s\n", b);
    return 0;
}
```

2. Now, we begin with compiling it using the C99 standard and see what happens. More than one error message will be printed:

```
$> gcc -Wall -Wextra -pedantic -std=c99 \
> str-posix.c -o str-posix
str-posix.c: In function 'main':
str-posix.c:8:9: warning: implicit declaration of
function 'strdup'; did you mean 'strcmp'? [-Wimplicit-
function-declaration]
     b = strdup(a);
         ^~~~~~
         strcmp
str-posix.c:8:7: warning: assignment to 'char *' from
```

```
'int' makes pointer from integer without a cast [-Wint-
conversion]
      b = strdup(a);
```

3. That generated a pretty severe warning. The compilation succeeded, though. If we try to run the program, it will fail on some distributions but not others. This is what's called **undefined behavior**:

```
$> ./str-posix
Segmentation fault
```

   On another Linux distribution, we might see the following:

```
$> ./str-posix
b = Hello
```

4. Now comes the fascinating—and somewhat confusing—part. There is one reason why this program crashes sometimes, but there are several possible solutions to it. We will cover them all here. But first, the reason it failed is that `strdup()` isn't part of C99 (we will cover why it *sometimes* works in the *How it works...* section). The most straightforward solution is to look at the manual page, which clearly states that we need the `_XOPEN_SOURCE` feature test macro set to `500` or higher. For the sake of this experiment, let's set it to `700` (I'll explain why later). Add the following line at the very top of `str-posix.c`. It needs to be on the very first line before any `include` statement; otherwise, it won't work:

```
#define _XOPEN_SOURCE 700
```

5. Now that you have added the preceding line, let's try to recompile the program:

```
$> gcc -Wall -Wextra -pedantic -std=c99 \
> str-posix.c -o str-posix
```

6. No warnings this time, so let's run the program:

```
$> ./str-posix
b = Hello
```

7. So, that was one of the possible solutions and the most obvious one. Now, delete that first line again (the entire `#define` line).

8. Once you have deleted the `#define` line we'll recompile the program, but this time, we set the feature test macro at the command line instead. We use the `-D` flag in GCC to accomplish this:

```
$> gcc -Wall -Wextra -pedantic -std=c99 \
> -D_XOPEN_SOURCE=700 str-posix.c -o str-posix
```

9. Let's try to run it:

```
$> ./str-posix
b = Hello
```

10. That was the second solution. But if we read the manual page for feature test macros with `man feature_test_macros`, we see that `_XOPEN_SOURCE` with a value of 700 or greater has the same effect as defining `_POSIX_C_SOURCE` with a value of 200809L or greater. So, let's try to recompile the program using `_POSIX_C_SOURCE` instead:

```
$> gcc -Wall -Wextra -pedantic -std=c99 \
> -D_POSIX_C_SOURCE=200809L str-posix.c -o str-posix
```

11. That worked just fine. Now, for the final—and possibly dangerous—solution. This time, we'll recompile the program without setting any C-standard or any feature test macros at all:

```
$> gcc -Wall -Wextra -pedantic str-posix.c \
> -o str-posix
```

12. No warning, so let's try to run it:

```
$> ./str-posix
b = Hello
```

13. How on earth could that work when we just had to define all of these macros and standards? Well, it turns out that when we don't set any C-standard or any feature test macros, the compiler sets a couple of standards of its own. To prove this, and to know how your compiler works, let's write the following program. Name it `which-c.c`. This program will print the C-standard that is being used and any commonly defined feature test macros:

```
#include <stdio.h>

int main(void)
{
```

```
    #ifdef __STDC_VERSION__
       printf("Standard C version: %ld\n",
          __STDC_VERSION__);
    #endif
    #ifdef _XOPEN_SOURCE
       printf("XOPEN_SOURCE: %d\n",
          _XOPEN_SOURCE);
    #endif
    #ifdef _POSIX_C_SOURCE
       printf("POSIX_C_SOURCE: %ld\n",
          _POSIX_C_SOURCE);
    #endif
    #ifdef _GNU_SOURCE
       printf("GNU_SOURCE: %d\n",
          _GNU_SOURCE);
    #endif
    #ifdef _BSD_SOURCE
       printf("BSD_SOURCE: %d\n", _BSD_SOURCE);
    #endif
    #ifdef _DEFAULT_SOURCE
       printf("DEFAULT_SOURCE: %d\n",
          _DEFAULT_SOURCE);
    #endif

    return 0;
}
```

14. Let's compile and run this program without setting any C standard or feature test macros:

```
$> gcc -Wall -Wextra -pedantic which-c.c -o which-c
$> ./which-c
Standard C version: 201710
POSIX_C_SOURCE: 200809
DEFAULT_SOURCE: 1
```

15. Let's try to specify that we want to use C-standard C99, and recompile `which.c`. What will happen here is that the compiler will enforce a strict C standard mode and disable the default feature test macros it might otherwise have set:

```
$> gcc -Wall -Wextra -pedantic -std=c99 \
> which-c.c -o which-c
$> ./which-c
Standard C version: 199901
```

16. Let's see what happens when we set `_XOPEN_SOURCE` to `600`:

```
$> gcc -Wall -Wextra -pedantic -std=c99 \
> -D_XOPEN_SOURCE=600 which-c.c -o which-c
$> ./which-c
Standard C version: 199901
XOPEN_SOURCE: 600
POSIX_C_SOURCE: 200112
```

How it works...

In *Steps 1-10*, we saw what happened to our program when we used different standards and feature test macros. We also noticed that it surprisingly worked without specifying any C standard or feature test macro. That's because GCC—and other compilers as well—set a lot of these features and standards by default. But we can't count on it. It's always safer to specify it ourselves; that way, we know it will work.

In *Step 13*, we wrote a program to print out the feature test macros used at compile time. To prevent the compiler from generating errors if a feature test macro was not set, we wrapped all the `printf()` lines inside `#ifdef` and `#endif` statements. These statements are `if` statements for the compiler, not the resulting program. For example, let's take the following line:

```
#ifdef _XOPEN_SOURCE
    printf("XOPEN_SOURCE: %d\n", _XOPEN_SOURCE);
#endif
```

If `_XOPEN_SOURCE` is not defined, then this `printf()` line isn't included after the **preprocessing** stage of compilation. If `_XOPEN_SOURCE`, on the other hand, is defined, it will be included. We will cover what preprocessing is in the next recipe.

In *Step 14*, we saw that on my system, the compiler sets `_POSIX_C_SOURCE` to `200809`. But the manual said that we should set `_XOPEN_SOURCE` to `500` or greater. But it still worked—how come?

If we read the manual page for the feature test macros (`man feature_test_macros`), we see that `_XOPEN_SOURCE` of a value greater than `700` has the same effect as setting `_POSIX_C_STANARD` to `200809` or greater. And since GCC has set `_POSIX_C_STANDARD` to `200809` for us, this has the same impact as `_XOPEN_SOURCE 700`.

In *Step 15*, we learned that the compiler enforces a strict C standard when we specify a standard—for example, `-std=c99`. This is the reason why `str-posix.c` failed to run (and got warning messages during compilation). The `strdup()` function isn't a standard C function; it's a POSIX function. That's why we needed to include some POSIX standard to use it. When the compiler uses a strict C standard, no other features are enabled. This enables us to write code that is portable to all systems with a C compiler that supports C99.

In *Step 16*, we specified `_XOPEN_SOURCE 600` when we compiled the program—doing so also sets `_POSIX_C_STANDARD` to `200112`. We can read about this in the manual page (`man feature_test_macros`). From the manual: *"[When] _XOPEN_SOURCE is defined with a value greater than or equal to 500 [...] the following macros are implicitly defined, _POSIX_C_SOURCE [...]"*.

But what do feature macros do, then? How do they modify the code?

The header files on the system are full of `#ifdef` statements, enabling and disabling various functions and features, depending on which feature test macros are set. For example, in our case with `strdup()`, the `string.h` header file has the `strdup()` function wrapped in `#ifdef` statements. Those statements check if either `_XOPEN_SOURCE` or some other POSIX standard is defined. If no such standards are specified, then `strdup()` is not visible. That is how feature test macros work.

But why did the program end with a segmentation fault in *Step 3* on some Linux distribution and not others? As already mentioned, the `strdup()` function is there, but without the feature test macro there's no declaration for it. What happens then is *undefined*. It could work because of some specific implementation detail, but it could also not work. When we program, we should always avoid *undefined behavior*. Just because something works on this specific computer, on this Linux distribution, with this compiler version, on this particular night when it's a full moon, this doesn't guarantee that it will work on someone else's computer on some other night. Therefore, we should always strive to write correct code following a specific standard. That way, we avoid undefined behavior.

There's more...

All of these feature test macros we have defined correspond to a POSIX or other standard of some sort. The idea behind these standards is to create a uniform programming interface among the different Unix versions and Unix-like systems out there.

For anyone who wants to dig deep into standards and feature test macros, there are some excellent manual pages available. Just to mention a few:

- `man 7 feature_test_macros` (Here, you can read all about which feature test macros correspond to which standard, such as POSIX, Single Unix Specification, XPG (X/Open Portability Guide), and so on.)
- `man 7 standards` (Even more information about the standards)
- `man unistd.h`
- `man 7 libc`
- `man 7 posixoptions`

Looking at the four stages of compilation

When we generally speak of compilation, we mean the entire process of turning code into a running binary program. But there are actually four steps involved in compiling a source code file into a running binary program, and it's just one of these steps that's called compilation.

Knowing about these four steps, and how to extract the intermediate files, enables us to do everything from writing efficient Makefiles to writing shared libraries.

Getting ready

For this recipe, we will write three small C source code files. You can also download them from `https://github.com/PacktPublishing/Linux-System-Programming-Techniques/tree/master/ch3`. You'll also need the GCC compiler that we installed in *Chapter 1*, *Getting the Necessary Tools and Writing Our First Linux Programs*.

How to do it...

In this recipe, we will create a small program and then manually compile it by executing each step individually, using the compiler's flags. We will also look at the files generated from each step. The program we will write is intentionally small so that we can look at the resulting code without too much clutter. The program we will write will simply return a cubed number—in our case, 4 cubed.

1. The first source code file for this recipe is a file called `cube-prog.c`. This will be the source code file with the `main()` function in it:

```
#include "cube.h"
#define NUMBER 4

int main(void)
{
    return cube(NUMBER);
}
```

2. Now, we write the function for `cube()` in a file called `cubed-func.c`:

```
int cube(int n)
{
    return n*n*n;
}
```

3. And finally, we write the header file, `cube.h`. This is just the function prototype:

```
int cube(int n);
```

4. Before we build the program step by step, we first compile it as usual since we haven't covered how to compile a program that consists of several files yet. To compile a program that's made up of more than one source file, we simply list them at the GCC command line. Note, however, that we don't list the header file here. Since the header file is included with a `#include` line, the compiler already knows about it.

   This is how we compile a program with several files:

```
$> gcc -Wall -Wextra -pedantic -std=c99 \
> cube-prog.c cube-func.c -o cube
```

5. And then, let's run it, and also check the return value:

```
$> ./cube
$> echo $?
64
```

6. Now, we begin to build the program step by step instead. First, we delete the binary file already produced:

```
$> rm cube
```

7. Now, let's begin compiling the program step by step. The first step is what is called the **preprocessor**. The preprocessor makes textual changes to the code—for example, it places the content of `#include` files in the program itself:

```
$> gcc -E -P cube-prog.c -o cube-prog.i
$> gcc -E -P cube-func.c -o cube-func.i
```

8. Now, we have two *preprocessed* files (`cube-prog.i` and `cube-func.i`). Let's take a look at them with `cat` or an editor. I have highlighted the changes in the following code snippet. Note how the `#include` statement has been replaced by the code from the header file, and how the `NUMBER` macro has been replaced by a `4`.

   First, we take a look at `cube-prog.i`:

```
int cube(int n);
int main(void)
{
    return cube(4);
}
```

   Then, let's look at `cube-func.i`. Nothing has changed here:

```
int cube(int n)
{
    return n*n*n;
}
```

9. The second step is the **compilation**. It is here that our preprocessed files are translated into *assembly language*. The resulting assembly files will look different on different machines and architectures:

```
$> gcc -S cube-prog.i -o cube-prog.s
$> gcc -S cube-func.i -o cube-func.s
```

10. Let's take a look at these files as well, but do note that these files can be different on your machine.

    First, we take a look at `cube-prog.s`:

```
        .file "cube-prog.i"
        .text
        .globl      main
        .type main, @function
main:
.LFB0:
        .cfi_startproc
        pushq %rbp
        .cfi_def_cfa_offset 16
        .cfi_offset 6, -16
        movq  %rsp, %rbp
        .cfi_def_cfa_register 6
        movl  $4, %edi
        call  cube@PLT
        popq  %rbp
        .cfi_def_cfa 7, 8
        ret
        .cfi_endproc
.LFE0:
        .size main, .-main
        .ident      "GCC: (Debian 8.3.0-6) 8.3.0"
        .section    .note.GNU-stack,"",@progbits
```

    Now, we take a look at `cube-func.s`:

```
        .file "cube-func.i"
        .text
        .globl      cube
        .type cube, @function
cube:
.LFB0:
        .cfi_startproc
        pushq %rbp
        .cfi_def_cfa_offset 16
        .cfi_offset 6, -16
        movq  %rsp, %rbp
        .cfi_def_cfa_register 6
        movl  %edi, -4(%rbp)
        movl  -4(%rbp), %eax
```

```
        imull -4(%rbp), %eax
        imull -4(%rbp), %eax
        popq  %rbp
        .cfi_def_cfa 7, 8
        ret
        .cfi_endproc
.LFE0:
        .size cube, .-cube
        .ident      "GCC: (Debian 8.3.0-6) 8.3.0"
        .section    .note.GNU-stack,"",@progbits
```

11. The third step is called **assembly**. This step is where the assembly source code files are built to what are called **object files**:

```
$> gcc -c cube-prog.s -o cube-prog.o
$> gcc -c cube-func.s -o cube-func.o
```

12. Now, we have two object files. We can't look at them since they are binary files, but we can use the `file` command to see what they are. The description here can also differ on different architectures—for example, 32-bit x86 machines, ARM64, and so on:

```
$> file cube-prog.o
cube-prog.o: ELF 64-bit LSB relocatable, x86-64, version
1 (SYSV), not stripped
$> file cube-func.o
cube-func.o: ELF 64-bit LSB relocatable, x86-64, version
1 (SYSV), not stripped
```

13. Now, we are at the fourth and final step. This is where we combine all the object files into a single binary file. This step is called the **linker**:

```
$> gcc cube-prog.o cube-func.o -o cube
```

14. Now, we have a binary file ready, called `cube`. Let's see what `file` has to say about it:

```
$> file cube
cube: ELF 64-bit LSB pie executable, x86-64,
version 1 (SYSV), dynamically linked, interpreter /
lib64/ld-linux-x86-64.so.2, for GNU/Linux 3.2.0,
BuildID[sha1]=53054824b4a495b7941cbbc95b550e7670481943,
not stripped
```

15. And finally, let's run it to verify that it works:

```
$> ./cube
$> echo $?
64
```

How it works...

In *Step 7* (the first step in the process), we used the `-E` and `-P` options to produce *preprocessed files*. The `-E` option makes GCC stop after preprocessing the files— that is, creating preprocessed files. The `-P` option is an option for the preprocessor not to include line markers in the preprocessed files. We want clean output files.

All `#include` statements include the content of those files in the preprocessed files. Likewise, any macros—such as `NUMBERS`—are replaced by the actual number. Preprocessed files usually have a `.i` extension.

In *Step 9* (the second step in the process), we compiled the preprocessed files. The compilation step creates assembly language files. For this step, we used the `-S` option, which tells GCC to stop after the compilation process is complete. Assembly files usually have a `.s` extension.

In *Step 11* (the third step in the process), we *assembled* the files. This step is also called the *assembly* stage. This step takes the assembly language files and makes *object files*. We will use object files later in this book when we create libraries. The `-c` option tells GCC to stop after the assembly stage (or after compiling). Object files usually have a `.o` extension.

Then, in *Step 13* (the fourth and final step), we *linked* the files, creating a single binary file that we can execute. No options were needed for this since the default action GCC takes is to run through all the steps and, finally, link the files to a single binary file. After we linked the files, we got a running binary file called `cube`:

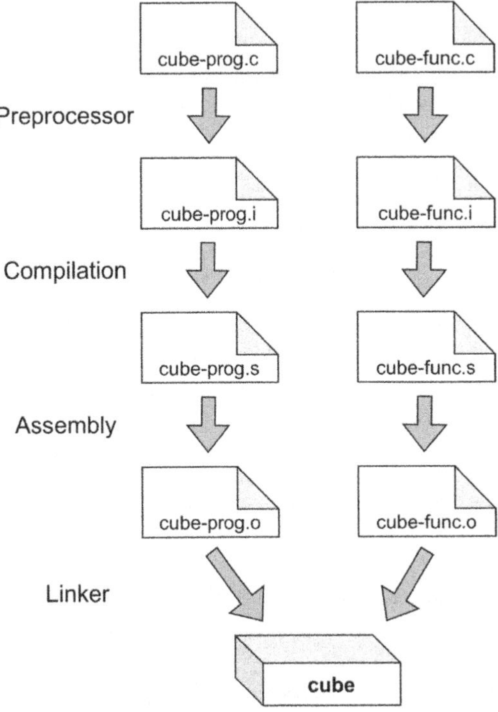

Figure 3.2 – The four stages of compilation

Compiling with Make

We have already seen some example usage with **Make**. Here, we will recap on what Make is and how we can use it to compile programs so that we don't have to type GCC commands.

Getting ready

All you need for this recipe is the GCC compiler and Make. You have already installed these tools if you followed *Chapter 1, Getting the Necessary Tools and Writing Our First Linux Programs.*

How to do it…

We will write a small program that calculates the circumference of a circle, given the radius. We will then use the Make tool to compile it. The Make tool is smart enough to figure out the name of the source code file.

1. Write the following code and save it as `circumference.c`. This program is built on the same code as `mph-to-kph.c` from the previous chapter:

```
#include <stdio.h>
#include <stdlib.h>
#include <string.h>
#define PI 3.14159

int main(void)
{
   char radius[20] = { 0 };

   while(fgets(radius, sizeof(radius), stdin)
      != NULL)
   {
      /* Check if radius is numeric
       * (and do conversion) */
      if( strspn(radius,"0123456789.\n") ==
         strlen(radius) )
      {
         printf("%.5f\n", PI*(atof(radius)*2) );
      }
      /* If radius is NOT numeric, print error
       * and return */
      else
      {
         fprintf(stderr, "Found non-numeric "
            "value\n");
         return 1;
      }
   }
   return 0;
}
```

2. Now, let's compile it with Make:

```
$> make circumference
cc     circumference.c   -o circumference
```

3. If we try to recompile it, it will only tell us that the program is up to date:

```
$> make circumference
make: 'circumference' is up to date
```

4. Add some more decimal places to the PI macro, making it 3.14159265 instead. The fourth line in the code should now look like this:

```
#define PI 3.14159265
```

   Save the file once you have made the changes.

5. If we try to recompile the program now it will do so, since it notices that the code has changed:

```
$> make circumference
cc     circumference.c   -o circumference
```

6. Let's try out the program:

```
$> ./circumference
5
31.41593
10
62.83185
103.3
649.05304
Ctrl+D
```

How it works...

The Make tool is a tool to ease the compilation of larger projects, but it is useful even for small programs like this.

When we execute `make circumference`, it assumes that we want to build a program called `circumference` and that its source code file is `circumference.c`. It also assumes that our compiler command is `cc` (`cc` is a *link* to `gcc` on most Linux systems), and compiles the program using the `cc circumference.c -o circumference` command. This command is the same that we run for ourselves when we compile a program, except that we have used the real name—`gcc`—instead. In the next recipe, we will learn how to change this default command.

The Make tool is also smart enough not to recompile a program unless it's necessary. This feature comes in handy on massive projects, where it can take several hours to recompile. Only recompiling the changed files saves a lot of time.

Writing a generic Makefile with GCC options

In the previous recipe, we learned that Make compiles a program using the `cc prog.c -o prog` command. In this recipe, we will learn how to change that default command. To control the default command, we write a **Makefile** and place that file in the same directory as the source file.

Writing a generic Makefile for all your projects is an excellent idea since you can then enable `-Wall`, `-Wextra`, and `-pedantic` for all files you compile. With these three options enabled, GCC will warn you about many more errors and irregularities in your code, making your programs better. That is what we will do in this recipe.

Getting ready

In this recipe, we will use the `circumference.c` source code file that we wrote in the previous recipe. If you don't already have the file on your computer, you can download it from `https://github.com/PacktPublishing/Linux-System-Programming-Techniques/blob/master/ch3/circumference.c`.

How to do it...

Here, we will write a generic Makefile that you can use for all your projects to ensure your programs follow the C99 standard and don't contain any apparent errors.

1. Write the following code and save it as a file called `Makefile` in the same directory as `circumference.c`. This Makefile sets your default compiler and some common compiler options:

```
CC=gcc
CFLAGS=-Wall -Wextra -pedantic -std=c99
```

2. Now, remove the `circumference` binary file if you still have it from the previous recipe. If you don't have it, skip ahead.

3. Now, compile the `circumference` program with Make, and notice how the compilation command has changed from the previous recipe. The options we just specified in the Makefile should now be applied:

```
$> make circumference
gcc -Wall -Wextra -pedantic -std=c99    circumference.c
-o circumference
```

4. Run the program to make sure it works:

```
$> ./circumference
5
31.41590
10
62.83180
15
94.24770
Ctrl+D
```

How it works...

The Makefile we created controls the Make behavior. Since this Makefile isn't written for any particular project, it works for all programs in the same directory.

On the first line of the Makefile, we set the compiler to `gcc` using the special `CC` variable. On the second line, we set the flags to the compiler using the special `CFLAGS` variable. We set this variable to `-Wall -Wextra -pedantic -std=c99`.

When we execute `make`, it puts together the `CC` variable and the `CFLAGS` variable, which results in a `gcc -Wall -Wextra -pedantic -std=c99` command. And, as we learned in the previous recipe, Make assumes the binary name we wish to use is the name we gave it. It also assumes the source code file has the same name, but with a `.c` ending.

Even on a small project like this with only one file, Make saves us from typing a long GCC command every time we want to recompile it. And that is what Make is all about: saving us time and energy.

There's more...

If you want to learn more about Make, you can read `man 1 make`. There is even more detailed information in `info make`. If you don't have the `info` command, you'll need to install it first using your package manager as root. The package is called `info` on most Linux distributions.

Writing a simple Makefile

In this recipe, we will learn how to write a Makefile for a specific project. The Makefile we wrote in the previous recipe was generic, but this will be for a single project only. Knowing how to write Makefiles for your projects will save you a lot of time and energy as you start making more complex programs.

Also, including a Makefile in a project is considered good manners. The person downloading your project usually has no idea how to build it. That person only wants to use your program, not be forced to understand how things fit together and how to compile it. After downloading, for example, an open source project, they would expect to be able just to type `make` and `make install` (or possibly also some form of configuration script, but we won't cover that here). The program should then be ready to run.

Getting ready

For this recipe, we will use the `cube` program we made in the *Looking at the four stages of compilation* recipe in this chapter. The source code files we will use are `cube-prog.c`, `cube-func.c`, and `cube.h`. They can all be downloaded from `https://github.com/PacktPublishing/Linux-System-Programming-Techniques/tree/master/ch3`.

Save these three files in a new and separate directory, preferably called `cube`. Make sure you are inside that directory when you create the Makefile.

How to do it...

Before we start writing the code, make sure you are in the directory where you saved the source code files for the `cube` program.

1. Let's create the Makefile for the `cube` program. Save the file as `Makefile`. In this Makefile we have only one *target*, `cube`. Below the target, we have the command that compiles the program:

```
CC=gcc
CFLAGS=-Wall -Wextra -pedantic -std=c99

cube: cube.h cube-prog.c cube-func.c
	$(CC) $(CFLAGS) -o cube cube-prog.c cube-func.c
```

2. Now, it's time to try to build the program using Make:

```
$> make
gcc -Wall -Wextra -pedantic -std=c99 -o cube cube-prog.c
cube-func.c
```

3. And finally, we execute the program. Don't forget to also check the return value:

```
$> ./cube
$> echo $?
64
```

4. If we try to rebuild the program now, it will say that everything is up to date, which it is. Let's try it:

```
$> make
make: 'cube' is up to date.
```

5. But if we change something in one of the source code files, it will rebuild the program. Let's change the `NUMBER` macro to `2`. The second line in the `cube-prog.c` file should now look like this:

```
#define NUMBER 2
```

6. Now, we can recompile the program with Make:

```
$> make
gcc -Wall -Wextra -pedantic -std=c99 -o cube cube-prog.c
cube-func.c
```

7. And then, let's view the changes that are made to our program:

```
$> ./cube
$> echo $?
8
```

8. Now, delete the `cube` program so that we can try to recompile it in the next step:

```
$> rm cube
```

9. Rename one of the source code files—for example, `cube.h` to `cube.p`:

```
$> mv cube.h cube.p
```

10. If we try to recompile it now, Make will protest that it's missing `cube.h` and refuse to go any further:

```
$> make
make: *** No rule to make target 'cube.h', needed by
'cube'.  Stop.
```

How it works...

We have already seen the first two lines in the Makefile. The first one, `CC`, sets the default C compiler to `gcc`. The second one, `CFLAGS`, sets the flags we want to pass to the compiler.

The next line—the one that starts with `cube:`—is called a **target**. Right after the target, on the same line, we list all the files that this target is dependent upon, which are all the source code files and header files.

Below the target, we have an indented line with the following content:

```
$(CC) $(CFLAGS) -o cube cube-prog.c cube-func.c
```

This line is the command that will compile the program. `$(CC)` and `$(CFLAGS)` will be replaced with the content of those variables, which is `gcc` and `-Wall -Wextra -pedantic -std=c99`. Basically, we have just written what we would usually write at the command line, but in a Makefile instead.

In the next recipe, we will learn how to leverage some of the smarter stuff in Make.

Writing a more advanced Makefile

In the previous recipe, we wrote a basic Makefile without using any of its more advanced features. In this recipe, however, we will write a more advanced Makefile, using object files, more variables, dependencies, and other fancy things.

Here, we will create a new program. The program will calculate the area of three different objects: circles, triangles, and rectangles. Each calculation will be performed in its own function, and every function will reside in its own file. On top of that, we will have a function in a separate file for the help text. There will also be a header file that holds all of the function prototypes.

Getting ready

This project will consist of a total of seven files. If you want, you can choose to download all the files from the directory at `https://github.com/PacktPublishing/Linux-System-Programming-Techniques/tree/master/ch3/area`.

Since we will create a Makefile for this project, I really recommend that you place all of the project files in a new and separate directory.

You will also need the Make tool and the GCC compiler installed in *Chapter 1, Getting the Necessary Tools and Writing Our First Linux Programs*.

How to do it...

First of all, we write all of the code files required for this program. Then, we try to compile the program using Make, and finally, we try to run it. Follow along.

1. Let's start by writing a main program file called `area.c`. This is the main part of the program, and it contains the `main()` function:

```
#define _XOPEN_SOURCE 700
#include <stdio.h>
#include <unistd.h>
#include "area.h"

int main(int argc, char *argv[])
{
    int opt;
    /* Sanity check number of options */
    if (argc != 2)
    {
        printHelp(stderr, argv[0]);
        return 1;
    }
    /* Parse command-line options */
    while ((opt = getopt(argc, argv, "crth")) != -1)
    {
        switch(opt)
        {
            case 'c':
                if (circle() == -1)
                {
                    printHelp(stderr, argv[0]);
                    return 1;
                }
                break;
            case 'r':
                if (rectangle() == -1)
                {
                    printHelp(stderr, argv[0]);
                    return 1;
                }
                break;
            case 't':
                if (triangle() == -1)
```

```
                {
                    printHelp(stderr, argv[0]);
                    return 1;
                }
                break;
            case 'h':
                printHelp(stdout, argv[0]);
                return 0;
            default:
                printHelp(stderr, argv[0]);
                return 1;
        }
```

2. Next, we write the header file, called `area.h`. This file contains all of the function prototypes:

```
void printHelp(FILE *stream, char progname[]);
int circle(void);
int rectangle(void);
int triangle(void);
```

3. And now, add the `help` function in its own file, called `help.c`: (Shankar)

```
#include <stdio.h>
void printHelp(FILE *stream, char progname[ ])
{
      fprintf(stream, "\nUsage: %s [-c] [-t] [-r] "
      "[-h]\n"
      "-c calculates the area of a circle\n"
      "-t calculates the area of a triangle\n"
      "-r calculates the area of a rectangle\n"
      "-h shows this help\n"
      "Example: %s -t\n"
      "Enter the height and width of the "
      "triangle: 5 9\n"
      "22.500\n", progname, progname);
}
```

4. Now, let's write a function for calculating the area of a circle. We write this in a file called `circle.c`:

```
#define _XOPEN_SOURCE 700
#include <math.h>
#include <stdio.h>
```

```
int circle(void)
{
    float radius;
    printf("Enter the radius of the circle: ");
    if (scanf("%f", &radius))
    {
        printf("%.3f\n", M_PI*pow(radius, 2));
        return 1;
    }
    else
    {
        return -1;
    }
}
```

5. Next up is a function for calculating the area of a rectangle. We name this file `rectangle.c`:

```
#include <stdio.h>

int rectangle(void)
{
    float length, width;
    printf("Enter the length and width of "
        "the rectangle: ");
    if (scanf("%f %f", &length, &width))
    {
        printf("%.3f\n", length*width);
        return 1;
    }
    else
    {
        return -1;
    }
}
```

6. And the last function is for calculating the area of a triangle. We name this file `triangle.c`:

```
#include <stdio.h>

int triangle(void)
```

```
{
    float height, width;
    printf("Enter the height and width of "
        "the triangle: ");
    if (scanf("%f %f", &height, &width))
    {
        printf("%.3f\n", height*width/2);
        return 1;
    }
    else
    {
        return -1;
    }
}
```

7. Now comes the exciting part: the `Makefile`. Note that the indentations in a Makefile must be precisely one tab character. Note that the `area` target lists all the object files using the `OBJS` variable. The command for this target, `$(CC) -o area $(OBJS) $(LIBS)`, links together all the object files into a single binary, using what's called a linker. But since the linker depends on all the object files, Make builds them first before linking:

```
CC=gcc
CFLAGS=-std=c99 -Wall -Wextra -pedantic
LIBS=-lm
OBJS=area.o help.o rectangle.o triangle.o circle.o
DEPS=area.h
bindir=/usr/local/bin

area: $(OBJS)
	$(CC) -o area $(OBJS) $(LIBS)

area.o: $(DEPS)

clean:
	rm area $(OBJS)

install: area
	install -g root -o root area $(bindir)/area

uninstall: $(bindir)/area
	rm $(bindir)/area
```

8. Finally, we can try to compile this entire program by typing `make`. Note that you must be in the same directory as the source code files and the Makefile. Notice here that all the object files get compiled first, then they are linked in the final step:

```
$> make
gcc -std=c99 -Wall -Wextra -pedantic   -c -o area.o
area.c
gcc -std=c99 -Wall -Wextra -pedantic   -c -o help.o
help.c
gcc -std=c99 -Wall -Wextra -pedantic   -c -o rectangle.o
rectangle.c
gcc -std=c99 -Wall -Wextra -pedantic   -c -o triangle.o
triangle.c
gcc -std=c99 -Wall -Wextra -pedantic   -c -o circle.o
circle.c
gcc -o area area.o help.o rectangle.o triangle.o circle.o
-lm
```

9. And now, let's try out the program. Test all the different functions:

```
$> ./area -c
Enter the radius of the circle: 9
254.469
$> ./area -t
Enter the height and width of the triangle: 9 4
18.000
$> ./area -r
Enter the length and width of the rectangle: 5.5 4.9
26.950
$> ./area -r
Enter the length and width of the rectangle: abcde

Usage: ./area [-c] [-t] [-r] [-h]
-c calculates the area of a circle
-t calculates the area of a triangle
-r calculates the area of a rectangle
-h shows this help
Example: ./area -t
Enter the height and width of the triangle: 5 9
22.500
```

10. Now, let's pretend we have changed some part of the `circle.c` file by updating its timestamp. We can update the timestamp of a file by running `touch` on it:

```
$> touch circle.c
```

11. Now, we rebuild the program. Compare the output from *Step 8*, where all the object files were compiled. This time, the only file that gets recompiled is `circle.o`. After the recompilation of `circle.o`, the binary is relinked into a single binary:

```
$> make
gcc -std=c99 -Wall -Wextra -pedantic    -c -o circle.o
circle.c
gcc -o area area.o help.o rectangle.o triangle.o circle.o
-lm
```

12. Now, let's try to install the program on the system by using the `install` target. For this to succeed, you need to run it as root using either `su` or `sudo`:

```
$> sudo make install
install -g root -o root area /usr/local/bin/area
```

13. Let's uninstall the program from the system. It's good practice to include an `uninstall` target, especially if the `install` target installs lots and lots of files on the system:

```
$> sudo make uninstall
rm /usr/local/bin/area
```

14. Let's also try the target called `clean`. This will delete all the object files and the binary file. It's good practice to include a target for cleaning up object files and other temporary files:

```
$> make clean
rm area area.o help.o rectangle.o triangle.o circle.o
```

How it works...

Even though the program example for this recipe was rather big, it's a pretty straightforward program. There are some parts of it, though, that are worth commenting on.

All of the C files get compiled to object files independently of each other. That's the reason why we need to include `stdio.h` in every single file that uses `printf()` or `scanf()`.

In the `circle.c` file, we have included the `math.h` header file. This header file is for the `pow()` function. We also defined `_XOPEN_SOURCE` with a value of `700`. The reason is that the `M_PI` macro that holds the value of Pi isn't included in the C standard but it is, on the other hand, included in the **X/Open** standard.

The Makefile

Now, it's time to discuss the Makefile in greater detail. We have already seen the first two variables, `CC` and `CFLAGS`, in previous recipes, but notice that we haven't used the `CFLAGS` variable anywhere in the code. We don't need to. `CFLAGS` is automatically applied when compiling the object files. If we had applied the `CFLAGS` variable manually after the `CC` variable in the command for the `area` target, those flags would also have been used for the linking process. In other words, the command we have specified for the target called `area` is just for the linking stage. The compilation of the object files happens automatically. Since the object files are a dependency, Make tries to figure out how to build them all on its own.

When we run Make without specifying a target, Make will run the first target in the Makefile. That's the reason why we put the `area` target first in the file, so that when we simply type `make`, the program is built.

Then, we have `LIBS=-lm`. This variable is added to the end of the `area` target to link against the math library, but do note that it is only the linker that makes use of this. Look at the output in *Step 8*. All the object files are compiled as usual, but at the last stage, when the linker assembles all the object files in to a single binary, `-lm` is added at the end.

Then, we have the following line:

```
OBJS=area.o help.o rectangle.o triangle.o circle.o
```

This variable lists all the object files. This is where Make gets really smart. The first place where we use `OBJS` is the dependency for the `area` target. To put together the `area` binary program, we need all of the object files.

The next place where we use `OBJS` is in the build command for the `area` binary. Note that we don't specify the C files here, only the object files (via `OBJS`). Make is smart enough to figure out that to build the binary, we first need the object files, and to compile the object files, we need the C files with the same names as the object files. Therefore, we don't need to spell out the entire command with all the source code files. Make figures this out all on its own.

The next new variable is `DEPS`. In this variable, we list the header file required to build the `area.o` object file. We specify this dependency on the `area.o: $(DEPS)` line. This target doesn't contain any command; we just use it to verify the dependency.

The final variable is `bindir`, which contains the full path to where the binary file should be installed. This variable is used in the `install` and `uninstall` targets, which we will discuss next.

We have already covered the `area` and `area.o` targets in the discussion about variables. So, let's move on to the `clean`, `install`, and `uninstall` targets. These targets are common in most projects. It's considered good manners to include them. They have nothing to do with compiling and building the program, but they help the end user to install and uninstall the software on the system. The `clean` target helps the end user in keeping the source code directory clean from temporary files such as object files. The commands under each of these targets are typical Linux commands, combined with the variables we have already covered.

The `install` command used in the `install` target copies the `area` file to where `bindir` points (`/usr/local/bin` in our case). It also sets the user and group for the installed file.

Note that we have specified dependencies for the `install` and `uninstall` targets (the dependency is the file that is to be installed or removed). This makes sense; there is no need to run these commands if the file doesn't exist. But for the `clean` target, we didn't specify any dependency. It could happen that the user has already deleted *some* of the object files themself. When they run `make clean`, they don't want the entire target to fail but to continue removing any leftover files.

4 Handling Errors in Your Programs

In this chapter, we will learn about **error handling** in C programs in Linux—specifically, how to catch errors and print relevant information about them. We will also learn how to incorporate this knowledge with what we have previously learned about **stdin**, **stdout**, and **stderr**.

We will continue on the path of system calls and learn about a particular variable called **errno**. Most system calls use this variable to save specific error values when an error occurs.

Handling errors in your programs will make them more stable. Errors do occur; it's just a matter of handling them correctly. A well-handled error does not seem like an error to the end user. For example, instead of letting your program crash in some mysterious way when the hard drive is filled, it's better to catch the error and print a human-readable and friendly message about it. That way, it merely appears as information to the end user and not an error. That, in turn, will make your programs seem friendlier and, most of all, more stable.

In this chapter, we will cover the following recipes:

- Why error handling is important in system programming
- Handling some common errors

- Error handling and `errno`
- Handling more `errno` macros
- Using `errno` with `strerror()`
- Using errno with `perror()`
- Returning an error value

Let's get started!

Technical requirements

For this chapter, you'll need the GCC compiler, the Make tool, and all the manual pages (dev and POSIX) installed. We covered how to install GCC and Make in *Chapter 1, Getting the Necessary Tools and Writing Our First Linux Programs*, and the manual pages in *Chapter 3, Diving Deep into C in Linux*. You will also need the generic Makefile that we created in *Chapter 3, Diving Deep into C in Linux*. Place that file in the same directory as the code you are writing for this chapter. You'll find a copy of that file—along with all other source code files we will write here—in the GitHub folder for this chapter, at `https://github.com/PacktPublishing/Linux-System-Programming-Techniques/tree/master/ch4`.

Check out the following link to see the Code in Action video: `https://bit.ly/3iE1W17`

Why error handling is important in system programming

This recipe is a short introduction to what error handling is. We will also see an example of a common error: *insufficient access rights*. Knowing these basic skills will make you a better programmer in the long run.

Getting ready

For this recipe, you'll only need the GCC compiler, preferably installed via the meta-package or group install, as we covered in *Chapter 1, Getting the Necessary Tools and Writing Our First Linux Programs*. Make sure that the Makefile mentioned in the *Technical requirements* section is placed in the same directory as the source code for this recipe.

How to do it...

Follow these steps to explore a common error and how to handle it:

1. First, we will write the program without any **error handling** (except the usual sanity checks for the arguments). Write the following program and save it as `simple-touch-v1.c`. The program will create an empty file that the user specifies as an argument. The `PATH_MAX` macro is new to us. It contains the maximum number of characters we can use in a path on our Linux system. It's defined in the `linux/limits.h` header file:

```
#include <stdio.h>
#include <fcntl.h>
#include <string.h>
#include <linux/limits.h>

int main(int argc, char *argv[])
{
    char filename[PATH_MAX] = { 0 };
    if (argc != 2)
    {
        fprintf(stderr, "You must supply a filename "
            "as an argument\n");
        return 1;
    }
    strncpy(filename, argv[1], PATH_MAX-1);
    creat(filename, 00644);
    return 0;
}
```

2. Compile the program:

```
$> make simple-touch-v1
gcc -Wall -Wextra -pedantic -std=c99    simple-touch-v1.c
-o simple-touch-v1
```

3. Now, let's try to run the program and see what happens. If we don't give it any arguments, it will print an error message and return `1`. When we give it a file that doesn't exist, it will create it with the permissions 644 (we'll cover permissions in the next chapter):

```
$> ./simple-touch-v1
You must supply a filename as an argument
$> ./simple-touch-v1 my-test-file
```

```
$> ls -l my-test-file
-rw-r--r-- 1 jake jake 0 okt 12 22:46 my-test-file
```

4. Let's see what happens if we try to create a file outside of our home directory; that is, a directory where we don't have write permissions:

```
$> ./simple-touch-v1 /abcd1234
```

5. This seems to have worked since it didn't complain—but it hasn't. Let's try to check out the file:

```
$> ls -l /abcd1234
ls: cannot access '/abcd1234': No such file or directory
```

6. Let's rewrite the file so that it prints an error message—*Couldn't create file*—to stderr in case `creat()` fails to create a file. To accomplish this, we wrap the entire call to `creat()` in an `if` statement. Name the new version `simple-touch-v2.c`. The changes from the previous version are highlighted here:

```
#include <stdio.h>
#include <fcntl.h>
#include <string.h>
#include <linux/limits.h>

int main(int argc, char *argv[])
{
   char filename[PATH_MAX] = { 0 };
   if (argc != 2)
   {
      fprintf(stderr, "You must supply a filename "
         "as an argument\n");
      return 1;
   }
   strncpy(filename, argv[1], PATH_MAX-1);
   if ( creat(filename, 00644) == -1 )
   {
      fprintf(stderr, "Can't create file %s\n",
         filename);
      return 1;
   }
   return 0;
}
```

7. Compile the new version:

```
$> make simple-touch-v2
gcc -Wall -Wextra -pedantic -std=c99    simple-touch-v2.c
-o simple-touch-v2
```

8. Finally, let's rerun it, both with a file that we can create and one that we can't. When we try to create a file that we don't have permission to, we will get an error message stating *Couldn't create file*:

```
$> ./simple-touch-v2 hello123
$> ./simple-touch-v2 /abcd1234
Couldn't create file /abcd1234
```

How it works...

In this recipe, we used a system call, `creat()`, that creates a file on the filesystem. The function takes two arguments: the first is the file to be created, while the second is which file access mode the newly created file shall have. In this case, we set the file's **access mode** to `644`, which is read and write for the user who owns the file, and read for the owner's group and all others. We will cover file access modes in more depth in *Chapter 5, Working with File I/O and Filesystem Operations.*

Nothing "bad" will happen if it can't create the file we ask it to create. It just returns -1 to the calling function (`main()` in this case). This means that in the first version of our program, it seems like everything has worked just fine and that the file has been created when, in fact, it hasn't. It's up to us, as programmers, to catch that return code and act on it. We can find the return values of the function in its manual page, `man 2 creat`.

In the second version of the program, we added an `if` statement to check for `-1`. If the function returns -1, an error message is printed to stderr, and 1 is returned to the shell. We have now informed both the user and any programs that might depend on this program to create a file.

Fetching the return values of functions is the most common—and most straightforward—way to check for errors. We should all make this a habit.
As soon as we use some function, we should check its return value (as long as it's reasonable, of course).

Handling some common errors

In this recipe, we will look at some common errors we can handle. Knowing what errors to look for is step one of mastering error handling. A police officer can't catch the bad guys if they don't know which crimes to look for.

We will look at both errors that can occur due to resource limitations on a computer, permission errors, and mathematical errors. It's important to remember, though, that most functions return a special value (often -1 or some predefined value) when errors occur. The actual data is returned when no errors occur.

We will also briefly touch on the subject of handling buffer overflows. Buffer overflows are a vast subject that deserves a book of its own, but some short examples can help.

Getting ready

In this recipe, we'll write shorter code samples and compile them with GCC and Make. We'll also read some man pages from the *POSIX Programmer's Manual*. If you are using Debian or Ubuntu, you have to install these manual pages first, which we did in the *Getting information about Linux- and Unix-specific header files* section of *Chapter 3, Diving Deep into C in Linux*.

How to do it...

The easiest way to find errors that are most likely to occur when using a specific function is to read the **RETURN VALUE** section of the function's manual page. Here, we will look at some examples:

1. Most **system calls** return -1 when an error occurs, and most—but not all—of these errors have something to do with resource limitations or access rights. For example, take a look at the manual pages for these system call functions: `creat()`, `open()`, and `write()`. Look under the **RETURN VALUE** heading. Note that all of these return -1 on an error and set something called `errno` with more specific information. We will cover `errno` later in this chapter.

2. Now, take a look at the manual page for the power function, `pow()`. Scroll down to the **RETURN VALUE** header. There are a lot of different possible return values. But since the `pow()` function returns the answer to a calculation, it can't return 0 or -1 if an error occurs; this could be the answer to some calculation. Instead, some special numbers are defined that are referred to as `HUGE_VAL`, `HUGE_VALF`, and `HUGE_VALL`. On most systems, though, these are defined as infinity. However, we can still use these macros to test for them, as shown in the following example. Name the file `huge-test.c`:

```
#include <stdio.h>
#include <math.h>

int main(void)
{
    int number = 9999;
    double answer;
    if ( (answer = pow(number, number)) == HUGE_VAL )
    {
        fprintf(stderr, "A huge value\n");
        return 1;
    }
    else
    {
        printf("%lf\n", answer);
    }
    return 0;
}
```

3. Compile the program and test it. Remember to link to the `math` library with `-lm`:

```
$> gcc -Wall -Wextra -pedantic huge-test.c \
> -o huge-test -lm
$> ./huge-test
A huge value
```

4. Other errors that can occur that don't give us return values are mostly overflow errors. This is especially true when handling **user input**. User input should always be handled carefully. Most string functions have an equivalent *n* function, which is safer. For example, `strcat()` has `strncat()`, `strdup()` has `strndup()`, and so on. Use these whenever possible. Write the following program and name it `str-unsafe.c`:

```
#include <stdio.h>
#include <string.h>

int main(int argc, char *argv[])
{
    char buf[10] = { 0 };
    strcat(buf, argv[1]);
    printf("Text: %s\n", buf);
    return 0;
}
```

5. Now, compile it using Make (and the Makefile that we have placed in this directory). Notice that we will get a warning from the compiler here since we aren't using the `argc` variable. This warning comes from the `-Wextra` option to GCC. However, this is just a warning stating that we never used `argc` in our code, so we can ignore this message. Always read the warning messages; sometimes, things may be more severe:

```
$> make str-unsafe
gcc -Wall -Wextra -pedantic -std=c99    str-unsafe.c    -o 
str-unsafe
str-unsafe.c: In function 'main':
str-unsafe.c:4:14: warning: unused parameter 'argc' 
[-Wunused-parameter]
 int main(int argc, char *argv[])
          ~~~~^~~~
```

6. Now, test this with different input lengths. If we don't provide any input at all or if we give it too much input (more than 9 characters), a segmentation fault will occur:

```
$> ./str-unsafe
Segmentation fault
$> ./str-unsafe hello
Text: hello
$> ./str-unsafe "hello! how are you doing?"
```

```
Text: hello! how are you doing?
Segmentation fault
```

7. Let's rewrite the program. First, we must make sure the user typed in an argument; second, we must replace `strcat()` with `strncat()`. Name the new version `str-safe.c`:

```
#include <stdio.h>
#include <string.h>

int main(int argc, char *argv[])
{
    if (argc != 2)
    {
        fprintf(stderr, "Supply exactly one "
            "argument\n");
        return 1;
    }
    char buf[10] = { 0 };
    strncat(buf, argv[1], sizeof(buf)-1);
    printf("Test: %s\n", buf);
    return 0;
}
```

8. Compile it. This time, we won't get a warning about `argc` since we're using it in the code:

```
$> make str-safe
gcc -Wall -Wextra -pedantic -std=c99    str-safe.c   -o
str-safe
```

9. Let's run it with various input lengths. Notice how the long text gets cut off at the ninth character, preventing a segmentation fault. Also, note that we have handled the segmentation fault on an empty input by requiring precisely one argument:

```
$> ./str-safe
Supply exactly one argument
$> ./str-safe hello
Text: hello
$> ./str-safe "hello, how are you doing?"
Text: hello, ho
$> ./str-safe asdfasdfasdfasdfasdfasdfasdfasdf
Text: asdfasdfa
```

How it works...

In *Step 2*, we looked at some manual pages to get a feel for what kind of errors we can expect to handle when dealing with them. Here, we learned that most system calls return -1 on errors and that most errors have something to do with either permissions or system resources.

In *Steps 2* and *3*, we saw how math functions can return special numbers on errors (since the usual numbers—0, 1, and -1—can be valid answers to a calculation).

In *Steps 4* to *9*, we briefly touched on the subject of handling user input and **buffer overflows**. Here, we learned that functions such as `strcat()`, `strcpy()`, and `strdup()` are unsafe since they copy whatever they get, even though the destination buffer doesn't have enough space for it. When we gave the program a string longer than 10 characters (nine actually, since the `NULL` character takes up one place), the program crashed with a *segmentation fault*.

These *str* functions have equivalent functions with *n* characters in their name; for example, `strncat()`. These functions only copy the size given to them as the third argument. In our example, we specified the size as `sizeof(buf)-1`, which in our program is 9. The reason we used one less than the actual size of `buf` is to make room for the null-terminating character (`\0`) at the end. It's better to use `sizeof(buf)` than to use a literal number. If we would have used the literal number 9 here and then changed the size of the buffer to 5, we would most likely forget to update the number for `strncat()`.

Error handling and errno

Most of the system call functions in Linux and other UNIX-like systems set a special variable called **errno** when an error occurs. This way, we get a general error code from the return value (often -1) and then more specific information about what went wrong by looking at the `errno` variable.

In this recipe, we'll learn what `errno` is, how to read values from it, and when it is set. We'll also see an example use case of `errno`. Learning about `errno` is imperative to system programming, primarily since it's used in conjunction with system calls.

The next few recipes in this chapter are closely tied to this recipe. In this recipe, we'll learn about `errno`; in the following three recipes, we'll learn how to interpret the error codes we get from `errno` and print human-readable error messages.

Getting ready

You'll need the same components for this recipe that we used in the previous one; that is, the GCC compiler, the Make tool, and the *POSIX Programmer's Manual*, all of which we have already installed. If not, see *Chapter 1, Getting the Necessary Tools and Writing Our First Linux Programs*, and the *Getting information about Linux- and UNIX-specific header files* section of *Chapter 3, Diving Deep into C in Linux*.

How to do it...

In this recipe, we'll continue building on `simple-touch-v2.c` from the first recipe in this chapter. Here, we'll extend it so that it prints some more useful information if it can't create a file:

1. Write the following code into a file and save it as `simple-touch-v3.c`. In this version, we'll use the `errno` variable to check if the error is caused by a permission error (`EACCES`) or some other, unknown error. The changed code has been highlighted here:

```
#include <stdio.h>
#include <fcntl.h>
#include <string.h>
#include <errno.h>
#include <linux/limits.h>

int main(int argc, char *argv[])
{
    char filename[PATH_MAX] = { 0 };
    if (argc != 2)
    {
        fprintf(stderr, "You must supply a filename "
            "as an argument\n");
        return 1;
    }
    strncpy(filename, argv[1], sizeof(filename)-1);
    if ( creat(filename, 00644) == -1 )
    {
        fprintf(stderr, "Can't create file %s\n",
            filename);
        if (errno == EACCES)
        {
            fprintf(stderr, "Permission denied\n");
        }
```

```
        else
        {
            fprintf(stderr, "Unknown error\n");
        }
        return 1;
    }
    return 0;
}
```

2. Let's compile this version:

```
$> make simple-touch-v3
gcc -Wall -Wextra -pedantic -std=c99    simple-touch-v3.c
-o simple-touch-v3
```

3. Finally, let's run the new version. This time, the program gives us more information about what went wrong. If it's a permission error, it will tell us that. Otherwise, it will print `Unknown error`:

```
$> ./simple-touch-v3 asdf
$> ls -l asdf
-rw-r--r-- 1 jake jake 0 okt 13 23:30 asdf
$> ./simple-touch-v3 /asdf
Can't create file /asdf
Permission denied
$> ./simple-touch-v3 /non-existent-dir/hello
Can't create file /non-existent-dir/hello
Unknown error
```

How it works...

The first difference we'll notice in this version is that we now include a header file called `errno.h`. This file is required if we wish to use the `errno` variable and the many error **macros**. One of these macros is `EACCES`, which we used in our new version.

The next difference is that we now use `sizeof(filename)-1` instead of `PATH_MAX-1` for the size argument to `strncpy()`. This was something we learned in the previous recipe.

Then, we have the `if (errno == EACCES)` line, which checks the `errno` variable for `EACCES`. We can read about these macros, such as `EACCES`, in both `man errno.h` and `man 2 creat`. This particular macro means *permission denied*.

When we use `errno`, we should first check the return value from the function or system call, as we did here with the `if` statement around `creat()`. The `errno` variable is just like any other variable, meaning that it isn't cleared after the system call. If we were to check `errno` directly, before checking the function's return value, `errno` could contain an error code from a previous error.

In our version of `touch`, we only handle this specific error. Next, we have an `else` statement, which catches all other errors and prints an `Unknown error` message.

In *Step 3*, we generated an `Unknown error` message by trying to create a file in a directory that doesn't exist on our system. In the next recipe, we'll extend our program so that it can take more macros into account.

Handling more errno macros

We'll continue to handle more `errno` macros in our version of `touch` in this recipe. In the previous recipe, we managed to provoke an `Unknown error` message since we only handled permission denied errors. Here, we'll find out what exactly caused that error and what it is called. We'll then implement another `if` statement to handle it. Knowing how to find the correct `errno` macros will help you gain a deeper understanding of computing, Linux, system calls, and error handling.

Getting ready

Once again, we'll examine the manual pages to find the information we are looking for. The only things that are needed for this recipe are the manual pages, the GCC compiler, and the Make tool.

How to do it...

Follow these steps to complete this recipe:

1. Start by reading the manual page for `creat()` by using `man 2 creat`. Scroll down to the **ERRORS** heading. Read through the descriptions of the different macros. Eventually, you'll find one that talks about *pathname does not exist*. The name of that macro is `ENOENT` (short for *Error No Entry*).

2. Let's implement a new `if` statement that handles `ENOENT`. Name the new version `simple-touch-v4.c`. The complete program is as follows. The changes from the previous version are highlighted here. Also, note that we have removed the brackets for some of the `if` statements in the highlighted code:

```
#include <stdio.h>
#include <fcntl.h>
#include <string.h>
#include <errno.h>
#include <linux/limits.h>

int main(int argc, char *argv[])
{
   char filename[PATH_MAX] = { 0 };
   if (argc != 2)
   {
      fprintf(stderr, "You must supply a filename "
         "as an argument\n");
      return 1;
   }
   strncpy(filename, argv[1], sizeof(filename)-1);
   if ( creat(filename, 00644) == -1 )
   {
      fprintf(stderr, "Can't create file %s\n",
         filename);
      if (errno == EACCES)
         fprintf(stderr, "Permission denied\n");
      else if (errno == ENOENT)
         fprintf(stderr, "Parent directories does "
            "not exist\n");
      else
         fprintf(stderr, "Unknown error\n");
      return 1;
   }
   return 0;
}
```

3. Compile the new version:

```
$> make simple-touch-v4
gcc -Wall -Wextra -pedantic -std=c99    simple-touch-v4.c
-o simple-touch-v4
```

4. Let's run it and generate some errors. This time, it will print an error message when the directory does not exist:

```
$> ./simple-touch-v4 asdf123
$> ./simple-touch-v4 /hello
Can't create file /hello
Permission denied
$> ./simple-touch-v4 /non-existent/hello
Can't create file /non-existent/hello
Parent directories do not exist
```

How it works...

In this version, I removed the brackets from the inner `if`, `else if`, and `else` statements to save space. This is valid code if there is only one statement under each of the `if`, `else if`, and `else`. However, this is potentially dangerous since it's easy to make a mistake. If we were to write more statements in one of the `if` statements, those would not be a part of the `if` statement, even though it looks correct and compiles with no errors. The name for this is *misleading indentation*. The indentation fools the brain, thinking it's right.

The next new thing in the code is the `else if (errno == ENOENT)` line and the lines below it. This is where we handle the `ENOENT` error macro.

There's more...

Almost all of the functions listed in `man 2 syscalls` set the `errno` variable. Take a look at some of the manual pages for these functions and scroll down to **RETURN VALUE** and **ERRORS**. Here you'll find which `errno` macros the different functions sets.

Also, read `man errno.h`, which contains useful information about these macros.

Using errno with strerror()

Instead of looking up every possible errno macro and figuring out which ones apply and what they mean, it's easier to use a function called `strerror()`. This function converts the `errno` code into a readable message. Using `strerror()` is much faster than implementing everything ourselves. It's a lot safer, too, since there's less of a risk that we mess something up. Whenever there's a function available to ease the manual work for us, we should use it.

Do note that this function is meant to convert the `errno` macro into a readable error message. If we want to handle a particular error in some specific way, we still need to use the actual `errno` value.

Getting ready

The requirements from the previous recipe apply to this recipe. This means we need the GCC compiler, the Make tool (along with the Makefile), and the manual pages.

How to do it...

In this recipe, we'll continue developing our own version of `touch`. We'll continue from the previous version. This time, we will rewrite the `if` statements we made for the different macros and use `strerror()` instead. Let's get started:

1. Write the following code and save it as `simple-touch-v5.c`. Notice how the code has been smaller now that we have replaced the `if` statements with `strerror()`. This version is much cleaner. The changes from the previous version are highlighted here:

```
#include <stdio.h>
#include <fcntl.h>
#include <string.h>
#include <errno.h>
#include <linux/limits.h>

int main(int argc, char *argv[])
{
    int errornum;
    char filename[PATH_MAX] = { 0 };
    if (argc != 2)
    {
        fprintf(stderr, "You must supply a filename "
            "as an argument\n");
        return 1;
    }
    strncpy(filename, argv[1], sizeof(filename)-1);
    if ( creat(filename, 00644) == -1 )
    {
        errornum = errno;
        fprintf(stderr, "Can't create file %s\n",
            filename);
```

```
        fprintf(stderr, "%s\n", strerror(errornum));
        return 1;
    }
    return 0;
}
```

2. Compile this new version:

```
$> make simple-touch-v5
gcc -Wall -Wextra -pedantic -std=c99    simple-touch-v5.c
-o simple-touch-v5
```

3. Let's try it out. Notice how the program now prints error messages describing what has gone wrong. We didn't even have to check the errno variable against possible errors:

```
$> ./simple-touch-v5 hello123
$> ls hello123
hello123
$> ./simple-touch-v5 /asdf123
Can't create file /asdf123
Permission denied
$> ./simple-touch-v5 /asdf123/hello
Can't create file /asdf123/hello
No such file or directory
How it works…
```

All the `if`, `else if`, and `else` statements have now been replaced with a single line of code:

```
fprintf(stderr, "%s\n", strerror(error));
```

We have also saved the value from `errno` in a new variable called `errornum`. We did this because on the next error that occurs, the value in `errno` will be overwritten by the new error code. To safeguard against showing the wrong error message in case `errno` gets overwritten, it's safer to save it to a new variable.

We then used the error code stored in `errornum` as an argument to a new function called `strerror()`. This function translates the error code into a human-readable error message and returns that message as a string. That way, we don't have to create `if` statements ourselves for every possible error that can occur.

In *Step 3*, we saw how `strerror()` had translated the `EACCES` macros into *Permission denied*, and `ENOENT` into *No such file or directory*.

There's more...

In the `man 3 strerror` manual page, you'll find a similar function that can print error messages in the user's preferred locale.

Using errno with perror()

In the previous recipe, we used `strerror()` to get a string containing a human-readable error message from `errno`. There's another function similar to `strerr()` called `perror()`. Its name stands for **print error**, and that's what it does; it prints the error message directly to *stderr*.

In this recipe, we'll write the sixth version of our simple touch program. This time, we'll replace both of the `fprinf()` lines with `perror()`.

Getting ready

The only programs necessary for this recipe are the GCC compiler and the Make tool (along with the generic Makefile).

How to do it...

Follow these steps to create an even shorter and better version of `simple-touch`:

1. Write the following code into a file and save it as `simple-touch-v6.c`. This time, the program is even smaller. We have removed the two `fprintf()` statements and replaced them with `perror()` instead. The changes from the previous version are highlighted here:

```
#include <stdio.h>
#include <fcntl.h>
#include <string.h>
#include <errno.h>
#include <linux/limits.h>

int main(int argc, char *argv[])
{
   char filename[PATH_MAX] = { 0 };
   if (argc != 2)
   {
      fprintf(stderr, "You must supply a filename "
         "as an argument\n");
      return 1;
```

```
    }
    strncpy(filename, argv[1], sizeof(filename)-1);
    if ( creat(filename, 00644) == -1 )
    {
        perror("Can't create file");
        return 1;
    }
    return 0;
}
```

2. Compile it using Make:

```
$> make simple-touch-v6
gcc -Wall -Wextra -pedantic -std=c99    simple-touch-v6.c
-o simple-touch-v6
```

3. Run it and witness the change in the error message's output:

```
$> ./simple-touch-v6 abc123
$> ./simple-touch-v6 /asdf123
Can't create file: Permission denied
$> ./simple-touch-v6 /asdf123/hello
Can't create file: No such file or directory
How it works…
```

This time, we have replaced both the `fprintf()` lines with a single line:

```
perror("Can't create file");
```

The `perror()` function takes one argument, a string with a description or function name. In this case, I chose to give it the generic error message `Can't create file`. When `perror()` prints the error message, it grabs the last error code in `errno` (notice we didn't specify any error code variable) and applies that error message after the text `Can't create file`. Hence, we don't need the `fprintf()` lines anymore.

Even though `errno` isn't explicitly stated in the call to `perror()`, it still uses it. If another error occurs, then the next call to `perror()` will print that error message instead. The `perror()` function always prints the *last* error.

There's more…

There are some great tips in the manual page, `man 3 perror`. For example, it's a good idea to include the name of the function that caused the error. This makes it easier to debug the program when users are reporting bugs.

Returning an error value

Even though human-readable error messages are important, we must not forget to return a value to the shell that indicates an error. We have already seen that returning 0 means that everything is okay, while returning something else (most of the time, 1) means that some kind of error did occur. However, we can return more specific values if we want so that other programs relying on our program can read those numbers. For example, we can actually return the `errno` variable since it is just an integer. All the macros we have seen, such as `EACCES` and `ENOENT`, are integers (13 and 2 for `EACCES` and `ENOENT`, respectively).

In this recipe, we will learn how to return the `errno` numbers to the shell to provide more specific information.

Getting ready

The same set of programs mentioned in the previous recipe apply to this recipe.

How to do it...

In this recipe, we will make the seventh version of our `simple-touch` program. Let's get started:

1. We are only going to change a single line in this version from the previous one. Open up `simple-touch-v6.c` and change the `return` statement just below the `perror()` line to `return errno;`. Save the new file as `simple-touch-v7.c`. The latest version is as follows, with the changed line highlighted:

```
#include <stdio.h>
#include <fcntl.h>
#include <string.h>
#include <errno.h>
#include <linux/limits.h>

int main(int argc, char *argv[])
{
   char filename[PATH_MAX] = { 0 };
   if (argc != 2)
   {
      fprintf(stderr, "You must supply a filename "
         "as an argument\n");
      return 1;
   }
```

```
    strncpy(filename, argv[1], sizeof(filename)-1);
    if ( creat(filename, 00644) == -1 )
    {
       perror("Can't create file");
       return errno;
    }
    return 0;
}
```

2. Compile the new version:

```
$> make simple-touch-v7
gcc -Wall -Wextra -pedantic -std=c99    simple-touch-v7.c
-o simple-touch-v7
```

3. Run it and check the exit codes:

```
$> ./simple-touch-v7 asdf
$> echo $
0
$> ./simple-touch-v7 /asdf
Can't create file: Permission denied
$> echo $?
13
$> ./simple-touch-v7 /asdf/hello123
Can't create file: No such file or directory
$> echo $?
2
```

How it works...

The error macros defined in `errno.h` are regular integers. So, if we, for example, return `EACCES`, we return the number 13. So, what is happening here (when an error occurs) is that, first, `errno` is set behind the scenes. Then, `perror()` uses the value stored in `errno` to print a human-readable error message. Finally, the program returns to the shell with the integer stored in `errno`, indicating to other programs what went wrong. We should be a bit careful with this, though, since there are some reserved return values. For example, in the shell, the return value `2` often means *Missuse of shell builtins*. However, in `errno`, the return value `2` means *No such file or directory* (`ENOENT`). This shouldn't cause you too much trouble, but keep it in mind just in case.

There's more...

There is a small program called `errno` that can print all macros and their integers. This tool isn't installed by default, though. The name of the package is `moreutils`.

Once installed, you can print a list of all the macros by running the `errno -l` command, where the `l` option stands for *list*.

To install the package in *Debian* and *Ubuntu*, type `apt install moreutils` as root.

To install the package in *Fedora*, use `dnf install moreutils` as root.

On *CentOS* and *Red Hat*, you must first add the `epel-release` repository with `dnf install epel-release`, then install the package with `dnf install moreutils` as root. At the time of writing, there are some dependency issues with CentOS 8 regarding `moreutils`, so it might not work.

5
Working with File I/O and Filesystem Operations

File I/O is an important part of system programming since most programs must read or write data to and from files. Doing file I/O also requires the developer to know a thing or two about the filesystem.

Mastering file I/O and filesystem operations will make you not only a better programmer but also a better system administrator.

In this chapter, we will learn about the Linux filesystem and inodes. We will also learn how to read and write files on the system, using both streams and file descriptors. We will also look at system calls to create and delete files and change file permissions and ownership. At the end of the chapter, we will learn how to fetch information about files.

In this chapter, we will cover the following recipes:

- Reading inode information and learning the filesystem
- Creating soft links and hard links
- Creating files and updating the timestamp

- Deleting files
- Getting access rights and ownership
- Setting access rights and ownership
- Writing to files with file descriptors
- Reading from files with file descriptors
- Writing to files with streams
- Reading from files with streams
- Reading and writing binary data with streams
- Moving around inside a file with `lseek()`
- Moving around inside a file with `fseek()`

Technical requirements

For this chapter, you'll need the GCC compiler, the Make tool, and the generic Makefile we made in the *Writing a generic Makefile with GCC options* recipe in *Chapter 3, Diving Deep into C in Linux. Chapter 1, Getting the Necessary Tools and Writing Our First Linux Programs*, covers installing the compiler and the Make tool.

The generic Makefile, along with all the source code examples for this chapter, can be downloaded from GitHub at this URL: `https://github.com/PacktPublishing/Linux-System-Programming-Techniques/tree/master/ch5`.

We are going to look up functions and header files in the built-in manual in Linux. If you are using Debian or Ubuntu, the Linux Programmer's Manual is installed as part of the *build-essentials* meta-package, covered in *Chapter 1, Getting the Necessary Tools and Writing Our First Linux Programs*. You'll also need to install the *POSIX Programmer's Manual*, covered in the *Getting information about Linux and Unix-specific header files* recipe in *Chapter 3, Diving Deep into C in Linux*. If you are using CentOS or Fedora, these manuals are most likely already installed. Otherwise, check out the recipe in *Chapter 3, Diving Deep into C in Linux*, that I mentioned.

Check out the following link to see the Code in Action video:
`https://bit.ly/3u4OuWz`

Reading inode information and learning the filesystem

Understanding inodes is the key to understanding the filesystem in Linux at a deeper level. A filename isn't the actual file in a Linux or Unix system. It's just a **pointer** to an **inode**. The inode has information about where the actual data is stored and a lot of meta data about the file, such as the file mode, last modification date, and owner.

In this recipe, we'll get a general understanding of the **filesystem** and how inodes fit into this. We will also view inode information and learn a few commands for that. We will also write a small C program that reads inode information from a filename.

Getting ready

In this recipe, we'll use both commands and C programs to explore the concepts of inodes. Everything you need for this recipe is covered in the *Technical requirements* section of this chapter.

How to do it...

In this recipe, we'll begin by exploring the commands that already exist on the system to view inode information. Then, we'll create a small C program to print inode information:

1. We'll start by creating a small text file that we'll use throughout this recipe:

```
$> echo "This is just a small file we'll use" \
> > testfile1
$> cat testfile1
This is just a small file we'll use
```

2. Now, let's view the *inode number* for this file, along with its size, block count, and other information. The inode number will be different on every system and for every file:

```
$> stat testfile1
  File: testfile1
  Size: 36              Blocks: 8            IO Block:
262144 regular file
Device: 35h/53d Inode: 19374124    Links: 1
Access: (0644/-rw-r--r--)  Uid: ( 1000/    jake)   Gid: (
1000/    jake)
Access: 2020-10-16 22:19:02.770945984 +0200
Modify: 2020-10-16 22:19:02.774945969 +0200
```

```
Change: 2020-10-16 22:19:02.774945969 +0200
 Birth: -
```

3. The size is in bytes and is 36 bytes. Since no special characters are used in the text, this will be the same as the number of characters the file contains. We can count the number of characters with `wc`:

```
$> wc -c testfile1
36 testfile1
```

4. Now, let's build a small program that extracts some of this information; the inode number, the file size, and the number of **links** (we'll return to the number of links in the next recipe). Write the following code in a file and save it as `my-stat-v1.c`. The name of the system call function that we'll use to extract information has the same name as the command-line tool, `stat`. The system call function is highlighted in the code:

```
#include <stdio.h>
#include <sys/types.h>
#include <sys/stat.h>
#include <unistd.h>
#include <errno.h>
#include <string.h>

int main(int argc, char *argv[])
{
   struct stat filestat;
   if ( argc != 2 )
   {
      fprintf(stderr, "Usage: %s <file>\n",
         argv[0]);
      return 1;
   }
   if ( stat(argv[1], &filestat) == -1 )
   {
      fprintf(stderr, "Can't read file %s: %s\n",
         argv[1], strerror(errno));
      return errno;
   }
   printf("Inode: %lu\n", filestat.st_ino);
   printf("Size: %zd\n", filestat.st_size);
   printf("Links: %lu\n", filestat.st_nlink);
```

```
    return 0;
}
```

5. Now compile this program using Make and the generic `Makefile`:

```
$> make my-stat-v1
gcc -Wall -Wextra -pedantic -std=c99    my-stat-v1.c   -o
my-stat-v1
```

6. Let's try the program on `testfile1`. Compare the inode number, size, and number of links. These numbers should be the same as when we used the `stat` program:

```
$> ./my-stat-v1 testfile1
Inode: 19374124
Size: 36
Links: 1
```

7. If we don't type an argument, we'll get a usage message:

```
$> ./my-stat-v1
Usage: ./my-stat-v1 <file>
```

8. And if we try it on a file that doesn't exist, we'll get an error message:

```
$> ./my-stat-v1 hello123
Can't read file hello123: No such file or directory
```

How it works...

The filename of a file isn't the data or file. The filename is just a link to an inode. And that inode, in turn, contains information about where on the filesystem the actual data is stored. As we will see in the next recipe, an inode can have multiple names or *links*. A filename is also called a link sometimes. The following figure illustrates the concepts of filenames that point to the inode, and the inode contains information about where the **data blocks** are stored:

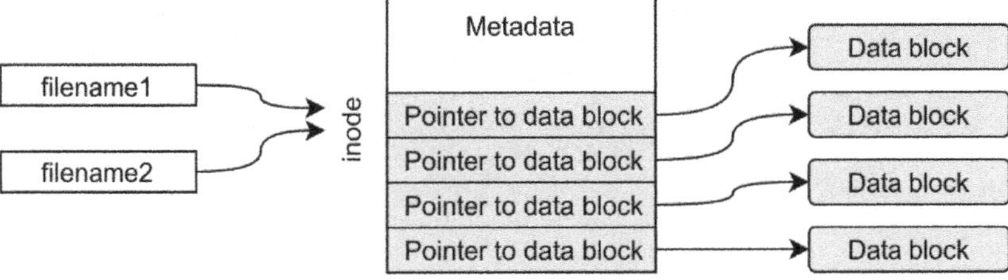

Figure 5.1 – Inodes and filenames

An inode also contains **metadata**, such as the creation date, date of last modification, total file size, owner and access rights, and more. In *step 2*, we extracted this metadata using the `stat` command.

In *step 4*, we created a small C program that reads this metadata using a system call function with the same name as the command, `stat()`. The `stat()` system call extracts much more data than what we printed here. We will print more of this information throughout this chapter. All of this information is stored in a struct called `stat`. We find all the information we need about this struct in the `man 2 stat` manual page. In that manual page, we also see what data types the variables are (`ino_t`, `off_t`, and `nlink_t`). And then, in `man sys_types.h`, under **Additionally**, we find what types these are.

The fields we use here are `st_ino` for the inode number, `st_size` for the file size, and `st_nlink` for the number of links to the file.

In *step 6*, we saw that the information we extracted using our C program was the same as the information from the `stat` command.

We also implemented error handling in the program. The `stat()` function is wrapped in an `if` statement, checking its return value for `-1`. And if an error does occur, we print an error message to *stderr* with the filename and the error message from `errno`. The program also returns the `errno` variable to the shell. We learned all about error handling and `errno` in *Chapter 4, Handling Errors in Your Programs*.

Creating soft links and hard links

In the previous recipe, we touched on the subject of links. In this recipe, we'll learn more about links and how they affect inodes. We'll also investigate the difference between **soft links** and **hard links**. In short, a hard link is a filename, and a soft link is like a shortcut to a filename.

On top of that, we'll write two programs, one that creates a hard link and one that creates a soft link. We'll then use the program we created in the previous recipe to check the **link count**.

Getting ready

Except for the requirements listed at the beginning of this chapter, you'll also need the program we created in the previous recipe, `my-stat-v1.c`. You'll also need the test file we created in the previous recipe, named `testfile1`. If you haven't created those files yet, you can also download them from GitHub at `https://github.com/PacktPublishing/Linux-System-Programming-Techniques/tree/master/ch5`.

You'll also need to compile the `my-stat-v1.c` program using Make so you'll be able to execute it, if you haven't done so already. You compile it with `make my-stat-v1`.

How to do it...

We will create both soft links and hard links, using both the built-in commands and writing simple C programs to do so:

1. We'll start by creating a new hard link to our test file, `testfile1`. We'll name the new hard link `my-file`:

```
$> ln testfile1 my-file
```

2. Now let's investigate this new filename. Note how the links have increased to `2`, but the rest is the same as for `testfile1`:

```
$> cat my-file
This is just a small file we'll use
$> ls -l my-file
-rw-r--r-- 3 jake jake 36 okt 16 22:19 my-file
$> ./my-stat-v1 my-file
Inode: 19374124
Size: 36
Links: 2
```

3. Now compare these numbers with the `testfile1` file. They should all be the same:

```
$> ls -l testfile1
-rw-r--r-- 3 jake jake 36 okt 16 22:19 testfile1
$> ./my-stat-v1 testfile1
Inode: 19374124
Size: 36
Links: 2
```

4. Let's create another hard link called `another-name`. We create this link using the name `my-file` as the target:

```
$> ln my-file another-name
```

5. We'll investigate this file as well:

```
$> ls -l another-name
-rw-r--r-- 2 jake jake 36 okt 16 22:19 another-name
$> ./my-stat-v1 another-name
Inode: 19374124
Size: 36
Links: 3
```

6. Now let's delete the `testfile1` filename:

```
$> rm testfile1
```

7. Now that we have deleted the first filename we created, we'll investigate the other two names:

```
$> cat my-file
This is just a small file we'll use
$> ls -l my-file
-rw-r--r-- 2 jake jake 36 okt 16 22:19 my-file
$> ./my-stat-v1 my-file
Inode: 19374124
Size: 36
Links: 2
$> cat another-name
This is just a small file we'll use
$> ls -l another-name
-rw-r--r-- 2 jake jake 36 okt 16 22:19 another-name
$> ./my-stat-v1 another-name
Inode: 19374124
Size: 36
Links: 2
```

8. It's time to create a soft link. We create a soft link called `my-soft-link` to the name `another-name`:

```
$> ln -s another-name my-soft-link
```

9. A soft link is a special file type, which we can see with the `ls` command. Note that we get a new timestamp here. Also, note that it's a special file, which can be seen by the first letter in the file mode field, the letter `l` for a link:

```
$> ls -l my-soft-link
lrwxrwxrwx 1 jake jake 12 okt 17 01:49 my-soft-link ->
another-name
```

10. Now let's check the link count of `another-name`. Note that the counter hasn't increased with the soft link:

```
$> ./my-stat-v1 another-name
Inode: 19374124
Size: 36
Links: 2
```

11. It's time to write our own program to create hard links. There exists an easy-to-use **system call** named `link()` that we'll use for this. Write the following code in a file and save it as `new-name.c`. The `link()` system call is highlighted in the code:

```
#include <stdio.h>
#include <unistd.h>
#include <string.h>
#include <errno.h>

int main(int argc, char *argv[])
{
    if (argc != 3)
    {
        fprintf(stderr, "Usage: %s [target] "
            "[new-name]\n", argv[0]);
        return 1;
    }
    if (link(argv[1], argv[2]) == -1)
    {
        perror("Can't create link");
        return 1;
    }
    return 0;
}
```

12. Compile the program:

```
$> make new-name
gcc -Wall -Wextra -pedantic -std=c99    new-name.c    -o
new-name
```

13. Create a new name to our previous `my-file` file. Name the new file `third-name`. We also try to generate some errors to see that the program prints the correct error messages. Note that the inode information for `third-name` is the same as for `my-file`:

```
$> ./new-name
Usage: ./new-name [target][new-name]
$> ./new-name my-file third-name
$> ./my-stat-v1 third-name
Inode: 19374124
Size: 36
Links: 3
$> ./new-name my-file /home/carl/hello
Can't create link: Permission denied
$> ./new-name my-file /mnt/localnas_disk2/
Can't create link: File exists
$> ./new-name my-file /mnt/localnas_disk2/third-name
Can't create link: Invalid cross-device link
```

14. Now let's create a program that creates a soft link. There's an easy-to-use system call for this as well, called `symlink()`, for **symbolic link**, which is another name for **soft link**. This program will be similar to the previous one. Write the following code in a file and save it as `new-symlink.c`. The `symlink()` system call is highlighted in the code. Notice how similar all of these system call functions are:

```
#define _XOPEN_SOURCE 700
#include <stdio.h>
#include <unistd.h>
#include <string.h>
#include <errno.h>

int main(int argc, char *argv[])
{
    if (argc != 3)
    {
        fprintf(stderr, "Usage: %s [target] "
            "[link]\n", argv[0]);
```

```
        return 1;
    }
    if (symlink(argv[1], argv[2]) == -1)
    {
        perror("Can't create link");
        return 1;
    }
    return 0;
}
```

15. Compile it:

```
$> make new-symlink
gcc -Wall -Wextra -pedantic -std=c99    new-symlink.c
-o new-symlink
```

16. And let's try it out, creating a new soft link called `new-soft-link` to `third-name`. Also, let's try generating some errors so we can verify that the error handling is working:

```
$> ./new-symlink third-name new-soft-link
$> ls -l new-soft-link
lrwxrwxrwx 1 jake jake 10 okt 18 00:31 new-soft-link ->
third-name
$> ./new-symlink third-name new-soft-link
Can't create link: File exists
$> ./new-symlink third-name /etc/new-soft-link
Can't create link: Permission denied
```

How it works...

There's a lot going on here, so let's take it from the top.

In steps 1 to 7, we created two new hard links to the `testfile1` file. But as we noticed, there's nothing special about a hard link; it's just another name to an inode. All filenames are hard links. A filename is just a link to an inode. We saw that when we deleted the `testfile1` filename. The two remaining names link to the same inode, and it contains the same text. There is nothing special about the first filename or link. There's no way to tell which of the hard links was created first. They are equal; they even share the same date, even though the other links were made at a later time. The date is for the inode, not the filenames.

As we created and deleted hard links, we saw how the link count increased and decreased. This is the inode keeping count of how many links—or names—it has.

The inode isn't deleted until the last name is deleted, that is, when the link counter reaches zero.

In *steps 8 to 10*, we saw that a soft link, on the other hand, is a special file type. A soft link doesn't count toward the inode's link counter. The file is denoted by an `l` at the start of the `ls -l` output. We can also see what file the soft link points to in the `ls -l` output. Think of a soft link as a shortcut.

In *steps 11 to 13*, we wrote a C program that creates a hard link—a new name—to an existing filename. Here we learned that the system calls for creating new names is called `link()` and takes two arguments, the target and the new name.

In *step 13*, we witnessed an interesting property for hard links. They cannot span across devices. When we think about it, it makes sense. The filename can't remain on a device separate from the inode. If the device is removed, there might not be any more names pointing to the inode, making it inaccessible.

For the remaining steps, we wrote a C program that creates soft links to existing files. This system call is similar to `link()` but is instead called `symlink()`.

There's more...

Please look at the manual pages for the system calls we covered in this recipe; they contain some great explanations of both hard links and soft links. The manual pages are `man 2 link` and `man 2 symlink`.

Creating files and updating the timestamp

Now that we understand the filesystem, inodes, and hard links, we'll learn how to create files by writing our own version of `touch` in C. We have already started writing a version of `touch` in *Chapter 4, Handling Errors in Your Programs,* where we learned about error handling. We will continue using the latest version of that program, which we named `simple-touch-v7.c`. The real version of `touch` updates the modification and access **timestamp** of a file if the file exists. In this recipe, we'll add that feature to our new version.

Getting ready

Everything you'll need for this recipe is listed in the *Technical requirements* section for this chapter. Although we will add on the latest version of `simple-touch`, we'll write the entire code in this recipe. But for complete comprehension of the program, it is wise to read through *Chapter 4, Handling Errors in Your Programs,* first.

How to do it...

In this eighth version of `simple-touch`, we will add the feature to update the access and modification date of a file:

1. Write the following code in a file and save it as `simple-touch-v8.c`. Here we will use the `utime()` system call to update a file's access and modification timestamps. The changes from the previous version are highlighted in the code (except for the added comments). Also, note how the `creat()` system call has moved into an `if` statement. The `creat()` system call is only called if the file doesn't already exist:

```
#include <stdio.h>
#include <fcntl.h>
#include <string.h>
#include <errno.h>
#include <utime.h>
#define MAX_LENGTH 100

int main(int argc, char *argv[])
{
   char filename[MAX_LENGTH] = { 0 };
   /* Check number of arguments */
   if (argc != 2)
   {
      fprintf(stderr, "You must supply a filename "
         "as an argument\n");
      return 1;
   }
   strncat(filename, argv[1], sizeof(filename)-1);

   /* Update the access and modification time */
   if ( utime(filename, NULL) == -1 )
   {
      /* If the file doesn't exist, create it */
      if (errno == ENOENT)
      {
         if ( creat(filename, 00644) == -1 )
         {
            perror("Can't create file");
            return errno;
         }
      }
```

```
        /* If we can't update the timestamp,
           something is wrong */
        else
        {
            perror("Can't update timestamp");
            return errno;
        }
    }
    return 0;
}
```

2. Compile the program using Make:

```
$> make simple-touch-v8
gcc -Wall -Wextra -pedantic -std=c99    simple-touch-v8.c
-o simple-touch-v8
```

3. Let's try it out and see how it works. We'll try it on the filenames we created in the previous recipe and see how each filename gets the same timestamp since they all point to the same inode:

```
$> ./simple-touch-v8 a-new-file
$> ls -l a-new-file
-rw-r--r-- 1 jake jake 0 okt 18 19:57 a-new-file
$> ls -l my-file
-rw-r--r-- 3 jake jake 36 okt 16 22:19 my-file
$> ls -l third-name
-rw-r--r-- 3 jake jake 36 okt 16 22:19 third-name
$> ./simple-touch-v8 third-name
$> ls -l my-file
-rw-r--r-- 3 jake jake 36 okt 18 19:58 my-file
$> ls -l third-name
-rw-r--r-- 3 jake jake 36 okt 18 19:58 third-name
$> ./simple-touch-v8 /etc/passwd
Can't change filename: Permission denied
$> ./simple-touch-v8 /etc/hello123
Can't create file: Permission denied
```

How it works...

In this recipe, we added the feature to update the timestamp of a file—or inode, as we have learned that it is.

To update the access and modification time, we use the `utime()` system call. The `utime()` system call takes two arguments, a filename and a timestamp. But if we give the function `NULL` as the second argument, it will use the current time and date.

The call to `utime()` is wrapped in an `if` statement, which checks whether the return value is -1. If it is, then something is wrong, and `errno` is set (see *Chapter 4, Handling Errors in Your Programs*, for an in-depth explanation of `errno`). We then use `errno` to check whether it was a *File not found* error (`ENOTENT`). If the file doesn't exist, we create it using the `creat()` system call. The call to `creat()` is also wrapped in an `if` statement. If something goes wrong while creating a file, the program prints an error message and return the `errno` value. If the program managed to create the file, it continues down to `return 0`.

If the `errno` value from `utime()` wasn't `ENOENT`, it continues down to the `else` statement, prints an error message, and returns `errno`.

When we tried the program, we noticed that both `my-file` and `third-name` got an updated timestamp when we updated one of them. This is because the filenames are just links to the same inode. And the timestamp is metadata in the inode.

There's more...

There's a lot of useful information in `man 2 creat` and `man 2 utime`. If you are interested in learning more about time and dates in Linux, I recommend you read `man 2 time`, `man 3 asctime`, and `man time.h`.

Deleting files

In this recipe, we learn how to **delete files** using a system call and where the name—`unlink()`—comes from. This recipe will enhance your understanding of links and close the circle. This will improve your overall knowledge of Linux and its filesystem. Knowing how to delete files using the system call will enable you to remove files directly from within your programs.

Here we will write our own version of `rm`, which we will call `remove`. After this recipe, we know how to create and delete files and how to make links. These are some of the most common filesystem operations.

Getting ready

In this recipe, we will use the `my-stat-v1` program, which we wrote in the *Reading inode information and learning the filesystem* recipe. We will also continue experimenting on the filenames we created in the previous recipes, `my-file`, `another-name`, and `third-name`. Except for that, you'll need what's listed under *Technical requirements* for this chapter, that is, the GCC compiler, the Make tool, and the generic Makefile.

How to do it...

Follow along here to write a simple version of `rm`:

1. Write the following code in a file and save it as `remove.c`. This program uses the `unlink()` system call to remove a file. The system call is highlighted in the code:

```
#include <stdio.h>
#include <unistd.h>
#include <errno.h>

int main(int argc, char *argv[])
{
    if (argc != 2)
    {
        fprintf(stderr, "Usage: %s [path]\n",
            argv[0]);
        return 1;
    }
    if ( unlink(argv[1]) == -1 )
    {
        perror("Can't remove file");
        return errno;
    }
    return 0;
}
```

2. Compile it using the **Make** tool:

```
$> make remove
gcc -Wall -Wextra -pedantic -std=c99    remove.c    -o
remove
```

3. And let's try it out:

```
$> ./my-stat-v1 my-file
Inode: 19374124
Size: 36
Links: 3
$> ./remove another-name
$> ./my-stat-v1 my-file
Inode: 19374124
Size: 36
Links: 2
```

How it works...

The system call to remove a file is called `unlink()`. The name comes from the fact that when we remove a filename, we only remove a hard link to that inode; hence we **unlink** a filename. If it happens to be the last filename to an inode, then the inode is also removed.

The `unlink()` system calls only takes one argument: the filename that we want to remove.

Getting access rights and ownership

In this recipe, we'll write a program that reads the access rights and ownership of a file using the `stat()` system call we have seen previously in this chapter. We will continue to build upon the `my-stat-v1` program that we built in the first recipe in this chapter. Here we will add the features to show ownership and access rights as well. Knowing how to get the owner and access rights programmatically is key to working with files and directories. It will enable you to check whether the user has the appropriate permissions and print an error message if they haven't.

We will also learn how access rights are interpreted in Linux and how to convert between numerical representation and letter representation. Understanding access rights in Linux is key to being a Linux system programmer. Every file and directory on the entire system has access rights and an owner and a group assigned to them. It doesn't matter whether it's a log file, a system file, or just a text file that a user owns. Everything has access rights.

Getting ready

For this recipe, you'll only need what's listed in the *Technical requirements* section of this chapter.

How to do it...

We will write a new version of `my-stat-v1` in this recipe. We will write the entire program here, though, so you don't need the previous version:

1. Write the following code in a file and save it as `my-stat-v2.c`. In this version, we'll pull information about the owner and the group of the file and the file mode. To translate the **user-ID** number into a username, we use `getpwuid()`. To get the group name for a **group-ID**, we use `getgrgid()`. The changes are highlighted in the code:

```
#include <stdio.h>
#include <sys/types.h>
#include <sys/stat.h>
#include <unistd.h>
#include <errno.h>
#include <string.h>
#include <pwd.h>
#include <grp.h>

int main(int argc, char *argv[])
{
    struct stat filestat;
    struct passwd *userinfo;
    struct group *groupinfo;
    if ( argc != 2 )
    {
        fprintf(stderr, "Usage: %s <file>\n",
            argv[0]);
        return 1;
    }
    if ( stat(argv[1], &filestat) == -1 )
    {
        fprintf(stderr, "Can't read file %s: %s\n",
            argv[1], strerror(errno));
        return errno;
    }
    if ( (userinfo = getpwuid(filestat.st_uid)) ==
```

```
            NULL )
        {
            perror("Can't get username");
            return errno;
        }
        if ( (groupinfo = getgrgid(filestat.st_gid)) ==
            NULL )
        {
            perror("Can't get groupname");
            return errno;
        }
        printf("Inode: %lu\n", filestat.st_ino);
        printf("Size: %zd\n", filestat.st_size);
        printf("Links: %lu\n", filestat.st_nlink);
        printf("Owner: %d (%s)\n", filestat.st_uid,
            userinfo->pw_name);
        printf("Group: %d (%s)\n", filestat.st_gid,
            groupinfo->gr_name);
        printf("File mode: %o\n", filestat.st_mode);
        return 0;
}
```

2. Compile the program:

```
$> make my-stat-v2
gcc -Wall -Wextra -pedantic -std=c99    my-stat-v2.c   -o
my-stat-v2
```

3. Try out the program on some different files:

```
$> ./my-stat-v2 third-name
Inode: 19374124
Size: 36
Links: 2
Owner: 1000 (jake)
Group: 1000 (jake)
File mode: 100644
$> ./my-stat-v2 /etc/passwd
Inode: 4721815
Size: 2620
Links: 1
Owner: 0 (root)
Group: 0 (root)
```

```
File mode: 100644
$> ./my-stat-v2 /bin/ls
Inode: 3540019
Size: 138856
Links: 1
Owner: 0 (root)
Group: 0 (root)
File mode: 100755
```

How it works...

In this version of `my-stat`, we have added features to retrieve the file access mode, or actually, the **file mode**. The file's complete file mode consists of six octal numbers. The first two (to the left) is the file type. In this case, it's a regular file (10 equals a regular file). The fourth octal digit is for the **set-user-ID bit**, the **set-group-ID bit**, and the **sticky bit**. The last three octal digits are for the **access mode**.

In the output from `ls -l`, all these bits are instead represented as letters. But when we write programs, we must set and read these as numbers. Before we move on, let's examine the letter-version of the file mode, so we truly understand it:

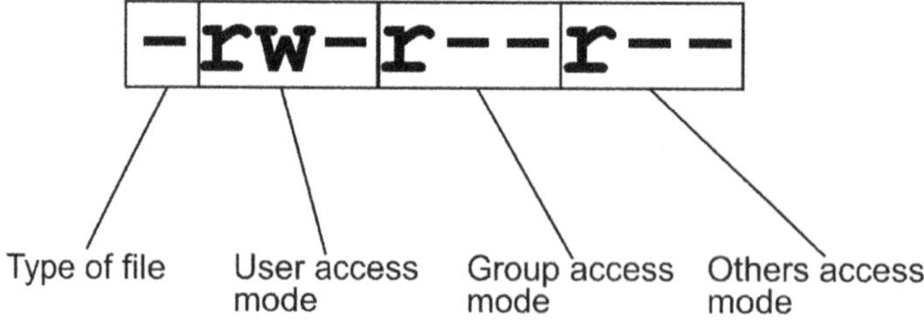

Figure 5.2 – File access mode

The set-user-ID bit is a bit that allows a process to run as the owner of the binary file, even though it is executed as a different user. Setting the set-user-ID bit is potentially dangerous and *not* something we should set on our programs. One program that does use the set-user-ID bit is the `passwd` program. The `passwd` program must update the `/etc/passwd` and `/etc/shadow` files when a user changes his or her password, even though those files are owned by root. Under normal circumstances, we can't even read the `/etc/shadow` file as a regular user, but with the set-user-ID bit set on the `passwd` program, it can even write to it. If the set-user-ID bit is set, it's denoted by an `s` in the third place of the user's access mode.

The set-group-ID has a similar effect. When a program is executed, and the set-group-ID bit is set, it is executed as that group. When the set-group-ID is set, it's denoted by an `s` in the third place of the group's access mode.

The sticky bit was historically used to *stick* a program to the swap space for faster loading time. Nowadays, it's used entirely differently. Now, the name—as well as the meaning—has changed to *restricted deletion flag*. When a directory has the sticky bit set, only a file's owner, the directory owner, or the root user can remove a file, even if the directory is writeable by anybody. For example, the `/tmp` directory usually has the sticky bit set. A sticky bit is denoted by a `t` in the last position of the last group.

File access mode

When we run `ls -l` on a file, we always see two names. The first name is the user (the owner), and the second name is the group that owns the file. Take this, for example:

```
$> ls -l Makefile
-rw-r--r-- 1 jake devops 134 okt 27 23:39 Makefile
```

In this case, `jake` is the user (owner), and `devops` is the group.

The file access modes are easier to understand than the special flags we just covered. Take a look at *Figure 5.2*. The first three letters are the user's access mode (the owner of the file). This particular example has `rw-`, which means that the user can read and write the file but not execute it. If the user were to be able to execute it, that would be denoted by an `x` in the last place.

The middle three letters are for the group access mode (the group that owns the file). In this case, the group can only read the file since the group is missing both the `w` for write and the `x` for execution.

The last three letters are for all others (not the owner and not in the owner group). In this case, everybody else can just read the file.

A full set of permissions would be `rwxrwxrwx`.

Converting access modes between letters and numeric

An **octal number** represents the file access mode. Until we get used to it, the easiest way to convert from letters to octal is to use a pen and paper. We add all the numbers together in each group where that access bit is set. If it is not set (a dash), then we don't add that number. When we're finished adding each group, we have the access mode:

```
rw- r-- r—
421 421 421
 6   4   4
```

The preceding octal access mode is therefore 644. Let's do another example:

```
rwx rwx r-x
421 421 421
 7   7   5
```

The preceding access mode turns out to be 775. Let's take one more example:

```
rw- --- ---
421 421 421
 6   0   0
```

This access mode is 600.

The other way around can also be done by using a pen and paper. Let's say we have the access mode 750, and we want to convert that into letters:

```
 7   5   0
421 401 000
rwx r-x ---
```

Hence, 750 becomes `rwxr-x---`.

When you have been doing it for a while, you learn the most commonly used access modes and don't need a pen and paper anymore.

The file mode in octal

The same principle applies here as with the file access mode. Remember that the set-user-ID is denoted by an `s` in the user's execute position, and the set-group-ID is denoted by an `s` in the group's execute bit. A `t` character denotes the sticky bit in the last execute bit position (the "others"). If we write it in a row, we get this:

```
s s t
4 2 1
```

So if only the set-user-ID bit is set, we get a 4. If both the set-user-ID and set-group-ID is set, we get *4+2=6*. If only the set-group-ID bit is set, we get a 2. If only the sticky bit is set, we get a 1, and so forth. And if all the bits are set, we get a *7 (4+2+1)*.

These file modes are represented by a number before the file access mode. For example, the octal file mode `4755` has the set-user-ID bit set (the 4).

When we program under Linux, we can even encounter two more numbers, as we saw with the output from our `my-stat-v2` program. There, we had this:

```
File mode: 100755
```

The two first numbers, `10` in this example, are the file type. Exactly what these two first numbers mean is something we'll have to look up in the `man 7 inode` manual page. There we have a nice table telling us what it means. I have made a simplified list here, showing only the first two numbers we are interested in and what file type it represents:

```
14    socket
12    symbolic link
10    regular file
06    block device
04    directory
02    character device
01    FIFO
```

That means that our example file is a regular file (10).

If we add up everything we just learned and translate the file mode *100755* from the preceding example output from `my-stat-v2`, we get this:

```
10  = a regular file
0   = no set-user-ID, set-group-ID or sticky bit is set
755 = the user can read, write, and execute it. The group can
read and execute it, and all others can also read and execute
it.
```

The file type is also denoted by a letter at the very first position (see *Figure 5.2*). The letters are as follows:

```
s    socket
l    symbolic link
-    regular file
b    block device
d    directory
c    character device
p    FIFO
```

Setting access rights and ownership

In the previous recipe, we learned how to read the **access rights** of files and folders. In this recipe, we'll learn how to set access rights, using both the `chmod` command and the `chmod()` system call. We will also learn how to change the owner and group of a file, using both the `chown` command and the `chown()` system call.

Knowing how to set access rights properly will help you keep your systems and files secure.

Getting ready

For this recipe, you'll only need what's listed in the *Technical requirements* section of this chapter. It's also a good idea to read the previous recipe to understand permissions in Linux. You will also need the `my-stat-v2` program from the previous recipe.

How to do it...

These steps will teach us how to change the access rights and ownership of files and directories.

Access rights

We will start by setting the access rights of a file by using the `chmod` command. We will then write a simple C version of the `chmod` command, using the `chmod()` system call:

1. Let's start by removing the execute permission from our `my-stat-v2` program, using the `chmod` command. The `-x` in the following command means *remove eXecute*:

```
$> chmod -x my-stat-v2
```

2. Now let's try to execute the program. This should now fail with permission denied:

```
$> ./my-stat-v2
bash: ./my-stat-v2: Permission denied
```

3. Now we change it back again, but this time we set the *absolute* permission using octal numbers. Suitable permissions for executable files are 755, which translates to `rwxr-xr-x`. That, in turn, means that the user has full permissions and, the group can read and execute the file. The same goes for all others; they can read and execute it:

```
$> chmod 755 my-stat-v2
```

4. After this command, we can once again execute the program:

```
./my-stat-v2
Usage: ./my-stat-v2 <file>
```

5. Now it's time to write a simple version of the `chmod` command, using the `chmod()` system call. Write the following code in a file and save it as `my-chmod.c`. The `chmod()` system call takes two arguments, the path to the file or directory and the file permission expressed as an octal number. Before we get to the `chmod()` system call, we perform some checks to ensure that the permission seems reasonable (an octal number that is either three or four digits long). After the checks, we convert the number to an octal number with `strtol()`. The third argument to `strtol()` is the base, in this case, `8`:

```
#include <stdio.h>
#include <sys/stat.h>
#include <string.h>
#include <stdlib.h>

void printUsage(FILE *stream, char progname[]);

int main(int argc, char *argv[])
{
    long int accessmode; /*To hold the access mode*/
    /* Check that the user supplied two arguments */
    if (argc != 3)
    {
        printUsage(stderr, argv[0]);
        return 1;
    }
    /* Simple check for octal numbers and
        correct length */
    if( strspn(argv[1], "01234567\n")
            != strlen(argv[1])
            || ( strlen(argv[1]) != 3 &&
                strlen(argv[1]) != 4 ) )
    {
        printUsage(stderr, argv[0]);
        return 1;
    }
    /* Convert to octal and set the permissions */
    accessmode = strtol(argv[1], NULL, 8);
```

```
    if (chmod(argv[2], accessmode) == -1)
    {
       perror("Can't change permissions");
    }
    return 0;
}

void printUsage(FILE *stream, char progname[])
{
     fprintf(stream, "Usage: %s <numerical "
         "permissions> <path>\n", progname);
}
```

6. Now compile the program:

```
$> make my-chmod
gcc -Wall -Wextra -pedantic -std=c99    my-chmod.c    -o
my-chmod
```

7. Test the program using different permissions. Don't forget to check the result using `ls -l`:

```
$> ./my-chmod
Usage: ./my-chmod <numerical permissions> <path>
$> ./my-chmod 700 my-stat-v2
$> ls -l my-stat-v2
-rwx------ 1 jake jake 17072 Nov  1 07:29 my-stat-v2
$> ./my-chmod 750 my-stat-v2
$> ls -l my-stat-v2
-rwxr-x--- 1 jake jake 17072 Nov  1 07:29 my-stat-v2
```

8. Let's also try to set the set-user-ID bit. This set-user-ID bit (and set-group-ID and sticky bit) is the fourth digit in front of the access mode. A `4` here sets the set-user-ID bit. Note the `s` (highlighted in the following code) in the user field:

```
$> chmod 4755 my-stat-v2
$> ls -l my-stat-v2
-rwsr-xr-x 1 jake jake 17072 Nov  1 07:29 my-stat-v2
```

9. Let's try to set all bits (set-user-ID, set-group-ID, sticky bit, and all permissions):

```
$> chmod 7777 my-stat-v2
$> ls -l my-stat-v2
-rwsrwsrwt 1 jake jake 17072 Nov  1 07:29 my-stat-v2
```

10. And finally, change it back to something more sensible:

```
$> chmod 755 my-stat-v2
$> ls -l my-stat-v2
-rwxr-xr-x 1 jake jake 17072 Nov  1 07:29 my-stat-v2
```

Ownership

But we also need to know how to change the **ownership** of a file, not just the file access mode. This is done with the `chown` command or the `chown()` system call:

1. To change the owner of a file, we must be root. Regular users cannot give away ownership of their files. Likewise, they cannot claim ownership of someone else's files. Let's try to change the owner of `my-stat-v2` to root using the `chown` command:

```
$> sudo chown root my-stat-v2
$> ls -l my-stat-v2
-rwxr-xr-x 1 root jake 17072 Nov  1 07:29 my-stat-v2
```

2. If we want to change both the owner and the group, we separate the user and the group using a colon. The first field is the owner, and the second field is the group:

```
$> sudo chown root:root my-stat-v2
$> ls -l my-stat-v2
-rwxr-xr-x 1 root root 17072 Nov  1 07:29 my-stat-v2
```

3. And now it's our turn to write a simplified version of `chown`, using the `chown()` system call. The `chown()` system call only takes user IDs as numerical values. To be able to use names instead, we must first look up the username using `getpwnam()`. This will give us the numerical value in the `passwd` struct, in the `pw_uid` field. The same goes for the group. We must get the numerical group-ID using its name, using the `getgrnam()` system call. Now that we know all the system calls, let's write the program. Name it `my-chown.c`. This program is a bit longer, so I have split it up into several steps. Keep in mind that all steps should go into a single file (`my-chown.c`). You can also download the entire code from `https://github.com/PacktPublishing/Linux-System-Programming-Techniques/blob/master/ch5/my-chown.c` if you wish. Let's start with all the header files, the variables, and the arguments check:

```
#include <stdio.h>
#include <stdlib.h>
#include <unistd.h>
```

```
#include <sys/types.h>
#include <pwd.h>
#include <grp.h>
#include <string.h>
#include <errno.h>

int main(int argc, char *argv[])
{
   struct passwd *user; /* struct for getpwnam */
   struct group *grp; /* struct for getgrnam */
   char *username = { 0 }; /* extracted username */
   char *groupname = { 0 }; /*extracted groupname*/
   unsigned int uid, gid; /* extracted UID/GID */

   /* Check that the user supplied two arguments
      (filename and user or user:group) */
   if (argc != 3)
   {
      fprintf(stderr, "Usage: %s [user][:group]"
         " [path]\n", argv[0]);
      return 1;
   }
```

4. Since we write the username and group as `username:group` in the argument, we need to extract the username part and the group part. We do this with a string function called `strtok()`. We only provide the first argument (the string) in the first call to `strtok()`. After this, we get the **User-ID** (**UID**) from the `user` struct and the **Group-ID** (**GID**) from the `grp` struct. We also check whether the user and group exist:

```
  /* Extract username and groupname */
   username = strtok(argv[1], ":");
   groupname = strtok(NULL, ":");

   if ( (user = getpwnam(username)) == NULL )
   {
      fprintf(stderr, "Invalid username\n");
      return 1;
   }
   uid = user->pw_uid; /* get the UID */

   if (groupname != NULL) /* if we typed a group */
```

```
    {
        if ( (grp = getgrnam(groupname)) == NULL )
        {
            fprintf(stderr, "Invalid groupname\n");
            return 1;
        }
        gid = grp->gr_gid; /* get the GID */
    }
    else
    {
        /* if no group is specifed, -1 won't change
           it (man 2 chown) */
        gid = -1;
    }
```

5. Finally, we update the user and group of the file using the `chown()` system call:

```
    /* update user/group (argv[2] is the filename)*/
    if ( chown(argv[2], uid, gid) == -1 )
    {
        perror("Can't change owner/group");
        return 1;
    }
    return 0;
}
```

6. Let's compile the program so that we can try it:

```
$> make my-chown
gcc -Wall -Wextra -pedantic -std=c99    my-chown.c    -o
my-chown
```

7. Now we test the program on a file. Remember that we need to be root to change a file's owner and group:

```
$> ls -l my-stat-v2
-rwxr-xr-x 1 root root 17072 nov  7 19:59 my-stat-v2
$> sudo ./my-chown jake my-stat-v2
$> ls -l my-stat-v2
-rwxr-xr-x 1 jake root 17072 nov  7 19:59 my-stat-v2
$> sudo ./my-chown carl:carl my-stat-v2
$> ls -l my-stat-v2
-rwxr-xr-x 1 carl carl 17072 nov  7 19:59 my-stat-v2
```

How it works...

Every file and directory on the system has access rights and an owner/group pair. The access rights are changed with the `chmod` command or the `chmod()` system call. The name is short for *change mode bits*. In the previous recipe, we covered how to translate access rights between the more human-readable text format and the numerical octal form. In this recipe, we wrote a program that changed the mode bits using the `chmod()` system call using the numerical form.

To convert the numerical form into an octal number, we used `strtol()` with `8` as the third argument, which is the numeral system base. Base 8 is octal; base 10 is the regular decimal system we use in everyday life; base 16 is hexadecimal, and so on.

We wrote the program so that the user can choose whatever they want to set, whether that's only the access mode bits (three digits) or also the special bits such as set-user-ID, set-group-ID, and sticky bit (four digits). To determine the number of digits the user typed, we use `strlen()`.

In the next program we wrote, we used `chown()` to update the owner and group of a file or directory. Since we want to update the user and group using the names, not the numerical UID and GID, the program got more complex. The `chown()` system call only takes the UID and GID, not names. That means we need to look up the UID and GID before we can call `chown()`. To look up the UID and GID, we use `getpwnam()` and `getgrnam()`. Each of these functions gives us a `struct` containing all information available for the respective user or group. From those structs, we extract the UID and GID, which we then use in the call to `chown()`.

To separate the username and group part from the command line (the colon), we use the `strtok()` function. In the first call to the function, we specify the string as the first argument (in this case, `argv[1]`) and the separator (a colon). In the next call to `strtok()`, we leave out the string by setting it to `NULL`, but we still specify the separator. The first call gives us the username and the second call gives us the group name.

After that, we check whether the username and group name exist when we call `getpwnam()` and `getgrnam()`. If the username or group name don't exist, the functions return `NULL`.

There's more...

There are several similar functions to `getpwnam()` and `getgrnam()`, depending on what information you have and what information you have. If you have the UID, you instead use `getpwuid()`. Likewise, if you have the GID, you use `getgrgid()`. There is more information—and more functions—if you read the `man 3 getpwnam` and `man 3 getgrnam` manual pages.

Writing to files with file descriptors

We have already seen some uses of **file descriptors** in previous chapters, for example, 0, 1, and 2 (*stdin*, *stdout*, and *stderr*). But in this recipe, we will use file descriptors to write text to files from a program.

Knowing how to use file descriptors to write to files both gives you a deeper understanding of the system and enables you to do some low-level stuff.

Getting ready

For this recipe, you only need what is listed under the *Technical requirements* section.

How to do it...

Here we will write a small program that writes text to a file:

1. Write the following code in a file and save it as `fd-write.c`. The program takes two arguments: a string and a filename. To write to a file using file descriptors, we must first open the file with the `open()` system call. The `open()` system call returns a file descriptor, which is an integer. We then use that file descriptor (the integer) with the `write()` system call. We have already seen `write()` in *Chapter 3, Diving Deep into C in Linux*. In that chapter, we used `write()` to write a small text to stdout. This time, we use `write()` to write a text to a file. Notice that the `open()` system call takes three arguments: the path to the file, which mode the file shall open in (in this case, create the file if it doesn't exist, and open it in read-write mode), and the **access mode** (here `0644`):

```
#include <stdio.h>
#include <unistd.h>
#include <fcntl.h>
#include <string.h>
#include <sys/types.h>
#include <sys/stat.h>
```

```
int main(int argc, char *argv[])
{
   int fd; /* for the file descriptor */

   if (argc != 3)
   {
      fprintf(stderr, "Usage: %s [path] [string]\n",
         argv[0]);
      return 1;
   }

   /* Open the file (argv[1]) and create it if it
      doesn't exist and set it in read-write mode.
      Set the access mode to 644 */
   if ( (fd = open(argv[1], O_CREAT|O_RDWR, 00644))
      == -1 )
   {
      perror("Can't open file for writing");
      return 1;
   }
   /* write content to file */
   if ( (write(fd, argv[2], strlen(argv[2])))
      == -1 )
   {
      perror("Can't write to file");
      return 1;
   }
   return 0;
}
```

2. Let's compile the program:

```
$> make fd-write
gcc -Wall -Wextra -pedantic -std=c99    fd-write.c    -o
fd-write
```

3. And let's try to write some text to a file. Remember that if the file already exists, the content will be overwritten! If the new text is smaller than the old content of the file, only the beginning will be overwritten. Also note that if the text doesn't contain a new line, the text in the file won't contain a new line either:

```
$> ./fd-write testfile1.txt "Hello! How are you doing?"
$> cat testfile1.txt
Hello! How are you doing?$>Enter
$> ls -l testfile1.txt
-rw-r--r-- 1 jake jake 2048 nov  8 16:34 testfile1.txt
$> ./fd-write testfile1.txt "A new text"
$> cat testfile1.txt
A new text are you doing?$>
```

4. We can even give it input from another file if we use `xargs`, a program that allows us to take the output of a program and parse it as a command-line argument to another program. Notice that this time, `testfile1` will have a new line at the end. The `-0` option to `xargs` makes it ignore new lines and will instead use the null character to indicate the end of the argument:

```
$> head -n 3 /etc/passwd | xargs -0 \
> ./fd-write testfile1.txt
$> cat testfile1.txt
root:x:0:0:root:/root:/bin/bash
daemon:x:1:1:daemon:/usr/sbin:/usr/sbin/nologin
bin:x:2:2:bin:/bin:/usr/sbin/nologin
```

How it works...

The `open()` system call returns a file descriptor, which we save in the `fd` variable. A file descriptor is just an integer, just as 0, 1, and 3 are *stdin*, *stdout*, and *stderr*.

The second argument we give to `open()` are macros with mode bits that are put together using *bitwise-or*. In our case, we use both `O_CREAT` and `O_RDWR`. The first one, `O_CREAT`, means that if the file doesn't exist, it is created. The second one, `O_RDWR`, means that the file should be open for both reading and writing.

To write the string to the file, we pass the file descriptor to `write()` as the first argument. As the second argument, we give it `argv[2]`, which contains the string that we want to write to the file descriptor. The last argument is the size of what we want to write. In our case, we get the size of `argv[2]` with `strlen`, a function from `string.h` to get the length of strings.

Just as in the previous recipes, we check all the system calls for `-1`. If they return `-1`, something has gone wrong, and we use `perror()` to print an error message, and then we return `1`.

There's more...

When a program returns normally, all open file descriptors are closed automatically. But if we want to close a file descriptor explicitly, we use the `close()` system call with the file descriptor as its argument. In our case, we could have added `close(fd)` just before the return.

There's a lot of good information about `open()`, `close()`, and `write()` in the manual pages. I suggest you read them for more in-depth information. You can read them with the following:

- `man 2 open`
- `man 2 close`
- `man 2 write`

Reading from files with file descriptors

In the previous recipe, we learned how to write to files using file descriptors. In this recipe, we will learn how to read from files using file descriptors. We will therefore write a small program that is similar to `cat`. It takes one argument—a filename—and prints its content to standard output.

Knowing how to read—and use—file descriptors enables you to read not only files but all sorts of data that comes through a file descriptor. File descriptors are a universal way to read and write data in Unix and Linux.

Getting ready

The only things you'll need for this recipe are listed under the *Technical requirements* section of this chapter.

How to do it...

Reading a file using a file descriptor is similar to writing to one. Instead of using the `write()` system call, we will instead use the `read()` system call. Before we can read the content, we must figure out the size of the file first. We can use the `fstat()` system call for this, which gives us information about a file descriptor:

1. Write the following code in a file and name it `fd-read.c`. Notice how we get the file information using `fstat()` and then read the data with `read()`. We still use the `open()` system call, but this time we have removed `O_CREATE` and changed `O_RDRW` to `O_RDONLY` to only allow reads. We will use a buffer size of 4,096 here so that we will be able to read some bigger files. This program is a bit longer, so I have split it up into several steps. All of the code in all of the steps goes into one file, though. First, we start by writing all the `include` lines, the variables, and the argument check:

```
#include <stdio.h>
#include <unistd.h>
#include <fcntl.h>
#include <sys/stat.h>
#include <sys/types.h>
#define MAXSIZE 4096

int main(int argc, char *argv[])
{
   int fd; /* for the file descriptor */
   int maxread; /* the maximum we want to read*/
   off_t filesize; /* for the file size */
   struct stat fileinfo; /* struct for fstat */
   char rbuf[MAXSIZE] = { 0 }; /* the read buffer*/

   if (argc != 2)
   {
      fprintf(stderr, "Usage: %s [path]\n",
         argv[0]);
      return 1;
   }
```

2. Now, we write the code that opens the file descriptor using the `open()` system call. We add some error handling to it as well by wrapping it in an `if` statement:

```
    /* open the file in read-only mode and get
       the file size */
    if ( (fd = open(argv[1], O_RDONLY)) == -1 )
    {
       perror("Can't open file for reading");
       return 1;
    }
```

3. Now, we write the code that fetches the file's size using the `fstat()` system call. Here we also check whether the file's size is bigger than `MAXSIZE`, in which case we set `maxread` to `MAXSIZE-1`. Otherwise, we set it to the file's size. Then, we read the file using the `read()` system call. And finally, we print the content using `printf()`:

```
    fstat(fd, &fileinfo);
    filesize = fileinfo.st_size;

    /* determine the max size we want to read
       so we don't overflow the read buffer */
    if ( filesize >= MAXSIZE )
       maxread = MAXSIZE-1;
    else
       maxread = filesize;

    /* read the content and print it */
    if ( (read(fd, rbuf, maxread)) == -1 )
    {
       perror("Can't read file");
       return 1;
    }
    printf("%s", rbuf);
    return 0;
}
```

4. Let's compile the program:

```
$> make fd-read
gcc -Wall -Wextra -pedantic -std=c99    fd-read.c    -o
fd-read
```

5. Let's try it on some files and see if we can read them:

```
$> ./fd-read testfile1.txt
root:x:0:0:root:/root:/bin/bash
daemon:x:1:1:daemon:/usr/sbin:/usr/sbin/nologin
bin:x:2:2:bin:/bin:/usr/sbin/nologin
$> ./fd-read Makefile
CC=gcc
CFLAGS=-Wall -Wextra -pedantic -std=c99
$> ./fd-read /etc/shadow
Can't open file for reading: Permission denied
$> ./fd-read asdfasdf
Can't open file for reading: No such file or directory
```

How it works...

When we read data from a file descriptor, we must specify how many characters should be read. Here we must be careful not to overflow the buffer. We also don't want to read any more than what the file actually contains. To solve all of this, we first find out the file's size by using `fstat()`. That function gives us the same information as we saw previously in the `my-stat-v2` program when we used `stat()`. These two functions, `stat()` and `fstat()`, do the same thing, but they operate on different things. The `stat()` function operates directly on a file, but `fstat()` operates on a file descriptor. Since we already have a file descriptor open to the correct file, it makes sense to use that instead. Both functions save their information to a struct called `stat`.

To not overflow the buffer, we check which is bigger, the file size or `MAXSIZE`. If the file size is bigger or equal to `MAXSIZE`, we use `MAXSIZE-1` as the maximum number of characters to read. Otherwise, we use the file's size as the maximum.

The `read()` system call takes the same arguments as `write()`, namely a file descriptor, a buffer, and the size we want to read (or write in the case of `write()`).

Since what we read in from a file is a bunch of characters, we can print the entire buffer to stdout using the regular `printf()`.

There's more...

If you look up `man 2 fstat`, you'll notice that it's the same manual page as `man 2 stat`.

Writing to files with streams

In this recipe, we will write to files using **file streams** instead of file descriptors, as we did in earlier recipes.

As with the previous recipes where we had already seen file descriptors 1, 2, and 3, and some of their system calls, we have already seen file streams too, such as some of the `printUsage()` functions we have created. Some of these functions we created took two arguments, the first one being declared as `FILE *stream`. The argument we provided was stderr or stdout.

But we can also use file streams to write to files, which we will do in this recipe.

As you probably have noticed by now, some things keep coming again and again, such as file descriptors and file streams.

Working with file streams instead of file descriptors has some advantages. For example, with file streams, we can use functions such as `fprintf()` to write to files. This means that there are more—and more powerful—functions to read and write data.

Getting ready

For this recipe, we only need what's listed under the *Technical requirements* section of this chapter.

How to do it...

Here we write a program that writes text to a file. The program will be similar to what we wrote previously using file descriptors. But this time, we will read the text from stdin instead of from the command line. We will also write the text using a file stream instead of a file descriptor:

1. Write the following code in a file and name it `stream-write.c`. Notice how much smaller this program is even though we have added a `while` loop to read everything from stdin. Since we can use all functions in C that operate on streams, we don't need to use any special system calls to read, write, and so on. We haven't even included any special header files, except `stdio.h`, which we always include anyway. We write the text to the file with `fprintf()`, as we have already seen many times when we write to stdout or stderr:

```
#include <stdio.h>

int main(int argc, char *argv[])
{
```

```
    FILE *fp; /* pointer to a file stream */
    char linebuf[1024] = { 0 }; /* line buffer */

    if ( argc != 2 )
    {
       fprintf(stderr, "Usage: %s [path]\n",
          argv[0]);
       return 1;
    }

    /* open file with write mode */
    if ( (fp = fopen(argv[1], "w")) == NULL )
    {
       perror("Can't open file for writing");
       return 1;
    }

    /*loop over each line and write it to the file*/
    while(fgets(linebuf, sizeof(linebuf), stdin)
       != NULL)
    {
       fprintf(fp, linebuf);
    }
    fclose(fp); /* close the stream */
    return 0;
}
```

2. Let's compile the program:

```
$> make stream-write
gcc -Wall -Wextra -pedantic -std=c99    stream-write.c
-o stream-write
```

3. Now let's try the program, both by typing in data to it and by redirecting data to it using a pipe. After we have redirected the entire password file into a new file using our program, we check that they are the same using `diff`, which they should be. We also try to write to a new file in a directory, which we haven't got permission to. When we press *Ctrl* + *D*, we send an **EOF** to the program, meaning **End Of File**, indicating no more data is to be received:

```
$> ./stream-write my-test-file.txt
Hello! How are you doing?
I'm doing just fine, thank you.
```

```
Ctrl+D
$> cat my-test-file.txt
Hello! How are you doing?
I'm doing just fine, thank you.
$> cat /etc/passwd | ./stream-write my-test-file.txt
$> tail -n 3 my-test-file.txt
telegraf:x:999:999::/etc/telegraf:/bin/false
_rpc:x:103:65534::/run/rpcbind:/usr/sbin/nologin
systemd-coredump:x:997:997:systemd Core Dumper:/:/usr/
sbin/nologin
$> diff /etc/passwd my-test-file.txt
$> ./stream-write /a-new-file.txt
Can't open file for writing: Permission denied
```

How it works...

As you might have noticed, this program is much shorter and easier than the corresponding file descriptor version we wrote earlier in this chapter.

We start by creating a pointer to a file stream using `FILE *fp`. Then we create a buffer that we use for each line.

Then, we open the file stream using `fopen()`. That function takes two arguments, the filename and the mode. Here the mode is also easier to set, just a `"w"` for write.

After that, we use a `while` loop to loop over each input line that comes into stdin. On each iteration, we write the current line to the file using `fprintf()`. As the first argument to `fprintf()` we use the file stream pointer, just as we did with stderr in the `if` statement at the top of the program.

Before the program returns, we close the file stream with `fclose()`. Closing the stream isn't strictly necessary, but it's a good thing to do, just in case.

See also

There's a lot of information in `man 3 fopen` if you want to dig deeper.

For a more in-depth explanation of the difference between file descriptors and file streams, see the GNU libc manual: `https://www.gnu.org/software/libc/manual/html_node/Streams-and-File-Descriptors.html`.

Another important aspect of streams is that they are buffered. There is more information about streams buffering in the GNU libc manual at this URL: `https://www.gnu.org/software/libc/manual/html_node/Buffering-Concepts.html`.

Reading from files with streams

Now that we know how to write to a file using streams, we will learn how to read a file using streams. In this recipe, we will write a similar program to that of the previous recipe. But this time, we will read line by line from a file instead and print it to stdout.

Mastering both the writing and reading of streams will enable you to do many things in Linux.

Getting ready

All you need for this recipe is listed under the *Technical requirements* section of this chapter.

How to do it…

Here we will write a program that will be very similar to the previous recipe, but it will read text from a file instead. The principle of the program is the same as the previous recipe:

1. Write the following code in a file and save it as `stream-read.c`. Notice how similar this program is. We have changed write mode (`"w"`) to read mode (`"r"`) when opening the stream with `fopen()`. In the `while` loop, we read from the file pointer `fp` instead of stdin. Inside the `while` loop, we print what is in the buffer, which is the current line:

```
#include <stdio.h>

int main(int argc, char *argv[])
{
   FILE *fp; /* pointer to a file stream */
   char linebuf[1024] = { 0 }; /* line buffer */

   if ( argc != 2 )
   {
      fprintf(stderr, "Usage: %s [path]\n",
         argv[0]);
      return 1;
   }

   /* open file with read mode */
   if ( (fp = fopen(argv[1], "r")) == NULL )
   {
```

```
        perror("Can't open file for reading");
        return 1;
    }

    /* loop over each line and write it to stdout */
    while(fgets(linebuf, sizeof(linebuf), fp)
        != NULL)
    {
        printf("%s", linebuf);
    }
    fclose(fp); /* close the stream */
    return 0;
}
```

2. Compile the program:

```
$> make stream-read
gcc -Wall -Wextra -pedantic -std=c99    stream-read.c
-o stream-read
```

3. And now we can try the program on some files. Here I try it on the test file we created earlier and the Makefile:

```
$> ./stream-read testfile1.txt
root:x:0:0:root:/root:/bin/bash
daemon:x:1:1:daemon:/usr/sbin:/usr/sbin/nologin
bin:x:2:2:bin:/bin:/usr/sbin/nologin

$> ./stream-read Makefile
CC=gcc
CFLAGS=-Wall -Wextra -pedantic -std=c99
```

How it works...

As you might have noticed, this program is very similar to that of the previous recipe. But instead of opening the file for writing (`"w"`), we instead open it for reading (`"r"`). The file pointer looks the same, as well as the linebuffer and the error handling.

To read each line, we loop over the file stream using `fgets()`. As you might have noticed in both this and the previous recipe, we don't use `sizeof(linebuf)-1`, only `sizeof(linebuf)`. That is because `fgets()` only reads *one less* than the size we give it.

There's more...

There are a lot of similar functions as `fgets()`. You can find all of them by reading the manual page for it with `man 3 fgets`.

Reading and writing binary data with streams

There comes a time when we must save variables or arrays in a program to a file. For example, if we make a stock-keeping program for a warehouse, we don't want to re-write the entire warehouse stocks every time we start the program. That would defeat the purpose of the program. With streams, it's easy to save variables as binary data in files for later retrieval.

In this chapter, we'll write two small programs: one that asks the user for two floats, saves them in an array, and writes them to a file, and another program that re-reads that array.

Getting ready

You only need the GCC compiler, the Make tool, and the generic Makefile for this recipe.

How to do it...

In this recipe, we'll write two small programs: one that writes and one that reads binary data. The data is an array of floats:

1. Write the following code in a file and save it as `binary-write.c`. Notice that we open the file in *write* mode and *binary* mode, indicated by `"wb"` as the second argument to `fopen()`. In binary mode, we can write variables, arrays, and structures to a file. The array in this program will be written to a file called `my-binary-file` in the current working directory. When we write binary data with `fwrite()`, we must specify the size of a single element (a `float` in this case) and how many of those elements we want to write. The second argument to `fwrite()` is the size of a single element and the third argument is the number of elements:

```
#include <stdio.h>

int main(void)
{
   FILE *fp;
   float x[2];
   if ( (fp = fopen("my-binary-file", "wb")) == 0 )
```

```
    {
        fprintf(stderr, "Can't open file for "
           "writing\n");
        return 1;
    }
    printf("Type two floating point numbers, "
        "separated by a space: ");
    scanf("%f %f", &x[0], &x[1]);
    fwrite(&x, sizeof(float),
        sizeof(x) / sizeof(float), fp);
    fclose(fp);
    return 0;
}
```

2. Before moving on, let's compile this program:

```
$> make binary-write
gcc -Wall -Wextra -pedantic -std=c99    binary-write.c
-o binary-write
```

3. Let's try out the program and verify that it writes the binary file. Since it's a binary file, we can't read it with programs such as `more`. But we can, however, look at it with a program called `hexdump`:

```
$> ./binary-write
Type two floating point numbers, separated by a space:
3.14159 2.71828
$> file my-binary-file
my-binary-file: data
$> hexdump -C my-binary-file
00000000  d0 0f 49 40 4d f8 2d 40              |..I@M.-@|
00000008
```

4. Now it's time to write the program that reads the array back from the file. Write the following code in a file and save it as `binary-ready.c`. Notice that we use `"rb"` here, for *read* and *binary*. The arguments to `fread()` are the same as `fwrite()`. Also, note that we need to create an array of the same type and length here. We will read the data from the binary file into that array:

```
#include <stdio.h>

int main(void)
{
```

```
    FILE *fp;
    float x[2];
    if ( (fp = fopen("my-binary-file", "rb")) == 0 )
    {
        fprintf(stderr, "Can't open file for "
            "reading\n");
        return 1;
    }
    fread(&x, sizeof(float),
        sizeof(x) / sizeof(float), fp);
    printf("The first number was: %f\n", x[0]);
    printf("The second number was: %f\n", x[1]);
    fclose(fp);
    return 0;
}
```

5. Now, let's compile this program:

```
$> make binary-read
gcc -Wall -Wextra -pedantic -std=c99    binary-read.c
-o binary-read
```

6. And finally, let's run the program. Notice that the numbers printed here are the same as those numbers we gave to `binary-write`:

```
$> ./binary-read
The first number was: 3.141590
The second number was: 2.718280
```

How it works...

What's important here is `fwrite()` and `fread()`, more specifically the sizes we specify:

```
fwrite(&x, sizeof(float), sizeof(x) / sizeof(float), fp);
```

First off, we have the `x` array. Next, we specify the size of a single element or item. In this case, we get the size by using `sizeof(float)`. Then, as the third argument, we specify how many of those elements or items. Instead of just typing a literal `2` here, we calculate the number of items by taking the full size of the array and dividing it by the size of a float. This is done with `sizeof(x) / sizeof(float)`. This gives us, in this case, 2.

The reason why it's better to calculate the items rather than just setting a number is to avoid errors when updating the code in the future. If we change the array to 6 items in a couple of months, chances are that we'll forget to update the arguments to `fread()` and `fwrite()`.

There's more...

If we didn't know beforehand how many floats the array contained, we could have figured it out with the following lines of code. We will learn more about `fseek()` later in this chapter:

```
fseek(fp, 0, SEEK_END); /* move to the end of the file */
bytes = ftell(fp); /* the total number of bytes */
rewind(fp); /* go back to the start of the file */
items = bytes / sizeof(float); /*number of items (floats)*/
```

Moving around inside a file with lseek()

In this recipe, we'll learn how to move around inside a file with `lseek()`. This function operates on **file descriptors**, so please note that we are now working with file descriptors, not streams. With `lseek()`, we can move around (or **seek**) freely inside a file descriptor. Doing so can be handy if we only want to read a specific part of a file or we want to go back and read some data twice and so on.

In this recipe, we will modify our previous program, called `fd-read.c`, to specify where we want to start reading. We also make it so that the user can specify how many characters should be read from that position.

Getting ready

To easier understand this recipe, I encourage you to read the recipe named *Reading from files with file descriptors* in this chapter before reading this one.

How to do it...

The program we will write here will read a file using file descriptors. The user must also set a starting position where the read should start. The user can also—optionally—specify how many characters to read from that position:

1. Write the following code and save it in a file called `fd-seek.c`. Notice the added `lseek()` before we do `read()`. We have also added an extra check (`else if`) to check that the user doesn't read more than what the buffer can hold. We have also added a newline character in `printf()` when we print the file to stdout. Otherwise, there won't be a new line when we specify how many characters to read, and the prompt would end up on the same line. This program is also rather long, so I have split it up into several steps. Keep in mind that all steps go into the same file. Let's begin with the variables and check the number of arguments:

```
#include <stdio.h>
#include <unistd.h>
#include <fcntl.h>
#include <sys/stat.h>
#include <sys/types.h>
#include <stdlib.h>
#define MAXSIZE 4096

int main(int argc, char *argv[])
{
   int fd; /* for the file descriptor */
   int maxread; /* the maximum we want to read*/
   off_t filesize; /* for the file size */
   struct stat fileinfo; /* struct for fstat */
   char rbuf[MAXSIZE] = { 0 }; /* the read buffer */

   if (argc < 3 || argc > 4)
   {
      fprintf(stderr, "Usage: %s [path] [from pos] "
         "[bytes to read]\n", argv[0]);
      return 1;
   }
```

2. Now we open the file using the `open()` system call. Just as before, we check the system call for errors by wrapping it in an `if` statement:

```
   /* open the file in read-only mode and get
      the file size */
```

```
if ( (fd = open(argv[1], O_RDONLY)) == -1 )
{
   perror("Can't open file for reading");
   return 1;
}
```

3. And now, we get the file's size using the `fstat()` system call. Here we also check whether the file is bigger than `MAXSIZE`, in which case we set `maxread` to `MAXSIZE-1`. In `else if`, we check whether the user has provided a third argument (how much to read), and set `maxread` to whatever the user typed:

```
fstat(fd, &fileinfo);
filesize = fileinfo.st_size;

/* determine the max size we want to read
   so we don't overflow the read buffer */
if ( filesize >= MAXSIZE )
{
   maxread = MAXSIZE-1;
}
else if ( argv[3] != NULL )
{
   if ( atoi(argv[3]) >= MAXSIZE )
   {
      fprintf(stderr, "To big size specified\n");
      return 1;
   }
   maxread = atoi(argv[3]);
}
else
{
   maxread = filesize;
}
```

4. And finally, we write the code to move the read position with `lseek()`. After that, we read the content with `read()` and print it with `printf()`:

```
/* move the read position */
lseek(fd, atoi(argv[2]), SEEK_SET);
/* read the content and print it */
if ( (read(fd, rbuf, maxread)) == -1 )
{
   perror("Can't read file");
```

```
        return 1;
    }
    printf("%s\n", rbuf);
    return 0;
}
```

5. Now compile the program:

```
$> make fd-seek
gcc -Wall -Wextra -pedantic -std=c99    fd-seek.c   -o
fd-seek
```

6. And let's try out the program. Here we read the password file and the generic Makefile in our current directory:

```
$> ./fd-seek /etc/passwd 40 100
:1:1:daemon:/usr/sbin:/usr/sbin/nologin
bin:x:2:2:bin:/bin:/usr/sbin/nologin
sys:x:3:3:sys:/dev:/usr
$> ./fd-seek Makefile 10
AGS=-Wall -Wextra -pedantic -std=c99
$> ./fd-seek Makefile
Usage: ./fd-seek [path] [from pos] [bytes to read]
```

How it works...

The `lseek()` function moves the *read head* (sometimes called a *cursor*) inside the file descriptor to the position we specify. The cursor then remains at that position until we start `read()`. To only read the number of characters that we specify as the third argument, we take that argument and assign the value to `maxread`. Since `read()` doesn't read any more than `maxread` (the third argument to `read()`), only those characters are read. If we don't give the program a third argument, `maxread` is set to the file's size or `MAXSIZE`, whichever is the smallest.

The third argument to `lseek()`, `SEEK_SET`, is where the cursor should be located in relation to the value we give as the second argument. In this case, with `SEEK_SET`, it means that the position should be set to whatever we specify as the second argument. If we wanted to move the position relative to our current position, we would have used `SEEK_CUR` instead. And if we wanted to move the cursor relative to the end of the file, we would have used `SEEK_END`.

Moving around inside a file with fseek()

Now that we have seen how to **seek** inside a file descriptor with `lseek()`, we can see how we can do so in file streams with `fseek()`. In this recipe, we will write a similar program to that of the previous recipe, but now we will use file streams instead. There will also be another difference here, namely, how we specify how long we want to read. In the previous recipe, we specified the third argument as the number of characters or bytes to read. But in this recipe, we will instead specify a position, that is, a *from position* and a *to position*.

Getting ready

I advise you to read the *Reading from files with streams* recipe earlier in this chapter before reading this one. That will give you a better understanding of what's going on here.

How to do it...

We will write a program that reads a file from a given position and optionally to an end position. If no end position is given, the file is read to the end:

1. Write the following code in a file and save it as `stream-seek.c`. This program is similar to `stream-read.c`, but with the added ability to specify the start position and optionally the end position. Notice that we have added `fseek()` to set the start position. To abort the read, when we have reached the end position, we use `ftell()` to tell us the current position. If the end position is reached, we break out of the `while` loop. Also, we no longer read entire lines but individual characters. We do this with `fgetc()`. We also print individual characters instead of an entire string (line). We do this with `putchar()`. After the loop, we print a newline character so that the prompt won't end up on the same line as the output:

```
#include <stdio.h>
#include <stdlib.h>

int main(int argc, char *argv[])
{
   int ch; /* for each character */
   FILE *fp; /* pointer to a file stream */
   if ( argc < 3 || argc > 4 )
   {
      fprintf(stderr, "Usage: %s [path] [from pos]"
         " [to pos]\n", argv[0]);
      return 1;
   }
```

```
    /* open file with read mode */
    if ( (fp = fopen(argv[1], "r")) == NULL )
    {
       perror("Can't open file for reading");
       return 1;
    }

    fseek(fp, atoi(argv[2]), SEEK_SET);
    /* loop over each line and write it to stdout */
    while( (ch = fgetc(fp)) != EOF )
    {
       if ( argv[3] != NULL)
       {
          if ( ftell(fp) >= atoi(argv[3]) )
          {
             break;
          }
       }
       putchar(ch);
    }
    printf("\n");
    fclose(fp); /* close the stream */
    return 0;
}
```

2. Now let's compile it:

```
$> make stream-seek
gcc -Wall -Wextra -pedantic -std=c99    stream-seek.c
-o stream-seek
```

3. And let's try it out on some files. We try with both possible combinations: only a starting position, and both start and end positions:

```
$> ./stream-seek /etc/passwd 2000 2100
24:Libvirt Qemu,,,:/var/lib/libvirt:/bin/false
Debian-exim:x:120:126::/var/spool/exim4:/bin/false
s
$> ./stream-seek Makefile 20
-Wextra -pedantic -std=c99
```

How it works...

The `fseek()` function works similarly to `lseek()`, as we saw in the previous recipe. We specify `SEEK_SET` to tell `fseek()` to seek an absolute position, and as the second argument, we specify the position.

The program is similar to `stream-read.c`, but we have changed how the program reads. Instead of reading the entire lines, we read individual characters. This is so that we can stop reading at the exact position we specify as the end position. That wouldn't be possible if we read line by line. Because we changed the behavior to read the file character by character, we have also changed how we print the file. Now we print each character with `putchar()` instead.

After each character, we check if we are on or above the specified end position. If we are, we `break` out of the loop and end the entire read.

There's more...

There exists a whole family of functions related to `fseek()`. You can find them all by reading the `man 3 fseek` manual page.

6
Spawning Processes and Using Job Control

In this chapter, we'll learn about how processes are created on the system, which process is the very first one, and how all processes are related to each other. We'll then learn the many terms involved in processes and process management in Linux. After that, we'll learn how to fork new processes and what **zombies** and **orphans** are. At the end of this chapter, we'll learn what a **daemon** is and how to create one, before learning about what signals are and how to implement them.

Knowing how processes are created on the system is key to implementing good daemons, dealing with security, and creating efficient programs. It will also give you a better understanding of the overall system. In this chapter, we will cover the following recipes:

- Exploring how processes are created
- Using job control in Bash
- Controlling and terminating processes using signals
- Replacing the program in a process with `execl()`

- Forking a process
- Executing a new program in a forked process
- Starting a new process with `system()`
- Creating a zombie process
- Learning about what orphans are
- Creating a daemon
- Implementing a signal handler

Let's get started!

Technical requirements

In this chapter, you'll need the GCC compiler and Make tool. We installed these tools in *Chapter 1, Getting the Necessary Tools and Writing Our First Linux Programs.*

You will also need a new program called `pstree` for this chapter. You can install it with your package manager. If you are using Debian or Ubuntu, you can install it with `sudo apt install psmisc`. If, on the other hand, you are using Fedora or CentOS, you can install it with `sudo dnf install psmisc`.

You will also need the generic `Makefile` we wrote in *Chapter 3, Diving Deep into C in Linux*. The Makefile is also available on GitHub, together with all the code samples for this chapter, at `https://github.com/PacktPublishing/Linux-System-Programming-Techniques/tree/master/ch6`.

Check out the following link to see the Code in Action video:
`https://bit.ly/3cxY0eQ`

Exploring how processes are created

Before we go into the details of creating processes and daemons, we need a general understanding of processes. The best way to get this understanding is by looking at the processes already running on your system, which is what we are going to do in this recipe.

Every process on the system has started its life by being *spawned*—forked—from another process. The very first process to be used on Unix and Linux systems has historically been **init**. The `init` process has been replaced in modern Linux distributions with **systemd**. They both serve the same purpose; to start the rest of the system.

A typical **process tree** may look like this, where a user has logged on via a terminal (that is, if we skip the complexity of X Window logons):

```
|- systemd (1)
  \- login (6384)
    \- bash (6669)
      \- more testfile.txt (7184)
```

The process IDs are the numbers in parenthesis. `systemd` (or `init` on some older systems) have a **process ID** (**PID**) of 1. Note that on some Linux systems, you can still see the name `init`, even though `systemd` is used. In this case, `init` is just a link to `systemd`. There are still Linux systems that use `init`, though.

Having a deep understanding of how processes **spawn** is essential when it comes to writing system programs. For example, when we want to create a daemon, we often spawn a new process. There are many other use cases where we must spawn processes or execute a new program from an existing process.

Getting ready

For this recipe, you'll need `pstree`. Installation instructions for `pstree` are listed in the *Technical requirements* section of this chapter.

How to do it...

In this recipe, we will look at our system and the processes it runs. We will use `pstree` to get a visual representation of these processes. Let's get started:

1. First, we need a way to get our current process ID. The `$$` environment variable contains the current shell's **PID**. Please note that the PID will differ on every system and also from one time to another:

   ```
   $> echo $$
   18817
   ```

2. Now, let's look at our current process, as well as its parent processes and child processes, with `pstree`. The parent process is what has started the process, while a child process is any process under it:

   ```
   $> pstree -A -p -s $$
   systemd(1)---tmux (4050)---bash(18817)---pstree(18845)
   ```

3. The output from the `pstree` command will most likely be different on your computer. Instead of `tmux`, you might have `xterm`, `konsole`, `mate-terminal`, or something similar. The `-A` option means to print the lines using ASCII characters, the `-p` option means to print the PID numbers, and the `-s` option means that we want to show the parent processes of the selected process (which is `$$` in our case). In my example, `tmux` is a child process of `systemd`, `bash` is a child process of `tmux`, and `pstree` is a child process of `bash`.

4. A process can also have several children. For example, we can start several processes in Bash. Here, we will start three sleep processes. Each sleep process will sleep for 120 seconds. We will then print another `pstree`. In this example, `pstree` and the three `sleep` processes are all children of `bash`:

```
$> sleep 120 &
[1] 21902
$> sleep 120 &
[2] 21907
$> sleep 120 &
[3] 21913
$> pstree -A -p -s $$
systemd(1)---tmux (4050)---bash(18817)-+-pstree(21919)
                                       |-sleep(21902)
                                       |-sleep(21907)
                                       `-sleep(21913)
```

5. At the beginning of this chapter, we provided a sample process tree that showed a process called `login`. That process originally started out as `getty`, a process that manages TTYs on the system. **TTY** stands for *Teletype*. Normally, a Linux computer has seven TTYs you can switch between by using the sequence *Ctrl+Alt+F1*, *Ctrl+Alt+F2*, and so on, all the way up to *Ctrl+Alt+F7*.

   To demonstrate the `getty/login` concept, switch over to TTY3 with *Ctrl+Alt+F3* to activate it. Then, go back to X (often on *Ctrl+Alt+F7* or *Ctrl+Alt+F1*). Here, we will use `grep` with `ps` to find TTY3 and make a note of its PID. The `ps` program is used to find and list processes on the system. Then, we will log in with a user on TTY3 (*Ctrl+Alt+F3*). After that, we will need to go back to our X Window session (and our terminal) again and use `grep` to find the PID we noted from TTY3. The program in that process has now been replaced with `login`. In other words, a process can swap out its program:

```
Ctrl+Alt+F3
login:
```

```
Ctrl+Alt+F7
$> ps ax | grep tty3
9124 tty3     Ss+    0:00 /sbin/agetty -o -p -- \u --
noclear tty3 linux
Ctrl+Alt+F3
login: jake
Password:
$>
Ctrl+Alt+F7
$> ps ax | grep 9124
9124 tty3     Ss     0:00 /bin/login -p -
```

How it works...

In this recipe, we learned about several important concepts regarding processes on Linux systems. We will need this knowledge moving forward. First off, we learned that all processes get spawned from an existing process. The very first process is `init`. On newer Linux distributions, this is a symbolic link to `systemd`. `systemd` then spawns several processes on the system, such as `getty`, to handle the terminals. When a user starts to log in on a TTY, `getty` is replaced with `login`, the program that handles logins. When the user finally logs in, the `login` process spawns a shell for the user, such as Bash. Every time the user then executes a program, Bash spawns a copy of itself and replaces it with the program the user executed.

To clarify the process/program terminology a bit: a **process** runs the **program code**. We often call a *running program* for a *process*, which is correct. However, the program code in the process can be swapped out, as we saw with the `getty/login` example.

The reason for using TTY3 in this recipe is that we get a *real* login process with `getty/login`, something we don't get when logging in via a X Window session or over SSH.

A process ID is denoted as PID. A parent process ID is denoted as **PPID**. Every process on the system has a parent (except for the very first process, **systemd**, which has a PID of `1`).

We also learned that a process can have several children, as with the example provided of the `sleep` processes. We started the `sleep` processes with an `&` symbol at the end. This ampersand tells the shell that we want to start the process in the background.

There's more...

The acronym TTY comes from the fact that, back in the old days, it was an actual *teletype* connected to the machine. A teletype is a typewriter-looking terminal. You type your commands on the typewriter and read the response on the paper. For anyone interested in teletypes, Columbia University has some exciting pictures and information at `http://www.columbia.edu/cu/computinghistory/teletype.html`.

Using job control in Bash

Not only will job control give you a better understanding of foreground and background processes, but it will also make you more efficient when working on a terminal. Being able to put a process in the background frees up your terminal to do other tasks.

Getting ready

Nothing particular is required for this recipe, except for the Bash shell. Bash is most often the default shell, so it's likely that you already have it installed.

How to do it...

In this recipe, we will start and stop several processes, send them to the background, and bring them back to the foreground. This will give us an understanding of background and foreground processes. Let's get started:

1. Previously, we have seen how to start a process in the background with an ampersand (`&`). We will repeat that here, but we will also list the current jobs running and bring one of them to the foreground. The first background process we'll start here is `sleep`, while the other will be a manual page:

   ```
   $> sleep 300 &
   [1] 30200
   $> man ls &
   [2] 30210
   ```

2. Now that we have two processes in the **background**, let's list them with `jobs`:

   ```
   $> jobs
   [1]-  Running                    sleep 300 &
   [2]+  Stopped                    man ls
   ```

3. The `sleep` process is in a running state, meaning that the seconds are ticking away in the program. The `man ls` command has been stopped, though. The `man` command is waiting for you to do something with it since it requires a terminal. So, right now, it doesn't do anything. We can bring it to the foreground by using the `fg` command (**fg** stands for **foreground**). The argument you give to the `fg` command is the job ID from the `jobs` list:

```
$> fg 2
```

4. Quit the manual page by hitting *Q*. `man ls` will appear on the screen.
5. Now, bring the sleep process to the foreground with `fg 1`. It only says `sleep 300`, nothing more. But now, the program is in the foreground. This means we can now stop the program by hitting *Ctrl+Z*:

```
sleep 300
Ctrl+Z
[1]+  Stopped                    sleep 300
```

6. With that, the program has been stopped, meaning it doesn't count down anymore. We can now once again bring it back to the foreground with `fg 1` and let it finish.
7. Now that the previous process has finished, let's start a new `sleep` process. This time, we can start it in the foreground (by omitting the ampersand). Then, we can stop the program by hitting *Ctrl+Z*. List the jobs and notice that the program is in a stopped state:

```
$> sleep 300
Ctrl+Z
[1]+  Stopped                    sleep 300
$> jobs
[1]+  Stopped                    sleep 300
```

8. Now, we can continue running the program in the background using the `bg` command (`bg` stands for *background*):

```
$> bg 1
[1]+ sleep 300 &
$> jobs
[1]+  Running                    sleep 300 &
```

9. We can also find the PID of the program by using a command called `pgrep`. The name `pgrep` stands for *Process Grep*. The `-f` option lets us specify the complete command, including its options, so that we get the correct PID:

```
$> pgrep -f "sleep 300"
4822
```

10. Now that we know the PID, we can kill the program using `kill`:

```
$> kill 4822
$> Enter
[1]+  Terminated                    sleep 300
```

11. We can also kill a program using `pkill`. Here, we will start another process and kill it with `pkill` instead. This command is used with the same options as `pgrep`:

```
$> sleep 300 &
[1] 6526
$> pkill -f "sleep 300"
[1]+  Terminated                    sleep 300
```

How it works…

In this recipe, we learned about background processes, foreground process, stopped and running jobs, killing processes, and much more. These are some basics concepts that are used in job control in Linux.

When we killed the process with `kill`, `kill` sent a signal to the process in the background. The default signal for `kill` is the `TERM` signal. **TERM** stands for **terminate**. A program may choose how to act on a `TERM` signal, though. The `TERM` signal is number 15. A signal that can't be handled—that always kills a program—is signal 9, or the `KILL` signal. We will cover signal handling in more depth in the next recipe.

Controlling and terminating processes using signals

Now that we know a bit more about processes, it's time to move on to signals and learn how we can kill and control a process using signals. In this recipe, we will also write our first C program, which will have a signal handler.

Getting ready

For this recipe, you'll only need what's listed in the *Technical requirements* section of this chapter.

How to do it...

In this recipe, we'll explore how to control and terminate processes with signals. Let's get started:

1. Let's start by listing the signals we can send to a process using the `kill` command. The list you get from this command is rather long, so it's not been included here. The most interesting—and used—signals are the first 31:

```
$> kill -L
```

2. Let's see how some of these signals work. We can send the `STOP` signal (number 19) to a process, which has the same effect as we saw when hitting *Ctrl+Z* in `sleep`. But here, we are sending the `STOP` signal to a background process directly:

```
$> sleep 120 &
[1] 16392
$> kill -19 16392

 [1]+  Stopped                    sleep 120
$> jobs
[1]+  Stopped                    sleep 120
```

3. Now, we can continue the process again by sending it the `CONT` signal (short for **continue**). We can type the name of the signal instead, if we wish, instead of its number:

```
$> kill -CONT 16392
$> jobs
[1]+  Running                    sleep 120 &
```

4. Now, we can kill the process by sending it the `KILL` signal (number 9):

```
$> kill -9 16392
$> Enter
[1]+  Killed                     sleep 120
```

5. Now, let's create a small program that acts upon different signals and ignores (or blocks) *Ctrl+C*, the interrupt signal. The `USR1` and `USR2` signals are perfect for this. Write the following code in a file and save it as `signals.c`. This code has been split up into multiple steps here, but all the code goes into this file. To register a signal handler in a program, we can use the `sigaction()` system call. We need to define `_POSIX_C_SOURCE` since `sigaction()` and its friends aren't included in strict C99. We also need to include the necessary headers files, write the handler function prototype, and begin the `main()` function:

```
#define _POSIX_C_SOURCE 200809L
#include <stdio.h>
#include <sys/types.h>
#include <signal.h>
#include <unistd.h>

void sigHandler(int sig);

int main(void)
{
```

6. Now, let's create some variables and structures that we need. The `sigaction` struct that we will create, `action`, is for the `sigaction()` system call. A bit further down in the code, we set its member. First, we must set `sa_handler` to our function, which will execute when the signal is received. Second, we set `sa_mask` to all signals using `sigfillset()`. This will ignore all the signals while our signal handler is being executed, preventing it from being interrupted. Third, we set `sa_flags` to `SA_RESTART`, meaning any interrupted systems calls will be restarted:

```
    pid_t pid; /* to store our pid in */
    pid = getpid(); /* get the pid */
    struct sigaction action; /* for sigaction */
    sigset_t set; /* signals we want to ignore */
    printf("Program running with PID %d\n", pid);
    /* prepare sigaction() */
    action.sa_handler = sigHandler;
    sigfillset(&action.sa_mask);
    action.sa_flags = SA_RESTART;
```

7. Now, it's time to register the signal handlers using `sigaction()`. The first argument to `sigaction()` is the signal we want to catch, the second argument is a struct for the new action that should be taken, and the third argument gives us the old action. If we are not interested in the old action, we set this to `NULL`. The actions must be a `sigaction` structs:

```
    /* register two signal handlers, one for USR1
       and one for USR2 */
    sigaction(SIGUSR1, &action, NULL);
    sigaction(SIGUSR2, &action, NULL);
```

8. Remember that we wanted the program to ignore *Ctrl+C* (the interrupt signal)? This can be achieved by calling `sigprocmask()` before the code that should ignore the signal. But first, we must create a *signal set* with all the signals it should ignore/block. First, we will empty the set with `sigemptyset()`, and then add the required signals with `sigaddset()`. The `sigaddset()` function can be called multiple times to add more signals. The first argument to `sigprocmask()` is the behavior, which is `SIG_BLOCK` here. The second argument is the signal set, while the third argument can be used to retrieve the old set. However, here, we will set it to `NULL`. After that, we start the infinite `for` loop. And after the loop, we unblock the signal set again. In this case, it's not necessary since we will just quit the program, but in other cases, it's advised to unblock the signals once we have moved past the section of code that should ignore them:

```
    /* create a "signal set" for sigprocmask() */
    sigemptyset(&set);
    sigaddset(&set, SIGINT);
    /* block SIGINT and run an infinite loop */
    sigprocmask(SIG_BLOCK, &set, NULL);
    /* infinite loop to keep the program running */
    for (;;)
    {
        sleep(10);
    }
    sigprocmask(SIG_UNBLOCK, &set, NULL);
    return 0;
}
```

9. Finally, let's write the function that will be executed on `SIGUSR1` and `SIGUSR2`. The function will print the received signal:

```
void sigHandler(int sig)
{
    if (sig == SIGUSR1)
    {
        printf("Received USR1 signal\n");
    }
    else if (sig == SIGUSR2)
    {
        printf("Received USR2 signal\n");
    }
}
```

10. Let's compile the program:

```
$> make signals
gcc -Wall -Wextra -pedantic -std=c99    signals.c   -o
 signals
```

11. Run the program, either in a separate terminal or in the same terminal in the background. Notice that we are using the signal names here with `kill`; it's a bit easier than keeping track of the numbers:

```
$> ./signals &
[1] 25831
$> Program running with PID 25831

$> kill -USR1 25831
Received USR1 signal
$> kill -USR1 25831
Received USR1 signal
$> kill -USR2 25831
$> kill -USR2 25831
Received USR2 signal
$> Ctrl+C
^C
$> kill -USR1 25831
Received USR1 signal
$> kill -TERM 25831
$> ENTER
[1]+  Terminated              ./signals
```

How it works...

First, we explored the many **signals** available in a Linux system, of which the first 31 are of interest and widely used. The most common ones are `TERM`, `KILL`, `QUIT`, `STOP`, `HUP`, `INT`, `STOP`, and `CONT`, as we saw here.

Then, we used the `STOP` and `CONT` signals to achieve the same effect that we achieved in the previous recipe; that is, to stop and continue running a background process. In the previous recipe, we used `bg` to continue running a process in the background, while to stop a process, we hit *Ctrl+Z*. This time, we didn't need to have the program open in the foreground to stop it; we just sent it the `STOP` signal with `kill`.

After that, we moved on and wrote a C program that catches two signals, `USR1` and `USR2`, and blocks the `SIGINT` signal (*Ctrl+C*). Depending on the signal we send to the program, different texts are printed. We did this by implementing a signal handler. A **signal handler** is a function that we write ourselves, just like any other function. Then, we registered that function as a signal handler with the `sigaction()` function.

Before calling the `sigaction()` system call, we had to populate the `sigaction` structure with information about the handler function, which signals to ignore during the handler's execution, and which behavior it should have.

The signal sets, both for sigaction's `sa_mask` and `sigprocmask()`, are created using the `sigset_t` type and manipulated with the following function calls (here, we're assuming a `sigset_t` variable with the name `s` is being used:

- `sigemptyset(&s);` clears all signals from `s`
- `sigaddset(&s, SIGUSR1);` adds the `SIGUSR1` signal to `s`
- `sigdelset(&s, SIGUSR1);` removes the `SIGUSR` signal from `s`
- `sigfillset(&s);` sets all signals in `s`
- `sigismember(&s, SIGUSR1);` finds out if `SIGUSR1` is a member of `s` (not used in our example code)

To print the PID of the process when it starts, we must fetch the PID with the `getpid()` system call. We store the PID in a variable of the `pid_t` type, as we have seen previously.

See also

There's a lot of useful information in the manual pages for `kill`, `pkill`, `sigprocmask()`, and the `sigaction()` system call. I suggest you read them by using the following commands:

- `man 1 kill`
- `man 1 pkill`
- `man 2 sigprocmask`
- `man 2 sigaction`

There is a much simpler system call, called `signal()`, that is also used for signal handling. Nowadays, that system call is more or less considered deprecated. But if you're interested, you can read about it in `man 2 signal`.

Replacing the program in a process with execl()

At the beginning of this chapter, we saw how `getty` gets replaced by `login` when a user logs in. In this recipe, we will write a small program that does exactly that—replaces its program with a new one. The system call for this is called `execl()`.

Knowing how to use `execl()` enables you to write programs that execute new programs inside the existing process. It also enables you to start a new program in a spawned process. When we start a new process, we probably want to replace that copy with a new program. So, understanding `execl()` is paramount.

Getting ready

You will need to have read the first three recipes in this chapter to understand this one fully. The other requirements for this recipe are mentioned in the *Technical requirements* section of this chapter; for example, you'll need the `pstree` tool.

You will also need two terminals or two terminal windows for this recipe. In one of these terminals, we will be running the program, while in the other terminal, we'll be looking at `pstree` for the process.

How to do it...

In this recipe, we will write a small program that replaces the program running inside the process. Let's get started:

1. Write the following code in a file and save it as `execdemo.c`:

```
#include <stdio.h>
#include <unistd.h>
#include <errno.h>
#include <sys/types.h>

int main(void)
{
    printf("My PID is %d\n", getpid());
    printf("Hit enter to continue ");
    getchar(); /* wait for enter key */
    printf("Executing /usr/bin/less...\n");
    /* execute less using execl and error check it */
    if ( execl("/usr/bin/less", "less",
        "/etc/passwd", (char*)NULL) == -1 )
    {
        perror("Can't execute program");
        return 1;
    }
    return 0;
}
```

2. Compile the program using Make:

```
$> make execdemo
gcc -Wall -Wextra -pedantic -std=c99    execdemo.c    -o
execdemo
```

3. Now, run the program in your *current* terminal:

```
$> ./execdemo
My PID is 920
Hit enter to continue
```

4. Now, start a *new* terminal and execute `pstree` with the PID from `execdemo`:

```
$> pstree -A -p -s 920
systemd(1)---tmux(4050)---bash(18817)---execdemo(920)
```

5. Now, go back to the first terminal, where `execdemo` is running, and hit *Enter*. This will print the password file with `less`.
6. Finally, go back to the second terminal—the one where you ran `pstree`. Rerun the same `pstree` command. Note that `execdemo` has been replaced with `less`, even though the PID is still the same:

```
$> pstree -A -p -s 920
systemd(1)---tmux(4050)---bash(18817)---less(920)
```

How it works...

The `execl()` function executes a new program and replaces the old one in the same process. To make the program pause its execution so that we had time to view it in `pstree`, we used `getchar()`.

The `execl()` function takes four mandatory arguments. The first one is the path to the program we want to execute. The second argument is the program's name, as it would be printed from `argv[0]`. Finally, the third and any following argument is the argument we want to pass to the program we are about to execute. To *terminate* this list of arguments that we want to pass to the program, we must end it with a pointer to `NULL`, cast as a `char`.

Another way to look at a process is to think of it as an execution environment. The program running inside that environment can be replaced. That's why we talk about processes and why we call them *Process IDs*, not Program IDs.

See also

There are several other `exec()` functions we can use, each with their own unique features and characteristics. These are often referred to as the "`exec()` family." You can read all about them by using the `man 3 execl` command.

Forking a process

Previously, we have been saying *spawned* when a program creates a new process. The correct terminology is to **fork** a process. What's happening is that a process creates a copy of itself—it *forks*.

In the previous recipe, we learned how to execute a new program inside a process using `execl()`. In this recipe, we'll learn how to fork a process using `fork()`. The forked process—the child—is a duplicate of the calling process—the parent.

Knowing how to fork a process enables us to create new processes on the system programmatically. Without being able to fork, we are limited to only a single process. For example, if we want to launch a new program from an existing one and still keep the original, we must fork.

Getting ready

Just as in the previous recipes, you'll need the `pstree` tool. The *Technical requirements* section covers how to install it. You'll also need the GCC compiler and the Make tool. You'll also need two terminals; one terminal to execute the program and another to view a process tree with `pstree`.

How to do it...

In this recipe, we'll use `fork()` to fork a process. We'll also view a process tree so that we can see what's going on. Let's get started:

1. Write the following code in a program and save it as `forkdemo.c`. The `fork()` system call is highlighted in this code. Before we `fork()`, we print the PID of the process:

```
#include <stdio.h>
#include <sys/types.h>
#include <unistd.h>

int main(void)
{
   pid_t pid;
   printf("My PID is %d\n", getpid());
   /* fork, save the PID, and check for errors */
   if ( (pid = fork()) == -1 )
   {
      perror("Can't fork");
      return 1;
   }
   if (pid == 0)
   {
      /* if pid is 0 we are in the child process */
      printf("Hello from the child process!\n");
      sleep(120);
   }
```

```
    else if(pid > 0)
    {
       /* if pid is greater than 0 we are in
        * the parent */
       printf("Hello from the parent process! "
          "My child has PID %d\n", pid);
       sleep(120);
    }
    else
    {
       fprintf(stderr, "Something went wrong "
          "forking\n");
       return 1;
    }
    return 0;
}
```

2. Now, compile the program:

```
$> make forkdemo
gcc -Wall -Wextra -pedantic -std=c99    forkdemo.c
-o forkdemo
```

3. Run the program in your *current* terminal and take note of the PID:

```
$> ./forkdemo
My PID is 21764
Hello from the parent process! My child has PID 21765
Hello from the child process!
```

4. Now, in a new terminal, run `pstree` with the PID of `forkdemo`. Here, we can see that `forkdemo` has forked and that the PID that we got from the program before the fork is the parent process. The forked process is the **child process**, and the child's PID matches what the parent told us. Also, notice that there are now two copies of `forkdemo` running:

```
$> pstree -A -p -s 21764
systemd(1)---tmux(4050)---bash(18817)---
forkdemo(21764)---forkdemo(21765)
```

How it works...

When a process forks, it creates a duplicate of itself. This duplicate becomes a child process of the process that called `fork()`—the **parent process**. The child process is identical to the parent process, except it has a new PID. Inside the parent process, `fork()` returns the PID of the child process. Inside the child process, `0` is returned. This is why the parent could print the PID of the child process.

Both processes contain the same program code, and both processes are running, but only the specific parts in the `if` statements get executed, depending on whether the process is the parent or the child.

There's more...

Generally speaking, both the parent and the child are identical except for the PID. There are, however, some other differences; for example, CPU counters are reset in the child. There are other such minor differences that you can read about in `man 2 fork`. However, the overall program code is the same.

Executing a new program in a forked process

In the previous recipe, we learned how to fork a process using the `fork()` system call. In the recipe before that, we learned how to replace the program in a process with `execl()`. In this recipe, we'll combine the two, `fork()` and `execl()`, to execute a new program in a forked process. This is what happens every time we run a program in Bash. Bash forks itself and executes the program we typed in.

Knowing how to use `fork()` and `execl()` enables you to write programs that start new programs. For example, you could write your own shell with this knowledge.

Getting ready

For this recipe, you'll need the `pstree` tool, the GCC compiler, and the Make tool. You can find installation instructions for these programs in the *Technical requirements* section of this chapter.

How to do it...

In this recipe, we'll write a program that `forks()` and executes a new program in the child process. Let's get started:

1. Write the following program code in a file and save it as `my-fork.c`. When we execute a new program inside a child process, we shall wait for the child process to finish. This is what we do with `waitpid()`. The `waitpid()` call also has another important function; to get the return status from the child process:

```
#include <stdio.h>
#include <unistd.h>
#include <sys/types.h>
#include <string.h>
#include <sys/wait.h>

int main(void)
{
   pid_t pid;
   int status;

   /* Get and print my own pid, then fork
      and check for errors */
   printf("My PID is %d\n", getpid());
   if ( (pid = fork()) == -1 )
   {
      perror("Can't fork");
      return 1;
   }
   if (pid == 0)
   {
      /* If pid is 0 we are in the child process,
         from here we execute 'man ls' */
      if ( execl("/usr/bin/man", "man", "ls",
         (char*)NULL) == -1 )
      {
         perror("Can't exec");
         return 1;
      }
   }
   else if(pid > 0)
   {
      /* In the parent we must wait for the child
```

```
            to exit with waitpid(). Afterward, the
            child exit status is written to 'status' */
         waitpid(pid, &status, 0);
         printf("Child executed with PID %d\n", pid);
         printf("Its return status was %d\n", status);
         printf("Its return status was %d\n", status);
      }
      else
      {
         fprintf(stderr, "Something went wrong "
            "forking\n");
         return 1;
      }
      return 0;
   }
```

2. Compile the program using Make:

```
$> make my-fork
gcc -Wall -Wextra -pedantic -std=c99    my-fork.c    -o
my-fork
```

3. In your current terminal, find the PID of the current shell and make a note of it:

```
$> echo $$
18817
```

4. Now, execute the program we compiled with `./my-fork`. This will display the manual page for `ls`.

5. Start a new terminal and look at the process tree for the shell in the other terminal. Note that `my-fork` has forked and replaced its content with `man`, which has forked and replaced its content with `pager` (to display the content):

```
$> pstree -A -p -s 18817
systemd(1)---tmux(4050)---bash(18817)---my-fork(5849)-
--man(5850)---pager(5861)
```

6. Quit the manual page in the first terminal by hitting Q. This will yield the following text. Compare the PID of the parent process and the child process from `pstree`. Notice that the child process is `5850`, which was the `man` command. It started out as a copy of `my-fork`, but then replaced its program with `man`:

```
My PID is 5849
Child executed with PID 5850
Its return status was 0
```

How it works...

The `fork()` system call is responsible for forking processes on Linux and Unix systems. `execl()` (or one of the other `exec()` functions) is then responsible for executing—and replacing its own—program with a new one. This is essentially how any program gets started on the system.

Note that we needed to tell the parent process to wait for the child process with `waitpid()`. If we needed to run a program that didn't require a terminal, we could have done without `waitpid()`. However, we should always wait for the child process. If we don't, the child will end up as an **orphan**. This is something we will discuss in great detail later on in this chapter, in the *Learning what orphans are* recipe.

But in this particular case, where we execute the `man` command, which requires a terminal, we need to wait for the child for everything to work. The `waitpid()` call also enables us to grab the *return status* of the child. We also prevent the child from becoming an orphan.

When we ran the program and looked at the process tree with `pstree`, we saw that the `my-fork` process had forked itself and replaced its program with `man`. We could see this because the PID of the `man` command was the same as the PID of the child process of `my-fork`. We also noticed that the `man` command, in turn, had forked itself and replaced its child with `pager`. The `pager` command is responsible for displaying the actual text on the screen, which is usually `less`.

Starting a new process with system()

What we just covered regarding using `fork()`, `waitpid()`, and `execl()` to start a new program in a forked process is the key to understanding Linux and processes at a deeper level. This understanding is key to becoming an excellent system developer. However, there is a shortcut. Instead of manually dealing with forking, waiting, and executing, we can use `system()`. The `system()` function does all these steps for us.

Getting ready

For this recipe, you only need what's listed in the *Technical requirements* section of this chapter.

How to do it...

In this recipe, we'll rewrite the previous program—`my-fork`—using the `system()` function instead. You'll notice how much shorter this program is compared to the previous one. Let's get started:

1. Write the following code in a file and save it as `sysdemo.c`. Notice how much smaller (and easier) this program is. The `system()` function does all the complex stuff for us:

```
#include <stdio.h>
#include <stdlib.h>

int main(void)
{
    if ( (system("man ls")) == -1 )
    {
        fprintf(stderr, "Error forking or reading "
            "status\n");
        return 1;
    }
    return 0;
}
```

2. Compile the program:

```
$> make sysdemo
gcc -Wall -Wextra -pedantic -std=c99    sysdemo.c    -o
sysdemo
```

3. Make a note of the shell's PID using the `$$` variable:

```
$> echo $$
957
```

4. Now, run the program in the current terminal. This will display the manual page for the `ls` command. Leave it running:

```
$> ./sysdemo
```

5. Start a new terminal and execute `pstree` on the PID from *step 3*. Notice that we have an additional process here called `sh`. This is because the `system()` function executes the `man` command from `sh` (the basic Bourne Shell):

```
$> pstree -A -p -s 957
systemd(1)---tmux(4050)---bash(957)---sysdemo(28274)--
-sh(28275)---man(28276)---pager(28287)
```

How it works...

This program was much smaller and easier to write. However, as we saw with `pstree`, there is an extra process compared to the previous recipe: `sh` (shell). The `system()` function works by executing the `man` command from `sh`. The manual page (`man 3 system`) clearly states this. It executes the command we specify by using the following `execl()` call:

```
execl("/bin/sh", "sh", "-c", command, (char *) 0);
```

The result is the same, though. It performs a `fork()` and then an `execl()` call, and it waits for the child with `waitpid()`. This is also a great example of a higher-level function that uses lower-level system calls.

Creating a zombie process

To fully understand processes in Linux, we also need to look at what a zombie process is. And to fully understand what this is, we need to create one ourselves.

A **zombie** process is a child that has exited before the parent, and the parent process hasn't waited for the child's status. The name "zombie process" comes from the fact that the process is *undead*. The process has exited, but there is still an entry for it in the system process table.

Knowing what a zombie process is and how it's created will help you avoid writing bad programs that create zombie processes on the system.

Getting ready

For this recipe, you'll only need what's listed in the *Technical requirements* section of this chapter.

How to do it...

In this recipe, we will write a small program that creates a zombie process on the system. We will also view the zombie process using the `ps` command. To prove that we can avoid zombies by waiting for the child, we will also write a second version with `waitpid()`. Let's get started:

1. Write the following code in a file and name it `create-zombie.c`. This program is the same as the one we saw in the `forkdemo.c` file, except that the child exits using `exit(0)` before the parent exits. The parent sleeps for 2 minutes after the child has exited, without waiting for the child with `waitpid()`, thus creating a zombie process. The call to `exit()` is highlighted here:

```
#include <stdio.h>
#include <sys/types.h>
#include <unistd.h>
#include <stdlib.h>

int main(void)
{
   pid_t pid;
   printf("My PID is %d\n", getpid());
   /* fork, save the PID, and check for errors */
   if ( (pid = fork()) == -1 )
   {
      perror("Can't fork");
      return 1;
   }
   if (pid == 0)
   {
      /* if pid is 0 we are in the child process */
      printf("Hello and goodbye from the child!\n");
      exit(0);
      /* if pid is greater than 0 we are in
       * the parent */
      printf("Hello from the parent process! "
         "My child had PID %d\n", pid);
      sleep(120);
   }
   else
   {
      fprintf(stderr, "Something went wrong "
         "forking\n");
```

```
        return 1;
    }
    return 0;
}
```

2. Compile the program:

```
$> make create-zombie
gcc -Wall -Wextra -pedantic -std=c99    create-
zombie.c    -o create-zombie
```

3. Run the program in the current terminal. The program (the parent process) will stay alive for 2 minutes. In the meantime, the child is a zombie since the parent didn't wait for it or its status:

```
$> ./create-zombie
My PID is 2429
Hello from the parent process! My child had PID 2430
Hello and goodbye from the child!
```

4. While the program is running, open up another terminal and check out the child's PID with `ps`. You get the child's PID from the preceding output from `create-zombie`. Here, we can see that the process is a zombie because of its status, `Z+`, and the word `<defunct>` after the process name:

```
$> ps a | grep 2430
  2430 pts/18   Z+     0:00 [create-zombie] <defunct>
  2824 pts/34   S+     0:00 grep 2430
```

5. After 2 minutes—when the parent process has finished executing—rerun the `ps` command with the same PID. The zombie process will now be gone:

```
$> ps a | grep 2430
  3364 pts/34   S+     0:00 grep 2430
```

6. Now, rewrite the program so that it looks as follows. Name the new version `no-zombie.c`. The code that's been added is highlighted here:

```
#include <stdio.h>
#include <sys/types.h>
#include <unistd.h>
#include <stdlib.h>
#include <sys/wait.h>
```

```
int main(void)
{
   pid_t pid;
   int status;
   printf("My PID is %d\n", getpid());
   /* fork, save the PID, and check for errors */
   if ( (pid = fork()) == -1 )
   {
      perror("Can't fork");
      return 1;
   }
   if (pid == 0)
   {
      /* if pid is 0 we are in the child process */
      printf("Hello and goodbye from the child!\n");
      exit(0);
   }
   else if(pid > 0)
   {
      /* if pid is greater than 0 we are in
       * the parent */
      printf("Hello from the parent process! "
         "My child had PID %d\n", pid);
      waitpid(pid, &status, 0); /* wait for child */
      sleep(120);
   }
   else
   {
      fprintf(stderr, "Something went wrong "
         "forking\n");
      return 1;
   }
   return 0;
}
```

7. Compile this new version:

```
$> make no-zombie
gcc -Wall -Wextra -pedantic -std=c99    no-zombie.c
-o no-zombie
```

8. Run the program in the current terminal. Just as before, it will create a child process that will exit immediately. The parent process will continue running for 2 minutes, giving us enough time to search for the child's PID:

```
$> ./no-zombie
My PID is 22101
Hello from the parent process! My child had PID 22102
Hello and goodbye from the child!
```

9. While the `no-zombie` program is running, open a new terminal and search for the child's PID with `ps` and `grep`. As you will see, there is no process that matches the PID of the child. Hence, the child has exited correctly since the parent waited for its status:

```
$> ps a | grep 22102
22221 pts/34   S+     0:00 grep 22102
```

How it works...

We always want to avoid creating zombie processes on the system, and the best way to do that is to wait for the child processes to finish.

In *steps 1 to 5*, we wrote a program that creates a zombie process. The zombie process gets created by the fact that the parent didn't wait for the child with the `waitpid()` system call. The child does exit, but it remains in the system process table. When we searched for the process with `ps` and `grep`, we saw the child process's status as `Z+`, meaning zombie. The process doesn't exist since it has exited using the `exit()` system call. However, it's still in there according to the system process table; hence, it's undead—a zombie.

In *steps 6 to 9*, we rewrote the program using the `waitpid()` system call to wait for the child. The child still exists before the parent, but this time, the parent gets the child's status.

A zombie process doesn't use up any system resources since the process has terminated. It only resides in the system process table. However, every process on the system—including zombies—takes up a PID number. Since there are a finite number of PIDs available to the system, there's a risk of running out of PIDs if dead processes are taking up PID numbers.

There's more...

There are many details about child process and their state changes in the manual page for `waitpid()`. There's actually three `wait()` functions available in Linux. You can read about them all by using the `man 2 wait` command.

Learning about what orphans are

Understanding what orphans are in a Linux system is just as crucial as understanding zombies. This will give you a deeper understanding of the entire system and how processes get inherited by `systemd`.

An **orphan** is a child whose parent has died. However, as we have learned in this chapter, every process needs a parent process. So, even orphans need a parent process. To solve this dilemma, every orphan gets inherited by `systemd`, which is the first process on the system—PID `1`.

In this recipe, we'll write a small program that forks, thus creating a child process. The parent process will then exit, leaving the child as an orphan.

Getting ready

Everything you need for this recipe is listed in the *Technical requirements* section of this chapter.

How to do it...

In this recipe, we will write a short program that creates an orphan process that will be inherited by `systemd`. Let's get started:

1. Write the following code in a file and save it as `orphan.c`. The program will create a child process that will run for 5 minutes in the background. When we press *Enter*, the parent process will exit. This gives us time to investigate the child process with `pstree` both before and after the parent has exited:

```
#include <stdio.h>
#include <sys/types.h>
#include <unistd.h>
#include <stdlib.h>

int main(void)
{
   pid_t pid;
```

```
    printf("Parent PID is %d\n", getpid());
    /* fork, save the PID, and check for errors */
    if ( (pid = fork()) == -1 )
    {
        perror("Can't fork");
        return 1;
    }
    if (pid == 0)
    {
        /* if pid is 0 we are in the child process */
        printf("I am the child and will run for "
            "5 minutes\n");
        sleep(300);
        exit(0);
    }
    else if(pid > 0)
    {
        /* if pid is greater than 0 we are in
         * the parent */
        printf("My child has PID %d\n"
            "I, the parent, will exit when you "
            "press enter\n", pid);
        getchar();
        return 0;
    }
    else
    {
        fprintf(stderr, "Something went wrong "
            "forking\n");
        return 1;
    }
    return 0;
}
```

2. Compile this program:

```
$> make orphan
gcc -Wall -Wextra -pedantic -std=c99    orphan.c    -o
 orphan
```

3. Run the program in the current terminal and leave the program running. Don't press *Enter* just yet:

```
$> ./orphan
My PID is 13893
My child has PID 13894
I, the parent, will exit when you press enter
I am the child and will run for 2 minutes
```

4. Now, in a new terminal, run `pstree` with the PID of the child. Here, we will see that it looks just like it did in the previous recipes. The process has been forked, which has created a child process with the same content:

```
$> pstree -A -p -s 13894
systemd(1)---tmux(4050)---bash(18817)---orphan(13893)-
--orphan(13894)
```

5. Now, it's time to end the parent process. Go back and hit *Enter* in the terminal where `orphan` is still running. This will end the parent process.
6. Now, run `pstree` again in the second terminal. This is the same command that you just ran. As you can see, the child process has now been inherited by `systemd` since its parent has died. After 5 minutes, the child process will exit:

```
$> pstree -A -p -s 13894
systemd(1)---orphan(13894)
```

7. There are other, more standardized tools we can use to view the **Parent Process ID** (**PPID**). One of these is `ps`. Run the following `ps` command to view more detailed information about the child process. Here, we will see a lot more information. The most important to us is the PPID, PID, and the **Session ID** (**SID**). We will also see the **User ID** (**UID**) here, which specifies who owns the process:

```
$> ps jp 13894
PPID PID PGID  SID   TTY  TPGID STAT UID TIME COMMAND
1  13894 13893 18817 pts/18 18817 S 1000 0:00 ./orphan
```

How it works...

Every process needs a parent process. That's the reason why `systemd` inherits any processes on the system that end up as orphans.

The code inside `if (pid == 0)` continued to run for 5 minutes. That gave us enough time to check that the child process had been inherited by `systemd`.

In the last step, we used `ps` to view more details about the child process. Here, we saw the PPID, PID, PGID, and SID. Some new names have been mentioned here that are important to know. We already know about PPID and PID, but PGID and SID haven't been covered yet.

PGID stands for **Process Group ID** and is a way for the system to group processes. The PGID for the child process is the PID of the parent process. In other words, this PGID was created to group the parent and child process since they belong together. The system sets the PGID to the PID of the parent who created the group. We don't need to create these groups ourselves; that is something the system does for us.

SID stands for **Session ID**, and this is also a way for the system to group processes. However, a SID group is usually bigger and contains more processes— often a whole "session," hence the name. The SID of this group is `18817`, which is the PID of the Bash shell. The same rules apply here; the SID number will be the same as the PID of the process that started the session. This session consists of my user's shell and all the programs that I start from it. That way, the system can kill all the processes that belong to that session if I log off the system.

See also

There's a lot of information you can get with `ps`. I recommend that you at least skim through the manual with `man 1 ps`.

Creating a daemon

A common assignment when working with system programming is to create various daemons. A **daemon** is a background process that runs on the system and performs some tasks. The SSH daemon is a great example of this. Another great example is the NTP daemon, which takes care of synchronizing the computer clock and sometimes even distributing the time to other computers.

Knowing how to create a daemon will enable you to create server software; for example, web servers, chat servers, and more.

In this recipe, we will create a simple daemon to demonstrate some important concepts.

Getting ready

You'll only need the components listed in the *Technical requirements* section of this chapter.

How to do it...

In this recipe, we'll write a small daemon that will run in the background in our system. The only "work" the daemon will do is write the current date and time to a file. This proves that the daemon is alive and well. Let's get started:

1. The code for the daemon is rather long compared to our previous examples. Therefore, the code has been split into several steps. There are some new things here as well that we haven't covered yet. Write the code in a file and save it as `my-daemon.c`. Remember that all the code in all the steps goes into this file. We'll start with all the `include` files, the variables we'll need, and our `fork()`, as we have seen previously. This `fork()` will be the first of two:

```
#include <stdio.h>
#include <unistd.h>
#include <stdlib.h>
#include <sys/types.h>
#include <sys/stat.h>
#include <time.h>
#include <fcntl.h>

int main(void)
{
   pid_t pid;
   FILE *fp;
   time_t now; /* for the current time */
   const char pidfile[] = "/var/run/my-daemon.pid";
   const char daemonfile[] =
      "/tmp/my-daemon-is-alive.txt";

   if ( (pid = fork()) == -1 )
   {
      perror("Can't fork");
      return 1;
   }
```

2. Now that we've forked, we want the parent to exit. Once the parent has exited, we will be in the child process. In the child process, we will create a new session with `setsid()`. Creating a new session will free the process from the controlling terminal:

```
else if ( (pid != 0) )
{
    exit(0);
}
/* the parent process has exited, so this is the
 * child. create a new session to lose the
 * controlling terminal */
setsid();
```

3. Now, we want to `fork()` again. This second fork will create a new process just as before, but since it's a new process in an already existing session, it will not be a session leader, preventing it from obtaining a new controlling terminal. The new child process is referred to as a grandchild. Once again, we exit the parent process (the child process). However, before we exit the child, we write the PID of the grandchild to a **PID file**. This PID file is used to keep track of the daemon:

```
/* fork again, creating a grandchild,
 * the actual daemon */
if ( (pid = fork()) == -1 )
{
    perror("Can't fork");
    return 1;
}
/* the child process which will exit */
else if ( pid > 0 )
{
    /* open pid-file for writing and error
     * check it */
    if ( (fp = fopen(pidfile, "w")) == NULL )
    {
        perror("Can't open file for writing");
        return 1;
    }
    /* write pid to file */
    fprintf(fp, "%d\n", pid);
    fclose(fp); /* close the file pointer */
```

```
        exit(0);
    }
```

4. Now, set the default mode (*umask*) to something sensible for the daemon. We must also change the current working directory to / so that the daemon won't prevent a filesystem from unmounting or a directory from being deleted. Then, we must open the daemon file, which is what we will write our messages to. The messages will contain the current date and time and will let us know if everything is working. Normally, this would be a log file instead:

```
    umask(022); /* set the umask to something ok */
    chdir("/"); /* change working directory to / */
    /* open the "daemonfile" for writing */
    if ( (fp = fopen(daemonfile, "w")) == NULL )
    {
        perror("Can't open daemonfile");
        return 1;
    }
```

5. Since the daemon will only run detached in the background, we have no use for stdin, stdout, and stderr, so let's close them all. However, it's not safe to leave them closed. If something in the code would open a file descriptor at a later time, it will get file descriptor 0, which is usually stdin. File descriptors are assigned in sequence. If there are no open file descriptors, the first call to `open()` will get descriptor `0`; the second call will get descriptor `1`. Another problem might be that some parts might try to write to stdout, which no longer exists, making the program crash. Therefore, we must reopen them all, but to `/dev/null` (the black hole) instead:

```
    /* from here, we don't need stdin, stdout or,
     * stderr anymore, so let's close them all,
     * then re-open them to /dev/null */
    close(STDIN_FILENO);
    close(STDOUT_FILENO);
    close(STDERR_FILENO);
    open("/dev/null", O_RDONLY); /* 0 = stdin */
    open("/dev/null", O_WRONLY); /* 1 = stdout */
    open("/dev/null", O_RDWR); /* 2 = stderr */
```

6. Finally, we can start the daemon's work. This is just a `for` loop that writes a message to the daemon file saying the daemon is still alive. Notice that we must flush the file pointer after each `fprintf()` with `fflush()`. Usually, in Linux, things are *line buffered*, meaning only a single line is buffered before writing. However, since this is a file and not stdout, it's fully buffered instead, meaning it buffers all data until either the buffer is full or the file stream is closed. Without `fflush()`, we wouldn't see any text in the file until we have filled the buffer. By using `fflush()` after each `fprintf()`, we can see the text live in the file:

```
    /* here we start the daemons "work" */
    for (;;)
    {
        /* get the current time and write it to the
           "daemonfile" that we opened above */
        time(&now);
        fprintf(fp, "Daemon alive at %s",
           ctime(&now));
        fflush(fp); /* flush the stream */
        sleep(30);
    }
    return 0;
}
```

7. Now, it's time to compile the entire daemon:

```
$> make my-daemon
gcc -Wall -Wextra -pedantic -std=c99    my-daemon.c
-o my-daemon
```

8. Now, we can start the daemon. Since we are writing the PID file to `/var/run`, we need to execute the daemon as root. We won't get any output from the daemon; it will silently detach from the terminal:

```
$> sudo ./my-daemon
```

9. Now that the daemon is running, let's check out the PID number that's been written to `/var/run/my-daemon.pid`:

```
$> cat /var/run/my-daemon.pid
5508
```

10. Let's investigate the daemon process using both ps and pstree. If everything has worked out the way it should have, it should have systemd as its parent, and it should be in its own session (SID should be the same as the process ID):

```
$> ps jp 5508
PPID PID PGID SID TTY TPGID STAT UID TIME COMMAND
1    5508 5508 5508?    -1     Ss     0  0:00 ./my-daemon
$> pstree -A -p -s 5508
systemd(1)---my-daemon(5508)
```

11. Let's also take a look at the /tmp/my-daemon-is-alive.txt file. This file should contain some rows specifying the date and time, 30 seconds apart:

```
$> cat /tmp/my-daemon-is-alive.txt
Daemon alive at Sun Nov 22 23:25:45 2020
Daemon alive at Sun Nov 22 23:26:15 2020
Daemon alive at Sun Nov 22 23:26:45 2020
Daemon alive at Sun Nov 22 23:27:15 2020
Daemon alive at Sun Nov 22 23:27:45 2020
Daemon alive at Sun Nov 22 23:28:15 2020
Daemon alive at Sun Nov 22 23:28:45 2020
```

12. Finally, let's kill the daemon so that it doesn't continue to write to the file:

```
$> sudo kill 5508
```

How it works...

The daemon we have just written is a basic traditional daemon, but it demonstrates all the concepts we need to understand well. One of these new and important concepts is how to start a new session with setsid(). If we don't create a new session, the daemon will still be a part of the user's login session and die when the user logs off. But since we've created a new session for the daemon and it is inherited by systemd, it now lives on its own, unaffected by the user and process that started it.

The reason for forking the second time is that a session leader—which is what our first child after the setsid() call is—can acquire a new controlling terminal if it were to open a terminal device. When we do the second fork, that new child is just a member of the session that was created by the first child, not the leader, and hence it cannot acquire a **controlling terminal** anymore. The reason for avoiding a controlling terminal is that if that terminal would exit, so would the daemon. Forking twice when creating a daemon is often called the **double-fork** technique.

The reason we needed to start the daemon as root is that it needs to write to `/var/run/`. If we were to change the directory—or skip it entirely—the daemon would run just fine as a regular user. However, most daemons do run as root. There are, however, daemons that run as regular users; for example, daemons that handle user-related things, such as `tmux` (a **terminal multiplexer**).

We also changed the working directory to `/`. This is so that the daemon won't lock up a directory. The top root directory isn't going to be removed or unmounted, which makes it a safe working directory for the daemon.

There's more...

What we have written here is a traditional Linux/Unix daemon. These kinds of daemons are still used today, for example, for small and quick daemons like this one. However, since `systemd` came around, we no longer need to "daemonize" a daemon the way we just did. For example, it's advised to leave stdout and stderr open and send all log messages there instead. These messages will then show up in the *journal*. We will cover systemd and the journal in more depth in *Chapter 7, Using systemd to Handle Your Daemons.*

The type of daemon we have written here is called *forking* in systemd language, which we'll learn more about later on.

Just like `system()` simplified things for us when executing new programs, there is a function called `daemon()` that can create daemons for us. This function will do all the heavy lifting for us, such as forking, closing and reopening the file descriptors, changing the working directory, and more. However, please note that this function doesn't use the double-fork technique we used for our daemons in this recipe. This fact is clearly stated under the BUGS section in the `man 3 daemon` manual page.

Implementing a signal handler

In the previous recipe, we wrote a simple but functional daemon. However, there are some problems with it; for example, the PID file isn't removed when the daemon is killed. Likewise, the open file stream (`/tmp/my-daemon-is-alive.txt`) isn't closed when the daemon is killed. A proper daemon should clean up after itself when it exits.

To be able to clean up on exit, we need to implement a signal handler. The signal handler should then take care of all the cleanup before the daemon is terminated. We have already seen examples of signal handlers in this chapter, so this concept isn't new.

It's not only daemons that use signal handlers, though. This is a common way of controlling processes, especially processes that don't have a controlling terminal.

Getting ready

You should read the previous recipe before reading this one so that you understand what the daemon does. Other than that, you'll need the programs listed in the *Technical requirements* section of this chapter.

How to do it...

In this recipe, we'll add signal handlers to the daemon we wrote in the previous recipe. Since the code will be a bit longer, I have split it up into several steps. Remember, though, that all the code goes in the same file. Let's get started:

1. Write the following code in and file a name it `my-daemon-v2.c`. We'll start with the `#include` files and the variables, just as we did previously. However, notice that this time, we have moved some of the variables to the global space. We have done this so that the signal handler can access them. There is no way to pass extra arguments to a signal handler, so this is the best way to access them. Here, we must also define `_POSIX_C_SOURCE` for `sigaction()`. We must also create a prototype for our signal handler here, called `sigHandler()`. Also, notice the new `sigaction` struct:

```
#include <sys/types.h>
#include <sys/stat.h>
#include <time.h>
#include <fcntl.h>
#include <signal.h>

void sigHandler(int sig);

/* moved these variables to the global scope
   since they need to be access/deleted/closed
   from the signal handler */
FILE *fp;
const char pidfile[] = "/var/run/my-daemon.pid";

int main(void)
{
   pid_t pid;
   time_t now; /* for the current time */
   struct sigaction action; /* for sigaction */
   const char daemonfile[] =
      "/tmp/my-daemon-is-alive.txt";
```

```
if ( (pid = fork()) == -1 )
{
   perror("Can't fork");
   return 1;
}
else if ( (pid != 0) )
{
   exit(0);
}
```

2. Just as we did previously, we must create a new session after the first fork. After that, we must do the second fork to make sure it isn't a session leader anymore:

```
/* the parent process has exited, which makes
 * the rest of the code the child process */
setsid(); /* create a new session to lose the
             controlling terminal */

/* fork again, creating a grandchild, the
 * actual daemon */
if ( (pid = fork()) == -1 )
{
   perror("Can't fork");
   return 1;
}
/* the child process which will exit */
else if ( pid > 0 )
{
   /* open pid-file for writing and check it */
   if ( (fp = fopen(pidfile, "w")) == NULL )
   {
      perror("Can't open file for writing");
      return 1;
   }
   /* write pid to file */
   fprintf(fp, "%d\n", pid);
   fclose(fp); /* close the file pointer */
   exit(0);
}
```

3. Again, as we did previously, we must change the umask, the current working directory, and open the daemon file with `fopen()`. Next, we must close and reopen stdin, stdout, and stderr:

```
umask(022); /* set the umask to something ok */
chdir("/"); /* change working directory to / */
/* open the "daemonfile" for writing */
if ( (fp = fopen(daemonfile, "w")) == NULL )
{
   perror("Can't open daemonfile");
   return 1;
}
/* from here, we don't need stdin, stdout or,
 * stderr anymore, so let's close them all,
 * then re-open them to /dev/null */
close(STDIN_FILENO);
close(STDOUT_FILENO);
close(STDERR_FILENO);
open("/dev/null", O_RDONLY); /* 0 = stdin */
open("/dev/null", O_WRONLY); /* 1 = stdout */
open("/dev/null", O_RDWR); /* 2 = stderr */
```

4. Now, it's finally time to prepare and register the signal handlers. This is exactly what we covered earlier in this chapter, only here, we are registering handlers for all the common exit signals, such as terminate, interrupt, quit, and abort. Once we have dealt with the signal handlers, we will begin the daemon's work; that is, the `for` loop that will write messages to the daemon file:

```
/* prepare for sigaction */
   action.sa_handler = sigHandler;
   sigfillset(&action.sa_mask);
   action.sa_flags = SA_RESTART;
   /* register the signals we want to handle */
   sigaction(SIGTERM, &action, NULL);
   sigaction(SIGINT, &action, NULL);
   sigaction(SIGQUIT, &action, NULL);
   sigaction(SIGABRT, &action, NULL);

   /* here we start the daemons "work" */
   for (;;)
   {
      /* get the current time and write it to the
```

```
           "daemonfile" that we opened above */
        time(&now);
        fprintf(fp, "Daemon alive at %s",
           ctime(&now));
        fflush(fp); /* flush the stream */
        sleep(30);
     }
     return 0;
}
```

5. Finally, we must implement the function for the signal handler. Here, we clean up after the daemon by removing the PID file before exiting. We also close the open file stream to the daemon file:

```
void sigHandler(int sig)
{
    int status = 0;
    if ( sig == SIGTERM || sig == SIGINT
        || sig == SIGQUIT
        || sig == SIGABRT )
    {
        /* remove the pid-file */
        if ( (unlink(pidfile)) == -1 )
            status = 1;
        if ( (fclose(fp)) == EOF )
            status = 1;
        exit(status); /* exit with the status set*/
    }
    else /* some other signal */
    {
        exit(1);
    }
}
```

6. Compile the new version of the daemon:

```
$> make my-daemon-v2
gcc -Wall -Wextra -pedantic -std=c99    my-daemon-v2.c
-o my-daemon-v2
```

7. Start the daemon as root, just as we did previously:

```
$> sudo ./my-daemon-v2
```

8. Check out the PID in the PID file and make note of it:

```
$> cat /var/run/my-daemon.pid
22845
```

9. Check it out with `ps` to see that it's running as it should:

```
$> ps jp 22845
  PPID   PID  PGID   SID TTY TPGID STAT UID TIME
COMMAND
     1 22845 22845 22845 ?      -1 Ss     0 0:00 ./my
daemon-v2
```

10. Kill the daemon with the default signal, `TERM`:

```
$> sudo kill 22845
```

11. If everything has worked out as planned, the PID file will have been removed. See if you can access the PID file with `cat`:

```
$> cat /var/run/my-daemon.pid
cat: /var/run/my-daemon.pid: No such file or directory
```

How it works...

In this recipe, we implemented a signal handler that takes care of all the cleanup. It removes the PID file and closes the open file stream. To cover the most common "exit" signals, we registered the handler with four different signals: *terminate*, *interrupt*, *quit*, and *abort*. When one of these signals is received by the daemon, it triggers the `sigHandler()` function. This function then removes the PID file and closes the file stream. Finally, the function exits the entire daemon by calling `exit()`.

However, since we can't pass the filename or the file stream as an argument to the signal handler, we placed those variables in the global scope instead. This makes it possible for both `main()` and `sigHandler()` to reach them.

There's more...

Remember that we had to flush the stream for the time and date to show up in `/tmp/my-daemon-is-alive.txt`? Since we now close the file stream once the daemon exits, we don't need `fflush()` anymore. The data is written to the file when it closes. However, then we can't see the time and date "live" while the daemon is running. That's why we still have `fflush()` in the code.

7
Using systemd to Handle Your Daemons

Now that we know how to build our own daemons, it's time to see how we can get Linux to handle them using **systemd**. In this chapter, we will learn what systemd is, how to start and stop services, what unit files are, and how to create them. We will also learn how daemons are logged to systemd and how we read those logs.

We will then learn about different kinds of services and daemons that systemd can handle and put the daemon from the previous chapter under systemd control.

In this chapter, we'll cover the following recipes:

- Getting to know systemd
- Writing a unit file for a daemon
- Enabling and disabling a service—and starting and stopping it
- Creating a more modern daemon for systemd
- Making the new daemon a systemd service
- Reading the journal

Technical requirements

For this recipe, you'll need a computer with a Linux distribution that uses systemd—which, today, is pretty much every distribution, with some rare exceptions.

You'll also need the GCC compiler and the Make tool. Installation instructions for these tools are covered in *Chapter 1, Getting the Necessary Tools and Writing Our First Linux Programs*. You'll also need the generic Makefile for this chapter, which is found in this chapter's repository on GitHub, along with all the code samples for this chapter. The URL for this chapter's repository folder on GitHub is `https://github.com/PacktPublishing/Linux-System-Programming-Techniques/tree/master/ch7`.

Check out the following link to see the Code in Action video: `https://bit.ly/3cxmXab`

Getting to know systemd

In this recipe, we'll explore what systemd is, how it handles the system, and all of the system's services.

Historically, Linux has been managed with several smaller pieces. For example, `init` was the first process on the system, which started other processes and daemons to bring up the system. System daemons were handled by shell scripts, also called *init scripts*. Logging was done either by the daemon itself via files or `syslog`. Networking was also handled by multiple scripts (and still is in some Linux distributions).

Nowadays, though, the entire system is handled by systemd. For example, the first process on the system is now `systemd` (which we have seen in previous chapters). Daemons are handled by something called *unit files*, which create a unified way of controlling daemons on the system. Logging is handled by **journald**, systemd's logging daemon. But do note that **syslog** is still used by many daemons to do extra logging. Later in this chapter, in the *Making the new daemon a systemd service* section, we'll re-write the daemon from *Chapter 6, Spawning Processes and Using Job Control*, to log to the journal.

Knowing how systemd works will enable you to use it properly when, for example, writing unit files for daemons. It will also help you to write daemons in the "new" way, to make use of systemd's logging features. You will become a better system administrator as well as a better Linux developer.

Getting ready

For this recipe, you'll only need a Linux distribution that uses systemd, which most distributions do today.

How to do it...

In this recipe, we'll take a look at some of the components involved in systemd. This will give us a bird's eyes view of systemd, journald, its commands, and **unit files**. All the details will come in later recipes in this chapter:

1. Start by typing `systemctl` in a console window and hit *Enter*. This will show you all active *units* on your machine right now. If you skim through the list, you'll notice that a unit can be just about anything—hard drives, sound cards, mounted network drives, miscellaneous services, timers, and so on.
2. All the services we saw in the previous step reside as unit files in `/lib/systemd/system` or `/etc/systemd/system`. Navigate to those directories and look around at the files. These are all typical unit files.
3. Now it's time to take a look at the journal, the log of systemd. We need to run this command as **root**; otherwise, we won't see system logs. Either type the command `sudo journalctl`, or switch to root first with `su`, and then type `journalctl`. This will show you the entire log of systemd and all of its services. Hit *Spacebar* several times to scroll down in the log. To go to the end of the log, type a capital *G* while the log is displayed.

How it works...

These three steps give us an overview of systemd. In the coming recipes, we'll cover the details in much more depth.

Installed packages place their unit files in `/lib/systemd/system` if it's a Debian/Ubuntu system, and in `/usr/lib/systemd/system` if it's a CentOS/Fedora system. On CentOS/Fedora, though, `/lib` is a symbolic link to `/usr/lib`, so `/lib/systemd/system` is universal.

So-called *local* unit files are placed in `/etc/systemd/system`. Local unit files mean unit files specific to this system, for example, modified by the administrator or manually added for some program.

There's more...

There have been other init systems for Linux before systemd. We have already mentioned the first one briefly, `init`. That init system, `init`, is often called *Sys-V-style init*, from UNIX version five (V).

After the Sys-V-style init came Upstart, a full replacement for `init` developed by Ubuntu. Upstart was also used by CentOS 6 and Red Hat Enterprise Linux 6.

Nowadays, though, most major Linux distributions use systemd. Since systemd is a huge part of Linux, this makes all the distributions pretty much alike. Fifteen years ago, it wasn't easy to jump from one distribution to another one. Nowadays, it's much easier.

See also

There are multiple manual pages on the system we can read to understand systemd, its commands, and the journal at a deeper level:

- `man systemd`
- `man systemctl`
- `man journalctl`
- `man systemd.unit`

Writing a unit file for a daemon

In this recipe, we will take the daemon we wrote in *Chapter 6*, *Spawning Processes and Using Job Control*, and make it a service under systemd. This daemon is what systemd calls a *forking daemon* because it does just that. It forks. This is traditionally how daemons have worked, and they are still widely used. Later in this chapter, in the *Making the new daemon a systemd service* section, we will modify it slightly to log to systemd's journal. But first things first, let's make our existing daemon into a service.

Getting ready

In this recipe, you'll need the file `my-daemon-v2.c` that we wrote in *Chapter 6*, *Spawning Processes and Using Job Control*. If you don't have that file, there is a copy of it in this chapter's directory on GitHub at `https://github.com/PacktPublishing/Linux-System-Programming-Techniques/blob/master/ch7/my-daemon-v2.c`.

Apart from `my-daemon-v2.c`, you'll need the GCC compiler, the Make tool, and the generic Makefile covered in the *Technical requirements* section of this chapter.

How to do it...

Here we will put our daemon under systemd's control:

1. If you haven't compiled `my-daemon-v2` yet, we'll need to begin with that. Compile it like any other program we have made so far:

   ```
   $> make my-daemon-v2
   gcc -Wall -Wextra -pedantic -std=c99    my-daemon-v2.c
   -o my-daemon-v2
   ```

2. For this to be a system daemon, we should place it in one of the directories for that purpose. A good place for this is `/usr/local/sbin`. The `/usr/local directory` is where we usually want to place things that we have added to the system ourselves, that is, third-party stuff. The `sbin` subdirectory is for system binaries or super-user binaries (hence the *s* before *bin*). To move our daemon here, we need to be root:

   ```
   $> sudo mv my-daemon-v2 /usr/local/sbin/
   ```

3. Now comes the exciting stuff, writing the *unit file* for the daemon. Create the file `/etc/systemd/system/my-daemon.service` as root. Use either `sudo` or `su` to become root. Write the content shown below in the file and save it. The unit file is divided into several sections. In this file, the sections are `[Unit]`, `[Service]`, and `[Install]`. The `[Unit]` section contains information about the unit, such as the description in our case. The `[Service]` section contains information about how this service should work and behave. Here, we have `ExecStart`, which contains the path to the daemon. We also have `Restart=on-failure`. This tells systemd to restart the daemon if it should crash. Then we have the `Type` directive, which in our case is forking. Remember that our daemon creates a fork of itself and the parent process exits. This is what the type *forking* means. We tell systemd the type so it knows how it should handle the daemon. Then we have `PIDFile`, which contains the path to our **PID file**, which the daemon creates on start. Finally, we have `WantedBy` set to `multi-user.target`. What this means is that this daemon should start when the system enters the multi-user stage:

   ```
   [Unit]
   Description=A small daemon for testing
   [Service]
   ExecStart=/usr/local/sbin/my-daemon-v2
   Restart=on-failure
   Type=forking
   PIDFile=/var/run/my-daemon.pid
   ```

```
[Install]
WantedBy=multi-user.target
```

4. For our new unit file to be recognized by the system, we need to *reload* the systemd daemon itself. This will read in our new file. This must be done as root:

```
$> sudo systemctl daemon-reload
```

5. We can now see if systemd recognizes our new daemon by using the `status` command for `systemctl`. Note that we see both the description here from the unit file and the actual unit file used. We also see that the daemon is currently *disabled* and *inactive*:

```
$> sudo systemctl status my-daemon
. my-daemon.service - A small daemon for testing
   Loaded: loaded (/etc/systemd/system/my-daemon.service;
disabled; vendor preset: enabled)
   Active: inactive (dead)
```

How it works...

It's not harder than this to create a service for a daemon in systemd. Once we have learned systemd and unit files, it's easier than writing *init scripts* as we did in the old days. With only nine lines, we have put the daemon under the control of systemd.

The unit file is mostly self-explanatory. In our case, with a traditional daemon that forks, we set the type to *forking* and specify a PID file. Systemd then uses the PID number from the PID file to track the daemon state. This way, systemd can restart the daemon if it notices that the PID has disappeared from the system.

In the status message, we saw that the service is *disabled* and *inactive*. **Disabled** means that it won't start automatically when the system boots. **Inactive** means that it hasn't started yet.

There's more...

If you are writing a unit file for a daemon that uses the network, for example, an internet daemon, you can explicitly tell systemd to wait with this daemon until the network is ready. To achieve this, we add these lines under the `[Unit]` section:

```
After=network-online.target
Wants=network-online.target
```

You can, of course, use `After` and `Wants` for other dependencies as well. There is also another dependency statement you can use, called `Requires`.

The difference between them is that `After` specifies the order of the units. A unit with `After` will wait to start after the unit required is started. `Wants` and `Requires`, however, only specify the dependency, not the ordering. With `Wants`, a unit will still start even if the other unit required isn't started successfully. But with `Requires`, the unit will fail to start if the required unit isn't started.

See also

In `man systemd.unit` is a lot of information about the different sections of a unit file and which directives we can use in each section.

Enabling and disabling a service – and starting and stopping it

In the previous recipe, we added our daemon as a service to systemd with a unit file. In this recipe, we'll learn how to enable it, start it, stop it, and disable it. There is a difference between enabling and starting and disabling and stopping a service.

Enabling a service means that it will start automatically when the system boots. Starting a service means that it will start right now, regardless of it being enabled or not. And disabling a service means that it will no longer start when the system boots. Stopping a service stops it right now, regardless of it being enabled or disabled.

Knowing how to do all of this enables you to control the system's services.

Getting ready

For this recipe to work, you'll first need to complete the previous recipe, *Writing a unit file for a daemon*.

How to do it...

1. Let's start by checking out the daemon status again. It should be both disabled and inactive:

```
$> systemctl status my-daemon
. my-daemon.service - A small daemon for testing
```

```
   Loaded: loaded (/etc/systemd/system/my-daemon.service;
disabled; vendor preset: enabled)
   Active: inactive (dead)
```

2. Now we'll *enable* it, meaning it will start automatically on boot (when the system enters *multi-user mode*). We must issue this command as root since it's a command that modifies the system. Notice also what's happening when we enable it. There's no arcane stuff going on; it just creates a symbolic link from our unit file to `/etc/systemd/system/multi-user.target.wants/my-daemon.service`. Remember that `multi-user.target` was the target we specified in the unit file. So when the system reaches the multi-user level, systemd will start all services in that directory:

```
$> sudo systemctl enable my-daemon
Created symlink /etc/systemd/system/multi-user.target.
wants/my-daemon.service → /etc/systemd/system/my-daemon.
service.
```

3. Let's check out the status of the daemon now that we have enabled it. It should now say *enabled* instead of *disabled*. However, it is still *inactive* (not started):

```
$> sudo systemctl status my-daemon
. my-daemon.service - A small daemon for testing
   Loaded: loaded (/etc/systemd/system/my-daemon.service;
enabled; vendor preset: enabled)
   Active: inactive (dead)
```

4. Now it's time to start the daemon:

```
$> sudo systemctl start my-daemon
```

5. And let's check out the status one more time. It should be both enabled and active (that is, started). This time, we'll get more information about the daemon than before. We'll see its PID, its status, its memory usage, and so on. We'll also see a snippet from the log at the end:

```
$> sudo systemctl status my-daemon
. my-daemon.service - A small daemon for testing
   Loaded: loaded (/etc/systemd/system/my-daemon.service;
enabled; vendor preset: enabled)
   Active: active (running) since Sun 2020-12-06 14:50:35
CET; 9s ago
  Process: 29708 ExecStart=/usr/local/sbin/my-daemon-v2
(code=exited, status=0/SUCCESS)
 Main PID: 29709 (my-daemon-v2)
```

```
     Tasks: 1 (limit: 4915)
    Memory: 152.0K
    CGroup: /system.slice/my-daemon.service
            └─29709 /usr/local/sbin/my-daemon-v2
dec 06 14:50:35 red-dwarf systemd[1]: Starting A small
daemon for testing...
dec 06 14:50:35 red-dwarf systemd[1]: my-daemon.service:
Can't open PID file /run/my-daemon.pid (yet?) after start
dec 06 14:50:35 red-dwarf systemd[1]: Started A small
daemon for testing.
```

6. Let's verify that systemd restarts the daemon if it crashes or gets killed. First, we check out the process with `ps`. Then we kill it with the `KILL` signal, so it has no chance of exiting normally. Then we check it out again with `ps` and notices that it has a new PID since it's a new process. The old one got killed, and systemd started a new instance of it:

```
$> ps ax | grep my-daemon-v2
  923 pts/12   S+     0:00 grep my-daemon-v2
29709 ?        S      0:00 /usr/local/sbin/my-daemon-v2
$> sudo kill -KILL 29709
$> ps ax | grep my-daemon-v2
 1103 ?        S      0:00 /usr/local/sbin/my-daemon-v2
 1109 pts/12   S+     0:00 grep my-daemon-v2
```

7. We can also check out the file that the daemon writes to in the `/tmp` directory:

```
$> tail -n 5 /tmp/my-daemon-is-alive.txt
Daemon alive at Sun Dec  6 15:24:11 2020
Daemon alive at Sun Dec  6 15:24:41 2020
Daemon alive at Sun Dec  6 15:25:11 2020
Daemon alive at Sun Dec  6 15:25:41 2020
Daemon alive at Sun Dec  6 15:26:11 2020
```

8. And finally, let's stop the daemon. We'll also check its status and check that the process is gone with `ps`:

```
$> sudo systemctl stop my-daemon
$> sudo systemctl status my-daemon
. my-daemon.service - A small daemon for testing
   Loaded: loaded (/etc/systemd/system/my-daemon.service;
enabled; vendor preset: enabled)
   Active: inactive (dead) since Sun 2020-12-06 15:27:49
CET; 7s ago
```

```
   Process: 1102 ExecStart=/usr/local/sbin/my-daemon-v2
 (code=exited, status=0/SUCCESS)
  Main PID: 1103 (code=killed, signal=TERM)
dec 06 15:18:41 red-dwarf systemd[1]: Starting A small
daemon for testing...
dec 06 14:50:35 red-dwarf systemd[1]: my-daemon.service:
Can't open PID file /run/my-daemon.pid (yet?) after start
dec 06 15:18:41 red-dwarf systemd[1]: Started A small
daemon for testing.
dec 06 15:27:49 red-dwarf systemd[1]: Stopping A small
daemon for testing...
dec 06 15:27:49 red-dwarf systemd[1]: my-daemon.service:
Succeeded.
dec 06 15:27:49 red-dwarf systemd[1]: Stopped A small
daemon for testing.
$> ps ax | grep my-daemon-v2
  2769 pts/12   S+     0:00 grep my-daemon-v2
```

9. To prevent the daemon from starting when the system reboots, we must also *disable* the service. Notice what's happening here. The symbolic link that got created when we enabled the service is now removed:

```
$> sudo systemctl disable my-daemon
Removed /etc/systemd/system/multi-user.target.wants/
my-daemon.service.
```

How it works...

When we enable or disable a service, systemd creates a symbolic link in the *target* directory. In our case, the target was *multi-user*, that is, when the system has reached the multi-user level.

In step five, when we started the daemon, we saw the *Main PID* in the status output. This PID matches the PID from the `/var/run/my-daemon.pid` file that the daemon creates. This is how systemd keeps track of *forking* daemons. In the next recipe, we'll see how we can create a daemon for systemd without forking.

Creating a more modern daemon for systemd

Daemons that are handled by systemd don't need to fork or close their file descriptors. Instead, it's advised to use standard output and standard error to write the daemon's logs to the journal. The journal is systemd's logging facility.

In this recipe, we'll write a new daemon, one that doesn't fork and leaves **stdin**, **stdout**, and **stderr** open. It will also write messages to standard output every 30 seconds (instead of to the `/tmp/my-daemon-is-alive.txt file`, as before). This kind of daemon is sometimes referred to as a **new-style daemon**. The old **forking** type, for example, `my-daemon-v2.c`, is referred to as a **SysV-style daemon**. **SysV** was the name of the init system before systemd.

Getting ready

For this recipe, you'll only need what's listed in the *Technical requirements* section of this chapter.

How to do it...

In this recipe, we'll write a **new-style daemon**:

1. This program is a bit long, so I've split it up into several steps. Write the code in a file and save it as `new-style-daemon.c`. All the code goes into a single file, even though there are several steps. We'll start by writing all the `include` statements, the function prototype for the signal handler, and the `main()` function body. Notice that we don't fork here. We also don't close any file descriptors or streams. Instead, we write the "*Daemon alive*" text to standard output. Note that we need to *flush* stdout here. Normally, streams are line-buffered, meaning they get flushed on each new line. But when stdout is redirected to something else, like with systemd, it's instead fully buffered. To be able to see the text as it gets printed, we need to flush it; otherwise, we wouldn't see anything in the log until we stop the daemon or the buffer gets filled:

```
#define _POSIX_C_SOURCE 200809L
#include <stdio.h>
#include <unistd.h>
#include <stdlib.h>
#include <signal.h>
#include <time.h>

void sigHandler(int sig);

int main(void)
{
    time_t now; /* for the current time */
    struct sigaction action; /* for sigaction */
```

```
    /* prepare for sigaction */
    action.sa_handler = sigHandler;
    sigfillset(&action.sa_mask);
    action.sa_flags = SA_RESTART;

    /* register the signal handler */
    sigaction(SIGTERM, &action, NULL);
    sigaction(SIGUSR1, &action, NULL);
    sigaction(SIGHUP, &action, NULL);

    for (;;) /* main loop */
    {
        time(&now); /* get current date & time */
        printf("Daemon alive at %s", ctime(&now));
        fflush(stdout);
        sleep(30);
    }
    return 0;
}
```

2. Now we'll write the function for the signal handler. Note that we catch both `SIGHUP` and `SIGTERM` here. `SIGHUP` is often used to reload any configuration files without restarting the entire daemon. `SIGTERM` is caught so that the daemon can clean up after itself (close all open file descriptors or streams and remove any temporary files). We don't have any configuration files or temporary files here, so we print a message to standard output instead:

```
void sigHandler(int sig)
{
    if (sig == SIGUSR1)
    {
        printf("Hello world!\n");
    }
    else if (sig == SIGTERM)
    {
        printf("Doing some cleanup...\n");
        printf("Bye bye...\n");
        exit(0);
    }
    else if (sig == SIGHUP)
    {
```

```
            printf("HUP is used to reload any "
                "configuration files\n");
        }
    }
```

3. Now it's time to compile the daemon so we can use it:

```
$> make new-style-daemon
gcc -Wall -Wextra -pedantic -std=c99    new-style-
daemon.c    -o new-style-daemon
```

4. We can run it interactively to verify that it's working:

```
$> ./new-style-daemon
Daemon alive at Sun Dec  6 18:51:47 2020
Ctrl+C
```

How it works...

This daemon works pretty much like any other program we have written. There's no need to do any forking, change the working directory, close file descriptors or streams, or anything like that. It's just a regular program.

Note that we don't flush the stdout buffer in the signal handler. Every time the program receives a signal and prints a message, the program goes back into the `for` loop, prints another "*Daemon alive*" message, and then flushes when the program reaches `fflush(stdout)` in the `for` loop. If the signal is `SIGTERM`, all buffers are flushed on `exit(0)`, so we don't need to flush here either.

In the next recipe, we'll make this program a systemd service.

See also

You can get much more in-depth information about the **SysV-style** daemons and new-style daemons from the manual page at `man 7 daemon`.

Making the new daemon a systemd service

Now that we've made a **new-style daemon** in the previous recipe, we'll see that it's even easier to make a unit file for this daemon.

Knowing how to write unit files to new-style daemons is important since more and more daemons are written this way. When making new daemons for Linux, we should make them in this new style.

Getting ready

For this recipe, you'll need to complete the previous one. It's the daemon from that recipe that we'll use here.

How to do it...

Here, we will make the **new-style daemon** a systemd service:

1. Let's begin by moving the daemon to `/usr/local/sbin`, just as we did with the traditional daemon. Remember, you'll need to be root for this:

```
$> sudo mv new-style-daemon /usr/local/sbin/
```

2. Now we'll write the new unit file. Create the `/etc/systemd/system/new-style-daemon.service` file and give it the following content. Remember, you'll need to be root to create that file. Notice that we don't need to specify any PID file here. Also, note that we have changed `Type=forking` to `Type=simple`. Simple is the default type for systemd services:

```
[Unit]
Description=A new-style daemon for testing
[Service]
ExecStart=/usr/local/sbin/new-style-daemon
Restart=on-failure
Type=simple
[Install]
WantedBy=multi-user.target
```

3. Reload the systemd daemon, so the new unit file gets recognized:

```
$> sudo systemctl daemon-reload
```

4. Start the daemon, and check out its status. Notice that we'll also see a "*Daemon alive*" message here. This is a snippet from the journal. Notice that we don't *enable* the service this time. We don't need to enable the service unless we want it to start automatically:

```
$> sudo systemctl start new-style-daemon
$> sudo systemctl status new-style-daemon
. new-style-daemon.service - A new-style daemon for
testing
   Loaded: loaded (/etc/systemd/system/new-style-daemon.
service; disabled; vendor preset: enabled
```

```
   Active: active (running) since Sun 2020-12-06 19:51:25
CET; 7s ago
 Main PID: 8421 (new-style-daemo)
    Tasks: 1 (limit: 4915)
   Memory: 244.0K
   CGroup: /system.slice/new-style-daemon.service
           └─8421 /usr/local/sbin/new-style-daemon

dec 06 19:51:25 red-dwarf systemd[1]: Started A new-style
daemon for testing.
dec 06 19:51:25 red-dwarf new-style-daemon[8421]: Daemon
alive at Sun Dec  6 19:51:25 2020
```

5. Leave the daemon running, and we'll take a look at the journal in the next recipe.

How it works...

Since this daemon isn't forking, systemd can keep track of it without a PID file. For this daemon, we used `Type=simple`, which is the default type in systemd.

When we started the daemon in *Step 4* and checked out the status of it, we saw the first line of the "*Daemon alive*" message. We can see a daemon's status without using `sudo`, but then we can't see the journal's snippet (since it might contain sensitive data).

Since we flush the stdout buffer after each `printf()` in the `for` loop, the journal is updated live as each new entry is written to it.

In the next recipe, we'll take a look at the journal.

Reading the journal

In this recipe, we'll learn how to read the journal. The journal is systemd's logging facility. All messages that a daemon prints to either stdout or stderr gets added to the journal. But we can find more than just the system daemons logs here. There's also the system's boot messages, among other things.

Knowing how to read the journal enables you to find errors in the system and the daemons more easily.

Getting ready

For this recipe, you'll need to have the `new-style-daemon` service running. If you don't have it running on your system, go back to the previous recipe for information on how to start it.

How to do it...

In this recipe, we'll explore how to read the journal and what kind of information we can find in it. We'll also learn how to follow a particular service's log:

1. We'll start by examining the logs from our service, `new-style-daemon`. The `-u` option stands for *unit*:

   ```
   $> sudo journalctl -u new-style-daemon
   ```

   The log is probably pretty long by now, so you can scroll down in the log by hitting *Spacebar*. To quit the journal, press *Q*.

2. Remember that we implemented a signal handler for `SIGUSR1`? Let's try sending our daemon that signal and then view the log again. But this time, we'll only show the last five lines in the journal with `--lines 5`. Find the PID of the process by using `systemctl status`. Notice the "*Hello world*" message (it's highlighted in the following code):

   ```
   $> systemctl status new-style-daemon
   . new-style-daemon.service - A new-style daemon for
   testing
      Loaded: loaded (/etc/systemd/system/new-style-daemon.
   service; disabled; vendor preset: enabled
      Active: active (running) since Sun 2020-12-06 19:51:25
   CET; 31min ago
    Main PID: 8421 (new-style-daemo)
       Tasks: 1 (limit: 4915)
      Memory: 412.0K
      CGroup: /system.slice/new-style-daemon.service
              └─8421 /usr/local/sbin/new-style-daemon
   $> sudo kill -USR1 8421
   $> sudo journalctl -u new-style-daemon --lines 5
   -- Logs begin at Mon 2020-11-30 18:05:24 CET, end at Sun
   2020-12-06 20:24:46 CET. --
   dec 06 20:23:31 red-dwarf new-style-daemon[8421]: Daemon
   alive at Sun Dec  6 20:23:31 2020
   dec 06 20:24:01 red-dwarf new-style-daemon[8421]: Daemon
   alive at Sun Dec  6 20:24:01 2020
   dec 06 20:24:31 red-dwarf new-style-daemon[8421]: Daemon
   alive at Sun Dec  6 20:24:31 2020
   dec 06 20:24:42 red-dwarf new-style-daemon[8421]: Hello
   world!
   dec 06 20:24:42 red-dwarf new-style-daemon[8421]: Daemon
   alive at Sun Dec  6 20:24:42 2020
   ```

3. It's also possible to *follow* the journal for a service, that is, view it "live." Open up a second terminal and run the following command. The `-f` stands for *follow*:

```
$> sudo journalctl -u new-style-daemon -f
```

4. Now, in the first terminal, send another `USR1` signal with `sudo kill -USR1 8421`. You'll see the "*Hello world*" message in the second terminal right away without any delay. To quit the follow mode, you just hit *Ctrl* + *C*.

5. The `journalctl` command offers a wide range of filtering. For example, it's possible to select only log entries between two dates using `--since` and `--until`. It's also possible to leave out either one of them to view all messages since or until a particular date. Here, we show all messages between two dates:

```
$> sudo journalctl -u new-style-daemon \
> --since "2020-12-06 20:32:00" \
> --until "2020-12-06 20:33:00"
-- Logs begin at Mon 2020-11-30 18:05:24 CET, end at Sun 2020-12-06 20:37:01 CET. --
dec 06 20:32:12 red-dwarf new-style-daemon[8421]: Daemon alive at Sun Dec  6 20:32:12 2020
dec 06 20:32:42 red-dwarf new-style-daemon[8421]: Daemon alive at Sun Dec  6 20:32:42 2020
```

6. By leaving out the `-u` option and the unit name, we can see all log entries from all services. Try it out and scroll through it with *Spacebar*. You can also try to only view the last 10 lines as we did before with `--line 10`.

   Now it's time to stop the `new-style-daemon service`. We'll also view the last five lines from the log after we have stopped the service. Notice the goodbye message from the daemon. This is from the signal handler we made for the `SIGTERM` signal. When we stop a service in systemd, it sends the service a `SIGTERM` signal:

```
$> sudo systemctl stop new-style-daemon
$> sudo journalctl -u new-style-daemon --lines 5
-- Logs begin at Mon 2020-11-30 18:05:24 CET, end at Sun 2020-12-06 20:47:02 CET. --
dec 06 20:46:44 red-dwarf systemd[1]: Stopping A new-style daemon for testing...
dec 06 20:46:44 red-dwarf new-style-daemon[8421]: Doing some cleanup...
dec 06 20:46:44 red-dwarf new-style-daemon[8421]: Bye bye...
dec 06 20:46:44 red-dwarf systemd[1]: new-style-daemon.
```

```
service: Succeeded.
dec 06 20:46:44 red-dwarf systemd[1]: Stopped A new-style
daemon for testing.
```

How it works...

Since the journal takes care of all messages that go to stdout and stderr, we don't need to handle logging ourselves. This makes it easier to write daemons for Linux that are handled by systemd. As we saw when we viewed the journal, every message gets a timestamp. This makes it easy to filter out a specific day or time when looking for errors.

Following the log for a specific service with the `-f` option is common when experimenting with new or unknown services.

See also

The manual page at `man journalctl` has even more tips and tricks on how to filter the journal.

8
Creating Shared Libraries

In this chapter, we will learn what libraries are and why they are such a big part of Linux. We also learn the differences between static libraries and dynamic libraries. When we know what libraries are, we start to write our own—both static and dynamic ones. We also take a quick peek inside a dynamic library.

The use of libraries has many benefits—for example, a developer doesn't need to reinvent functions over and over again as there's often an existing function already in a library. A big advantage with dynamic libraries is that the resulting program gets much smaller in size, and the libraries are upgradable even after the program has been compiled.

In this chapter, we'll learn how to make our own libraries with useful functions and install them on the system. Knowing how to make and install libraries enables you to share your functions with others in a standardized way.

In this chapter, we'll cover the following recipes:

- The what and why of libraries
- Creating a static library
- Using a static library
- Creating a dynamic library

- Installing the dynamic library on the system
- Using the dynamic library in a program
- Compiling a statically linked program

Technical requirements

In this chapter, we'll need the **GNU Compiler Collection** (**GCC**) compiler and the Make tool. You'll find installation instructions for these tools in *Chapter 1, Getting the Necessary Tools and Writing Our First Linux Programs*. All the code samples for this chapter can be found in this chapter's GitHub directory at `https://github.com/PacktPublishing/Linux-System-Programming-Techniques/tree/master/ch8`.

Check out the following link to see the Code in Action video: `https://bit.ly/3zsrIeD`

The what and why of libraries

Before we go into the details of libraries, it's essential to understand what they are and why they matter to us. It's also important to understand the difference between static and dynamic libraries:

This knowledge will enable you to make smarter choices when making your own libraries.

A **dynamic library** is dynamically **linked** to the binary that uses it. What this means is that the library code isn't included in the binary. The library resides outside of the binary. This has several advantages. First, the resulting binary will be smaller in size since the library code isn't included. Second, the library can be updated without needing to recompile the binary. The disadvantage is that we can't move or delete the dynamic library from the system. If we do, the binary won't work anymore.

A **static library**, on the other hand, is included inside the binary file. The advantage of this is that the binary will be completely independent of the library once compiled. The disadvantage is that the binary will be bigger, and the library can't be updated without also recompiling the binary.

We have already seen a short example of a dynamic library in *Chapter 3, Diving Deep into C in Linux*.

In this recipe, we'll look at some common libraries. We'll also install a new one on the system via the package manager that we'll use in a program.

Getting ready

For this recipe, you'll need the GCC compiler. You'll also need root access to the system, either via `su` or `sudo`.

How to do it...

In this recipe, we'll both explore some common libraries and look at where they live on the system, and then install a new one and peek inside a library. In this recipe, we'll only deal with dynamic libraries.

1. Let's start by taking a look at the many libraries already on your system. The libraries will reside in one or more of these directories, depending on your distribution:

   ```
   /usr/lib
   /usr/lib64
   /usr/lib32
   ```

2. Now, we will install a new library on the system with the Linux distribution package manager. The library we will install is for **cURL**, an application and library to fetch files or data from the internet—for example, over **HyperText Transfer Protocol** (**HTTP**). Follow these instructions, depending on your distribution:

   - **Debian/Ubuntu**:

   ```
       $> sudo apt install libcurl4-openssl-dev
   ```

   - **Fedora/CentOS/Red Hat**:

   ```
       $> sudo dnf install libcurl-devel
   ```

3. Now, let's take a look inside the library with `nm`. But first, we need to find it with `whereis`. The path to the library is different on different distributions. This example is from a Debian 10 system. The file we are looking for is the `.so` file. Notice that we use `grep` with `nm` to only list lines with `T`. These are the functions that the library provides. If we were to remove the `grep` part, we would also see functions that this library depends on. We also add `head` to the command since the list of functions is long. If you want to see all the functions, leave out `head`:

   ```
   $> whereis libcurl
   libcurl: /usr/lib/x86_64-linux-gnu/libcurl.la
   /usr/lib/x86_64-linux-gnu/libcurl.a /usr/lib/x86_64
   linux-gnu/libcurl.so
   $> nm -D /usr/lib/x86_64-linux-gnu/libcurl.so \
   ```

```
> | grep " T " | head -n 7
000000000002f750 T curl_easy_cleanup
000000000002f840 T curl_easy_duphandle
00000000000279b0 T curl_easy_escape
000000000002f7e0 T curl_easy_getinfo
000000000002f470 T curl_easy_init
000000000002fc60 T curl_easy_pause
000000000002f4e0 T curl_easy_perform
```

4. Now that we know a bit more about the library, we can use it in a program. Write the following code in a file and save it as `get-public-ip.c`. The program will send a request to the web server at `ifconfig.me` and give you your public **Internet Protocol** (**IP**) address. The complete manual for the cURL library can be found online at `https://curl.se/libcurl/c/`. Notice that we don't print anything from cURL. The library will automatically print the content it receives from the server:

```
#include <stdio.h>
#include <curl/curl.h>
int main(void)
{
    CURL *curl;

    curl = curl_easy_init();
    if(curl)
    {
        curl_easy_setopt(curl, CURLOPT_URL,
            "https://ifconfig.me");
        curl_easy_perform(curl);
        curl_easy_cleanup(curl);
    }
    else
    {
        fprintf(stderr, "Cannot initialize curl\n");
        return 1;
    }
    return 0;
}
```

5. Compile the code. Notice that we must also link against the cURL library using the `-l` option:

```
$> gcc -Wall -Wextra -pedantic -std=c99 \
> get-public-ip.c -o get-public-ip -lcurl
```

6. And now, finally, we can run the program to get our public IP address. My IP address is masked in the following output:

```
$> ./get-public-ip
158.174.xxx.xxx
```

How it works...

Here, we have looked at all the steps involved in using a library to add new functionality. We installed the library on the system using the package manager. We found its location using `whereis`, investigated which functions it contains using `nm`, and finally used it in a program.

The `nm` program provides a quick way to see which functions a library contains. The `-D` option, which we used in this recipe, is for dynamic libraries. We used `grep` to only view functions that the library provides; otherwise, we will also see functions that this library depends on (those lines start with a `U`).

Since this library is not part of `libc`, we needed to link against it with the `-l` option to `gcc`. The name of the library should be right after the `l`, without any spaces.

The `ifconfig.me` website is a site and service that returns the public IP of the client requesting the site.

There's more...

cURL is also a program. Many Linux distributions have it pre-installed. The cURL library provides a convenient way of using cURL functions in your own programs.

You can run `curl ifconfig.me` for the same result as the program we wrote, assuming you already have cURL installed.

Creating a static library

In *Chapter 3, Diving Deep into C in Linux*, we saw how to create a dynamic library and how it was linked from the current working directory. In this recipe, we'll make a **static library** instead.

A static library is included in the binary during compilation. The advantage is that the binary gets a bit more portable and independent. We can remove the static library after compilation, and the program will still work.

The downsides are that the binary will be slightly larger and that we can't update the library after it has been compiled into the program.

Knowing how to create static libraries will make it much easier to distribute and reuse your functions in new programs.

Getting ready

For this recipe, we'll need the GCC compiler. We will also use a tool called `ar` in this recipe. The `ar` program is almost always installed by default.

How to do it...

In this recipe, we'll make a small static library. The library will contain two functions: one for converting Celsius to Fahrenheit and one for converting Celsius to Kelvin:

1. Let's start by writing the library functions. Write the following code in a file and save it as `convert.c`. This file contains both of our functions:

```
float c_to_f(float celsius)
{
    return (celsius*9/5+32);
}
float c_to_k(float celsius)
{
    return (celsius + 273.15);
}
```

2. We also need a header file with the function prototypes for these functions. Create another file and write the following code in it. Save it as `convert.h`:

```
float c_to_f(float celsius);
float c_to_k(float celsius);
```

3. The first task in making the library is to compile `convert.c` into an **object file**. We do this by passing the `-c` option to GCC:

```
$> gcc -Wall -Wextra -pedantic -std=c99 -c convert.c
```

4. We should now have a file called `convert.o` in our current directory. We can verify this with the `file` command, which also tells us the type of file it is:

```
$> file convert.o
convert.o: ELF 64-bit LSB relocatable, x86-64, version 1
(SYSV), not stripped
```

5. The last step to making it a static library is to pack it in an **archive file**, with the `ar` command. The `-c` option stands for *creating* the archive; the `-v` option stands for *verbose* output; and the `-r` option stands for *replacing* members with the same name. The name `libconvert.a` is the resulting filename our library will get:

```
$> ar -cvr libconvert.a convert.o
a - convert.o
```

6. Let's take a look at our static library with `nm` before we move on:

```
$> nm libconvert.a
convert.o:
0000000000000000 T c_to_f
0000000000000037 T c_to_k
```

How it works...

As we have seen here, a static library is just an object file in an archive.

When we looked at the object file with the `file` command, we noticed it said *not stripped*, meaning that all the **symbols** are still in the file. *Symbols* are what expose the functions so that programs can access and use them. In the next recipe, we'll return to symbols and the meaning of *stripped* versus *not stripped*.

See also

There's a lot of good information about `ar` in its manual page, `man 1 ar`—for example, it's possible to modify and remove an already existing static library.

Using a static library

In this recipe, we'll use the static library created in the previous recipe in a program. Using a static library is a bit easier than using a dynamic library. We just add the static library (the archive file) to the list of files that will be compiled to a final binary.

Knowing how to use a static library will enable you to use other people's libraries and reuse your own code as static libraries.

Getting ready

For this recipe, you'll need both the `convert.h` file and the static library file, `libconvert.a`. You'll also need the GCC compiler.

How to do it...

Here, we will write a small program that uses our functions from the library we created in the previous recipe:

1. Write the following code in a file and save it as `temperature.c`. Notice the syntax for including header files from the current directory.

   The program takes two arguments: an option (either `-f` or `-k` for Fahrenheit or Kelvin) and a Celsius degree as a floating-point value. The program will then convert the Celsius degree into Fahrenheit or Kelvin, depending on the option chosen:

```
#include <stdio.h>
#include <stdlib.h>
#include <string.h>
#include "convert.h"
void printUsage(FILE *stream, char progname[]);
int main(int argc, char *argv[])
{
    if ( argc != 3 )
    {
        printUsage(stderr, argv[0]);
        return 1;
    }
    if ( strcmp(argv[1], "-f") == 0 )
    {
        printf("%.1f C = %.1f F\n",
            atof(argv[2]), c_to_f(atof(argv[2])));
    }
    else if ( strcmp(argv[1], "-k") == 0  )
    {
        printf("%.1f C = %.1f F\n",
            atof(argv[2]), c_to_k(atof(argv[2])));
    }
```

```
    else
    {
        printUsage(stderr, argv[0]);
        return 1;
    }

    return 0;
}

void printUsage(FILE *stream, char progname[])
{
    fprintf(stream, "%s [-f] [-k] [temperature]\n"
        "Example: %s -f 25\n", progname, progname);
}
```

2. Let's compile this program. To include the static library, we simply add it to the list of files to GCC. Also, make sure that the `convert.h` header file is in your current working directory:

```
$> gcc -Wall -Wextra -pedantic -std=c99 \
> temperature.c libconvert.a -o temperature
```

3. Now we can test the program with some different temperatures:

```
$> ./temperature -f 30
30.0 C = 86.0 F
$> ./temperature -k 15
15.0 C = 288.1 F
```

4. Finally, take a look at the resulting `temperature` binary with `nm`:

```
$> nm temperature
```

As you can see, we can view all of the functions in the binary—for example, we see `c_to_f`, `c_to_k`, `printUsage`, and `main` (the `Ts`). We also see which functions from dynamic libraries the program is depending on—for example, `printf` (preceded by a `U`). What we see here are called *symbols*.

5. Since this binary will be used as a standalone program, we don't need the symbols. It's possible to *strip* the symbols from the binary with the `strip` command. This makes the program a bit smaller in size. Once we have stripped the binary from its symbols, let's look at it again with `nm`:

```
$> strip temperature
$> nm temperature
nm: temperature: no symbols
```

6. We can see if a program or library is stripped or not with the `file` command. Remember that a static library can't be stripped; otherwise, the linker can't see the functions, and the linking will fail:

```
$> file temperature
temperature: ELF 64-bit LSB pie executable, x86-64,
version 1 (SYSV), dynamically linked, interpreter/
lib64/ld-linux-x86-64.so.2, for GNU/Linux 3.2.0,
BuildID[sha1]=95f583af98ff899c657ac33d6a014493c44c362b,
stripped
$> file convert.o
convert.o: ELF 64-bit LSB relocatable, x86-64, version 1
(SYSV), not stripped
```

How it works...

When we want to use the static library in a program, we give GCC the archive's filename and the program's `c` file, resulting in a binary that includes the static library.

In the last few steps, we examined the binary with `nm`, revealing all the symbols. Then we stripped—removed—those symbols, using the `strip` command. If we look at programs such as `ls`, `more`, `sleep`, and so on with the `file` command, we notice that these are also *stripped*. This means that the program has had its symbols removed.

A static library must have its symbols untouched. If they were removed—stripped—the linker wouldn't find the functions, and the linking process would fail. Therefore, we should never strip our static libraries.

Creating a dynamic library

While static libraries are convenient and easy to both create and use, **dynamic libraries** are more common. Just as we saw at the beginning of this chapter, many developers choose to provide a library and not only a program—for example, cURL.

In this recipe, we'll redo the library from the *Creating a static library* recipe that we covered earlier in this chapter so that it becomes a dynamic library.

Knowing how to create dynamic libraries enables you to distribute your code as easy-to-implement libraries for other developers to use.

Getting ready

For this recipe, you'll need the two `convert.c` and `convert.h` files from the *Creating a static library* recipe earlier in this chapter. You'll also need the GCC compiler.

How to do it...

Here, we make a dynamic library out of `convert.c` from the *Creating a static library* recipe earlier in this chapter:

1. First of all, let's remove the object file and the old static library we created earlier. This will make sure we don't use the wrong object file or the wrong library by mistake:

```
$> rm convert.o libconvert.a
```

2. The first thing we need to do is create a new object file from the `c` file. The `-c` option creates an object file, not the final binary. The `-fPIC` option tells GCC to generate what's called **Position-Independent Code** (**PIC**), allowing the code to execute at different addresses in different processes. We also check the resulting file with `file`:

```
$> gcc -Wall -Wextra -pedantic -std=c99 -c -fPIC \
> convert.c
$> file convert.o
convert.o: ELF 64-bit LSB relocatable, x86-64, version 1
(SYSV), not stripped
```

3. The next step is to create a `.so` file, a **shared object**, using GCC. The `-shared` option does what it says—it creates a shared object. The `-Wl` option means that we want to pass all the options separated by commas to the linker. In this case, the option passed to the linker is `-soname` with the argument `libconvert.so`, which sets the name of the dynamic library to *libconvert.so*. Finally, the `-o` option specifies the name of the output file. Then, we list the symbols that this shared library provides, using `nm`. The symbols preceded by a `T` are the symbols provided by this library:

```
$> gcc -shared -Wl,-soname,libconvert.so -o \
> libconvert.so.1 convert.o
$> nm -D libconvert.so.1
00000000000010f5 T c_to_f
000000000000112c T c_to_k
                 w __cxa_finalize
                 w __gmon_start__
                 w _ITM_deregisterTMCloneTable
                 w _ITM_registerTMCloneTable
```

How it works...

Creating a dynamic library involves two steps: creating an object file that's position-independent, and packaging that file in a `.so` file.

The code in a shared library gets loaded at runtime. Since it can't predict where it will end up in memory, it needs to be position-independent. That way, the code will work correctly, no matter where in memory it gets called.

The `-Wl,-soname,libconvert.so` GCC option might need some further explanation. The `-Wl` option tells GCC to treat any comma-separated words as options to the linker. Since we can't use a space—that would be treated as a new option—we separate `-soname` and `libconvert.so` with a comma instead. The linker, however, sees it as `-soname libconvert.so`.

`soname` is short for *shared object name*, which is an internal name in the library. It's this name that is used when referring to the library.

The actual filename specified with the `-o` option is sometimes called the *real name* of the library. It's a standard convention to use a real name that contains the version number of the library, such as `1` in this example. It's also possible to include a minor version—for example, `1.3`. In our example, it would look like this: `libconvert.so.1.3`. Both the *real name* and the *soname* must begin with `lib`, short for *library*. All in all, this gives us a total of five parts for the real name:

- `lib` (short for library)
- `convert` (the name of the library)
- `.so` (the extension, short for *shared object*)
- `.1` (the major version of the library)
- `.3` (the minor version of the library, optionally)

There's more...

Contrary to static libraries, dynamic libraries can be stripped and will still work. Note, however, that the stripping must then occur after creating the dynamic library on the `.so` file. If we were to strip the object (`.o`) file instead, we would lose all the symbols, making it useless for linking. But a `.so` file keeps the symbols in a special table called `.dynsym`, which the `strip` command won't touch. It's possible to view this table on a stripped dynamic library with the `readelf` command, using the `--symbols` option. So, if the `nm` command replies with *no symbols* on a dynamic library, you can try `readelf --symbols` instead.

See also

GCC is a massive piece of software with lots of options. There are PDF manuals available for each version of GCC on GNU's website. The manuals are about 1,000 pages long and can be downloaded from `https://gcc.gnu.org/onlinedocs/`.

Installing the dynamic library on the system

We have now seen how to create both static and dynamic libraries, and in *Chapter 3, Diving Deep into C in Linux*, we even saw how we could use a dynamic library from our home directory. But now, the time has come to install a dynamic library system-wide so that any user on your computer can use it.

Knowing how to install a dynamic library on a system will enable you to add libraries system-wide for any user to use.

Getting ready

For this recipe, you'll need the `libconvert.so.1` dynamic library we created in the previous recipe. You will also need root access to the system, either via `sudo` or `su`.

How to do it...

Installing a dynamic library is just a matter of moving the library file and header file to the correct directory and running a command. However, there are some conventions we should follow:

1. The first thing we need to do is to copy the library file to the correct place on the system. A common directory for user-installed libraries is `/usr/local/lib`, which we will use here. Since we are copying the file to a place outside of our home directory, we need to execute the command as the root user. We'll use `install` here to set the user, the group, and the mode in a single command, and since it's a system-wide install, we want it to be owned by root. It should also be executable since it will be included and executed at runtime:

```
$> sudo install -o root -g root -m 755 \
> libconvert.so.1 /usr/local/lib/libconvert.so.1
```

2. Now, we must run the `ldconfig` command, which will create the necessary links and update the cache.

> **Important note**
>
> On Fedora and CentOS, the `/usr/local/lib` directory isn't included in the `ldconfig` search path by default. Add it before moving forward by first switching to root with either `su` or `sudo -i` and then execute the command:
>
> `echo "/usr/local/lib" >> /etc/ld.so.conf.d/local.conf`

After we have executed `ldconfig`, we run `ls` on `libconvert*` in `/usr/local/lib` and see that `ldconfig` has created a symbolic link to our library file, without the version part:

```
$> sudo ldconfig
$> cd /usr/local/lib/
$> ls -og libconvert*
```

```
lrwxrwxrwx 1 15 dec 27 19:12 libconvert.so ->
libconvert.so.1
-rwxr-xr-x 1 15864 dec 27 18:16 libconvert.so.1
```

3. We must also copy the header file to a system directory; otherwise, the user would have to download and keep track of the header file manually, which is less than ideal. A good place for user-installed header files is `/usr/local/include`. The word *include* is from the C language `#include` line:

```
$> sudo install -o root -g root -m 644 convert.h \
> /usr/local/include/convert.h
```

4. Since we installed the library and the header file system-wide, we can go ahead and remove them from our current working directory. Doing so will make sure that we use the correct files in the next recipe:

```
$> rm libconvert.so.1 convert.h
```

How it works…

We installed the library file and header file using `install`. This program is excellent for tasks such as this since it sets the user (the `-o` option), the group (the `-g` option), and the mode (the `-m` option) in a single command. If we had used `cp` to copy the file, it would have been owned by the user who created it. We always want system-wide installation of binaries, libraries, and header files owned by the root user for security purposes.

The `/usr/local` directory is a good place for user-created stuff. We placed our library under `/usr/local/lib` and our header file under `/usr/local/include`. System libraries and header files are often placed in `/usr/lib` and `/usr/include`, respectively.

When we later use the library, the system will look for it in a file with a `.so` ending, and hence we need a symbolic link to the library with the name `libconvert.so`. But we didn't need to create that link ourselves; `ldconfig` took care of that for us.

Also, since we have placed the header file in `/usr/local/include`, we don't need to have that file in our current working directory anymore. We can now use the same syntax when including it like any other system header file. We'll see this in the next recipe.

Using the dynamic library in a program

Now that we have created a dynamic library and installed it on our system, it's time to try it out in a program. We have actually been using dynamic libraries without even thinking about it since the very beginning of this book. Functions such as `printf()` and so on are all part of the standard library. In the *The what and why of libraries* recipe from earlier in this chapter, we used another dynamic library called cURL. In this recipe, we'll use our very own library that we installed in the previous recipe.

Knowing how to use custom libraries will enable you to use other developers' code, which will speed up the development process. There's often no need to reinvent the wheel.

Getting ready

For this recipe, we'll need the `temperature.c` code from the *Using a static library* recipe earlier in this chapter. That program will use the dynamic library. You'll also need to complete the previous recipe before attempting this one.

How to do it…

In this recipe, we'll use the `temperature.c` code to make use of the library we installed in the previous recipe:

1. Since we will use the **header file** installed in `/usr/local/include`, we must modify the `#include` line in `temperature.c`. *Line 4* in `temperature.c` currently appears as this:

   ```
   #include "convert.h"
   ```

   Change the preceding code to this:

   ```
   #include <convert.h>
   ```

   Then, save it as `temperature-v2.c`.

2. We can now go ahead and compile the program. GCC will use the system-wide header file and library file. Remember that we need to link against the library using the `-l` option. When we do this, we must leave out the `lib` part and `.so` ending:

   ```
   $> gcc -Wall -Wextra -pedantic -std=c99 \
   > temperature-v2.c -o temperature-v2 -lconvert
   ```

3. Then, let's try it out with some different temperatures:

```
$> ./temperature-v2 -f 34
34.0 C = 93.2 F
$> ./temperature-v2 -k 21
21.0 C = 294.1 F
```

4. We can verify which libraries are dynamically linked with `ldd`. When we run this tool on our program, we see our `libconvert.so` library, `libc`, and something called `vdso` (*virtual dynamic shared object*):

```
$> ldd temperature-v2
        linux-vdso.so.1 (0x00007fff4376c000)
        libconvert.so => /usr/local/lib/libconvert.so
(0x00007faaeefe2000)
        libc.so.6 => /lib/x86_64-linux-gnu/libc.so.6
(0x00007faaeee21000)
        /lib64/ld-linux-x86-64.so.2 (0x00007faaef029000)
```

How it works...

When we include local header files from our current directory, the syntax is `#include "file.h"`. But for system-wide header files, the syntax is `#include <file.h>`.

Since the library is now installed in one of the system directories, we didn't need to specify the path to it. It was sufficient to link against the library with `-lconvert`. When doing so, all the common system-wide directories are being searched for the library. When we link with `-l`, we leave out both the `lib` part of the filename and the `.so` ending—the linker figures this out on its own.

In the last step, we verified that we are using the system-wide installation of `libconvert.so`, using `ldd`. Here, we also saw the standard C library, `libc`, and something called `vdso`. The standard C library has all the usual functions that we use time and time again, such as `printf()`. The `vdso` library, however, is a bit more arcane and is not something we are going to cover here. In short, it exports a small set of often-used system calls to userland to avoid too much context-switching, which would impair performance.

There's more...

Throughout this chapter, we've talked a lot about the **linker** and the linking process. The linker is a separate program called `ld`. To gain a deeper understanding of the linker, I suggest you read its manual page with `man 1 ld`.

See also

For more information about `ldd`, see `man 1 ldd`.

For the curious mind, there's a detailed explanation of `vdso` in `man 7 vdso`.

Compiling a statically linked program

Now that we have such a deep understanding of libraries and linking, we can create a **statically linked** program—that is, a program with all dependencies compiled into it. This makes the program—more or less—dependency-free. Making statically linked programs isn't common but sometimes it can be desirable—for example, if you for some reason need to distribute a single precompiled binary to many computers without worrying about installing all the libraries. But please note: it's not always possible to create completely dependency-free programs. If a program uses a library that depends on another library, this is not easily accomplished.

The downside of making and using statically linked programs is that they get a lot bigger in size. Also, it's no longer possible to update the program's libraries without recompiling the entire program. So, bear in mind that this is only used in rare cases.

But, by knowing how to compile statically linked programs, you not only enhance your knowledge but will also be able to distribute precompiled binaries to systems without the necessary libraries, on many different distributions.

Getting ready

For this recipe, you'll need to have completed the two previous recipes—in other words, you need to have installed the `libconvert.so.1` library on the system, and you need to have compiled `temperature-v2.c`. You also need the GCC compiler, as usual.

How to do it...

In this recipe, we'll compile a statically linked version of `temperature-v2.c`. We'll then remove the library from the system and notice that the statically linked program still works while the other doesn't:

> **Important note**
>
> On Fedora and CentOS, the static library for `libc` isn't included by default. To install it, run `sudo dnf install glibc-static`.

1. To link against the libraries statically, we need to have static versions of all the libraries. This means that we have to recreate the archive (`.a`) version of our library and install that as well. These steps are the same as from the *Creating a static library* recipe earlier in this chapter. First, we remove the object file, if we still have it. Then, we create a new one and create an archive from that:

```
$> rm convert.o
$> gcc -Wall -Wextra -pedantic -std=c99 -c convert.c
$> ar -cvr libconvert.a convert.o
a - convert.o
```

2. Next, we must install the static library on the system, preferably in the same location as the dynamic library. A static library doesn't need to be executable since it's included at compile time, not at runtime:

```
$> sudo install -o root -g root -m 644 \
> libconvert.a /usr/local/lib/libconvert.a
```

3. Now, compile a statically linked version of `temperature-v2.c`. The `-static` option makes the binary statically linked, meaning it will include the library code in the binary:

```
$> gcc -Wall -Wextra -pedantic -std=c99 -static \
> temperature-v2.c -o temperature-static -lconvert
```

4. Before we try the program, let's examine it with `ldd`, and also its size with `du`. Notice that on my system, the binary is now almost 800 kilobytes (on another system, it's 1.6 megabytes). Compare this to the dynamic version, which is only around 20 kilobytes:

```
$> du -sh temperature-static
788K    temperature-static
$> du -sh temperature-v2
```

```
20K        temperature-v2
$> ldd temperature-static
        not a dynamic executable
```

5. Now, let's try the program:

```
$> ./temperature-static -f 20
20.0 C = 68.0 F
```

6. Let's remove both the static and the dynamic libraries from the system:

```
$> sudo rm /usr/local/lib/libconvert.a \
> /usr/local/lib/libconvert.so \
> /usr/local/lib/libconvert.so.1
```

7. Now, let's try the dynamically linked binary, which shouldn't work since we have removed a library that it depends on:

```
$> ./temperature-v2 -f 25
./temperature-v2: error while loading shared
libraries: libconvert.so: cannot open shared object
file: No such file or directory
```

8. Finally, let's try the statically linked binary, which should work just as well as before:

```
$> ./temperature-static -f 25
25.0 C = 77.0 F
```

How it works...

A statically linked program includes all the code from all the libraries, which is why our binary got so huge in this example. To build a statically linked program, we need static versions of all the program's libraries. That's why we needed to recreate the static library and place it in one of the system directories. We also needed a static version of the standard C library, which we installed if we were using a CentOS or Fedora machine. On Debian/Ubuntu, it's already installed.

9
Terminal I/O and Changing Terminal Behavior

In this chapter, we learn what a **TTY** (short for **TeleTYpewriter**) and a **PTY** (short for **Pseudo-TeletYpewriter**) are and how to get information about them. We also learn how to set their attributes. Then, we write a small program that takes input without echoing the text—perfect for a password prompt. We also write a program that checks the size of the current terminal.

A terminal can take many forms—for example, a terminal window in X (the graphical frontend); the seven terminals accessed with *Ctrl* + *Alt* + *F1* through *F7*; an old serial terminal; a dial-up terminal; or a remote terminal such as **Secure Shell** (**SSH**).

A **TTY** is a hardware terminal, such as the consoles accessed with *Ctrl* + *Alt* + *F1* through *F7*, or a serial console.

A **PTY**, on the other hand, is a **pseudo-terminal**, meaning it's emulated in software. Examples of PTYs are programs such as `xterm`, `rxvt`, **Konsole**, **Gnome Terminal**, or a terminal multiplexer such as `tmux`. It could also be a remote terminal, such as SSH.

Since we all use terminals in our daily lives with Linux, knowing how to get information about them and control them can help us write better software. One such example is to hide the password in a password prompt.

In this chapter, we will cover the following recipes:

- Viewing terminal information
- Changing terminal settings with `stty`
- Investigating TTYs and PTYs and writing to them
- Checking if it's a TTY
- Creating a PTY
- Disabling echo for password prompts
- Reading the terminal size

Technical requirements

In this chapter, we'll need all the usual tools, such as the **GNU Compiler Collection** (**GCC**) compiler, the Make tool, and the generic Makefile, but we'll also need a program called `screen`. If you don't already have it, you can install it with your distribution's package manager—for example, `sudo apt-get install screen` for Debian/Ubuntu, or `sudo dnf install screen` for CentOS/Fedora.

All code samples for this chapter can be downloaded from `https://github.com/PacktPublishing/Linux-System-Programming-Techniques/tree/master/ch9`.

Check out the following link to see the Code in Action video:
`https://bit.ly/2O8j7Lu`

Viewing terminal information

In this recipe, we'll learn more about what TTYs and PTYs are and how to read their attributes and information. This will help us in our understanding of TTYs as we move forward in the chapter. Here, we learn how to find out which TTY or PTY we are using, where it lives on the filesystem, and how to read its attributes.

Getting ready

There are no special requirements for this recipe. We'll only use standard programs that are already installed.

How to do it...

In this recipe, we'll explore how to find your own TTY, what attributes it has, where its corresponding file lives, and what kind of TTY it is:

1. Start by typing `tty` in your terminal. This will tell you which TTY you are using on the system. There can be many TTYs and PTYs on a single system. Each of them is represented by a file on the system:

```
$> tty
/dev/pts/24
```

2. Now, let's examine that file. As we see here, it's a special file type, called *character special*:

```
$> ls -l /dev/pts/24
crw--w---- 1 jake tty 136, 24 jan  3 23:19 /dev/pts/24
$> file /dev/pts/24
/dev/pts/24: character special (136/24)
```

3. Now, let's examine the terminal's attributes with a program called `stty`. The `-a` option tells `stty` to display all attributes. The information we get is, for example, the size of the terminal (number of rows and columns); its speed (only important on serial terminals, dial-up, and so on); which *Ctrl* key combination is used for **EOF** (**End Of File**), suspend, kill, and so on. All options that start with a minus sign are disabled values, such as `-parenb`. All values without a minus sign, such as `cs8`, are enabled:

```
$> stty -a
speed 38400 baud; rows 14; columns 88; line = 0;
intr = ^C; quit = ^\; erase = ^?; kill = ^U; eof = ^D;
eol = M-^?; eol2 = M-^?;
swtch = <undef>; start = ^Q; stop = ^S; susp = ^Z; rprnt
= ^R; werase = ^W; lnext = ^V;
discard = ^O; min = 1; time = 0;
-parenb -parodd -cmspar cs8 hupcl -cstopb cread -clocal
-crtscts
-ignbrk brkint -ignpar -parmrk -inpck -istrip -inlcr
-igncr icrnl ixon -ixoff -iuclc
ixany imaxbel iutf8
opost -olcuc -ocrnl onlcr -onocr -onlret -ofill -ofdel
nl0 cr0 tab0 bs0 vt0 ff0
isig icanon iexten echo echoe echok -echonl -noflsh
-xcase -tostop -echoprt echoctl
echoke -flusho -extproc
```

4. It's also possible to view another terminal's attributes, assuming you own it, meaning the logged-in user must be you. If we try to view another user's terminal, we get a *Permission denied* error:

```
$> stty -F /dev/pts/33
speed 38400 baud; line = 0;
lnext = <undef>; discard = <undef>; min = 1; time = 0;
-brkint -icrnl ixoff -imaxbel iutf8
-icanon -echo
$> stty -F /dev/tty2
stty: /dev/tty2: Permission denied
```

How it works...

A single Linux system can have hundreds or thousands of logged-in users. Each of them is connected over a TTY or PTY. Back in the old days, this was often hardware terminals (TTYs) connected to the machine over serial lines. Nowadays, hardware terminals are pretty rare; instead, we log in over **SSH** or use terminal programs.

In our example, the current user is logged in on a **PTY** device with the number 24, but notice that the device said `/dev/pts/24`; that is *pts*, not *pty*. A PTY has two parts, a master and a slave. **PTS** stands for *pseudo-terminal slave*, and it's that part we connect to. The master part opens/creates the pseudo-terminal, but it's the slave that we use. We'll dig a bit deeper into this concept later in the chapter.

The settings we used as an example in *Step 3* (`-parenb` and `cs8`) mean that `parenb` is disabled since it has a minus sign, and `cs8` is enabled. The `parenb` option will generate a parity bit and expect one back in the input. Parity bits were widely used in dial-up connections and serial communication. The `cs8` option sets the character size to 8 bits.

The `stty` program can be used to both view and set attributes for a terminal. In the next recipe, we'll return to `stty` to change some values.

As long as we are the terminal device owner, we can read and write to it, as we saw in the last step of the recipe.

See also

There's a lot of useful information in `man 1 tty` and `man 1 stty`.

Changing terminal settings with stty

In this recipe, we'll learn how to change the settings (or attributes) of our terminal. In the previous recipe, we listed our current settings with `stty -a`. In this recipe, we'll change some of those settings, using the same `stty` program.

Knowing how to change your terminal settings will enable you to adapt it according to your preference.

Getting ready

No special requirements exist for this recipe.

How to do it...

Here, we will change some of the settings for our current terminal:

1. Let's start by turning off **echoing**. Doing so is common—for example, for password prompts—but it can also be done manually, as we'll see here. After you turn off the terminal echo, you won't see anything you write. Everything still works, though—for example, we can type `whoami`, and get an answer. Notice that you won't see the `whoami` command as you type it:

```
$> stty -echo
$> whoami jake
$>
```

2. To turn on echoing again, we type the same command again but without the minus sign. Notice that you won't see the `stty` command when you type it:

```
$> stty echo
$> whoami
jake
```

3. We can also change special key sequences—for example, usually, the EOF character is *Ctrl* + *D*. We can rebind that with a single dot (`.`) if we'd like:

```
$> stty eof .
```

4. Type a single dot (`.`) now, and your current terminal will quit or log out. When you start a new terminal or log back in, the settings are back to normal.

5. To save the settings for reuse later, we first make the necessary changes—for example, setting EOF to a dot. Then, we use `stty --save`. That option will print a long line of hexadecimal numbers—these numbers are the settings. So, to save them, we can redirect the output from `stty --save` to a file:

```
$> stty eof .
$> stty --save
5500:5:bf:8a3b:3:1c:7f:15:2e:0:1:0:11:13:1a:0:1
2:f:17:16:0:0:0:0:0:0:0:0:0:0:0:0:0:0:0:0
$> stty --save > my-tty-settings
```

6. Now, log out by pressing a dot.
7. Log back in (or re-open the terminal window). Try typing a dot, and nothing will happen. To reload our settings, we use the `my-tty-settings` file from the previous step. The `$()` sequence *expands* the command inside the parenthesis and is then used as an argument for `stty`:

```
$> stty $(cat my-tty-settings)
```

8. Now, we can once again try to log out by pressing a dot.

How it works...

A terminal is often a "dumb" device, and hence it requires lots of settings to make it work right. This is also one of those leftovers from the old days of hardware teletypewriters. The `stty` program is used to set attributes on a terminal device.

Options with a minus sign are negated—that is, disabled. Options without a minus sign are enabled. In our example, we first turned off echoing, a common practice for password prompts, and so on.

There is no real way of saving the settings for a TTY, except for the way we saw here by saving it to a file and re-reading it later.

Investigating TTYs and PTYs and writing to them

In this recipe, we'll learn how to list currently logged-in users, which TTYs they use, and which programs they are running. We'll also learn how to write to those users and terminals. As we'll see in this recipe, we can write to a **terminal device** just as if it were a file, assuming we have the correct permissions.

Knowing how to write to other terminals deepens understanding of how terminals work and what they are. It also enables you to write some interesting software and, above all, it will make you a better system administrator. It also teaches you about terminal security.

How to do it...

We'll start by investigating the logged-in users; then, we'll learn how to send messages to them:

1. To make things a bit more interesting, open up three to four terminal windows. If you're not using the **X-Window System**, log in on multiple TTYs. Or, if you are using a remote server, log in several times.
2. Now, type the `who` command in one of the terminals. You'll get a list of all the logged-in users, which TTY/PTY they are using, and the date and time they logged in. In my example, I've logged in several times over SSH. If you are using a local machine with multiple `xterm` applications, you'll see `(:0)` instead of the **Internet Protocol** (**IP**) address:

```
$> who
root     tty1         Jan  5 16:03
jake     pts/0        Jan  5 16:04 (192.168.0.34)
jake     pts/1        Jan  5 16:04 (192.168.0.34)
jake     pts/2        Jan  5 16:04 (192.168.0.34)
```

3. There's a similar command, w, that even shows which program the user on each terminal is currently using:

```
$> w
 16:09:33 up 7 min,  4 users,  load average: 0.00, 0.16, 0.13
USER   TTY    FROM          LOGIN@   IDLE   JCPU   PCPU WHAT
root   tty1   -             16:03    6:05   0.07s  0.07s -bash
jake   pts/0  192.168.0.34  16:04    5:25   0.01s  0.01s -bash
jake   pts/1  192.168.0.34  16:04    0.00s  0.04s  0.01s w
jake   pts/2  192.168.0.34  16:04    5:02   0.02s  0.02s -bash
```

4. Let's find out which terminal we are using:

```
$> tty
/dev/pts/1
```

5. Now that we know which terminal we are using, let's send a message to another user and terminal. At the beginning of this book, I mentioned that everything is just a file or a process. This is true even for terminals. That means we can send data to a terminal using regular redirections:

```
$> echo "Hello" > /dev/pts/2
```

   The text *Hello* will now appear in the PTS2 terminal.

6. Sending messages to a terminal using `echo` only works if it's the same user that's logged in on the other terminal. For example, if I try to send a message to TTY1 where root is logged in, it doesn't work—for a good reason:

```
$> echo "Hello" > /dev/tty1
-bash: /dev/tty1: Permission denied
```

7. However, there exists a program that allows users to write to each other's terminal, assuming they have allowed it. That program is called `write`. To allow or disallow messages, we use the `mesg` program. If you can log in as root (or some other user) on a terminal, do so, and then allow messages (the letter `y` stands for *yes*):

```
#> tty
/dev/tty1
#> whoami
root
#> mesg y
```

8. Now, from another user, we can write to that user and terminal:

```
$> write root /dev/tty1
Hello! How are you doing?
Ctrl+D
```

   That message will now appear on TTY1, where root is logged in.

9. There's another command that allows a user to write on *all* terminals. However, root is the only user that can write to users who have turned off messages. When logged in as root, issue the following command to write a message about a pending reboot to all logged-in users:

```
#> wall "The machine will be rebooted later tonight"
```

This will display a message, shown here, on all users' terminals:

```
Broadcast message from root (tty1) (Tue Jan  5 16:59:33)

The machine will be rebooted later tonight
```

How it works...

Since all the terminals are represented by files on the filesystem, it's easy to send messages to them. The regular permissions apply, however, to prevent users from writing to other users or snooping on their terminal.

With the `write` program, though, users can write messages to each other quickly, without needing any third-party software.

There's more...

The `wall` program is used to warn users of a pending reboot or shutdown. For example, if root issues the `shutdown -h +5` command to schedule a shutdown in 5 minutes, all users will receive a warning. That warning is sent automatically, using the `wall` program.

See also

For more information about the commands covered in this recipe, see the following manual pages:

- `man 1 write`
- `man 1 wall`
- `man 1 mesg`

Checking if it's a TTY

In this recipe, we'll start looking at some of the C functions to examine TTYs. Here, we mean TTY in the broadest sense, meaning both TTY and PTY.

The program we will write here will check if stdout is a terminal. If it's not, it will print an error message.

Knowing how to check if stdin, stdout, or stderr are terminal devices will enable you to write error checks for programs that require a terminal to work.

Getting ready

For this recipe, we'll need the GCC compiler, the Make tool, and the generic Makefile. The generic Makefile can be downloaded from this chapter's GitHub folder, at `https://github.com/PacktPublishing/Linux-System-Programming-Techniques/tree/master/ch9`.

How to do it...

Here, we'll write a small program that prints an error message if stdout is not a terminal:

1. Write the following small program in a file and save it as `ttyinfo.c`. We use two new functions here. The first one is `isatty()`, which checks if a **file descriptor** is a terminal. Here, we check if stdout is a terminal. The other function is `ttyname()`, which prints the terminal's name connected to stdout (or actually the path):

```
#include <stdio.h>
#include <unistd.h>
#include <errno.h>
int main(void)
{
    if ( (isatty(STDOUT_FILENO) == 1) )
    {
        printf("It's a TTY with the name %s\n",
            ttyname(STDOUT_FILENO));
    }
    else
    {
        perror("isatty");
    }
    printf("Hello world\n");
    return 0;
}
```

2. Compile the program:

```
$> make ttyinfo
gcc -Wall -Wextra -pedantic -std=c99    ttyinfo.c   -o
ttyinfo
```

3. Let's try out the program. First, we run it without any redirections. The program will print the name of the terminal and the text *Hello world*:

```
$> ./ttyinfo
It's a TTY with the name /dev/pts/10
Hello world
```

4. But if we were to redirect file descriptor 1 to a file, it's no longer a terminal (because that file descriptor is then pointing to a file and not a terminal). This will print an error message, but the *Hello world* message is still redirected to the file:

```
$> ./ttyinfo > my-file
isatty: Inappropriate ioctl for device
$> cat my-file
Hello world
```

5. To prove the point, we can "redirect" file descriptor 1 to `/dev/stdout`. Everything will then work as usual since file descriptor 1 is then once again stdout:

```
$> ./ttyinfo > /dev/stdout
It's a TTY with the name /dev/pts/10
Hello world
```

6. Another step to prove the point is to redirect to our own terminal device. This will be similar to what we saw in the previous recipe when we used `echo` to print a text to a terminal:

```
$> tty
/dev/pts/10
$> ./ttyinfo > /dev/pts/10
It's a TTY with the name /dev/pts/10
Hello world
```

7. For the sake of experimentation, let's open up a second terminal. Find the TTY name of the new terminal with the `tty` command (in my case, it's `/dev/pts/26`). Then, from the first terminal, run the `ttyinfo` program again, but redirect file descriptor 1 (stdout) to the second terminal:

```
$> ./ttyinfo > /dev/pts/26
```

No output will show up in the *current* terminal. However, on the *second* terminal, we see the program's output, with the name of the second terminal:

```
It's a TTY with the name /dev/pts/26
Hello world
```

How it works...

The `STDOUT_FILENO` macro, which we used with both `isatty()` and `ttyname()`, is just the integer 1—that is, file descriptor 1.

Remember that when we redirect stdout with a > sign, we redirect file descriptor 1.

Normally, file descriptor 1 is stdout, which is connected to your terminal. If we redirect file descriptor 1 with the > character to a file, it instead points to that file. Since the regular file isn't a terminal, we get an error message from the program (from the `isatty()` function's `errno` variable).

When we redirected file descriptor 1 back to `/dev/stdout`, it was once again stdout and no error message was printed.

In the last step, when we redirected the program's output to another terminal, all text got redirected to that terminal. Not only that—the name of the TTY printed by the program was indeed that second terminal's. The reason is that the terminal device connected to file descriptor 1 was indeed that terminal (`/dev/pts/26`, in my case).

See also

For more information about the functions we used in the recipe, I recommend that you read `man 3 isatty` and `man 3 ttyname`.

Creating a PTY

In this recipe, we'll create a **PTY** using a C program. A PTY consists of two parts: a master (referred to as a pseudo-terminal master, or **PTM**) and a slave, or **PTS**. The program will create a PTY and print the path to the slave on the current terminal. We can then connect to that PTS with an application called `screen` and type away, and the characters will be printed to both the master and the slave. The slave is where the `screen` program is connected to, which is our terminal in this case. The master is usually quiet and runs in the background, but for demonstration purposes, we'll print the characters on the master as well.

Knowing how to create a PTY enables you to write your own terminal applications, such as `xterm`, Gnome Terminal, `tmux`, and so on.

Getting ready

For this recipe, you'll need the GCC compiler, the Make tool, and the `screen` program. Installation instructions for `screen` are found in the *Technical requirements* section of this chapter.

How to do it...

Here, we'll write a small program that creates a PTY. We'll then connect to the slave end of this PTY—the PTS—using `screen`. We can then type characters, and they are printed back to us on the PTS:

1. We'll start by writing the program for this recipe. There are a lot of new concepts here, so the code is broken up into several steps. Write all of the code in a single file, called `my-pty.c`. We'll start by defining `_XOPEN_SOURCE` (for `posix_openpt()`), and include all the header files we need:

```
#define _XOPEN_SOURCE 600
#include <stdio.h>
#include <stdlib.h>
#include <fcntl.h>
#include <string.h>
#include <unistd.h>
```

2. Next, we'll start the `main()` function and define some variables we'll need:

```
int main(void)
{
    char rxbuf[1];
    char txbuf[3];
    int master; /* for the pts master fd */
    int c; /* to catch read's return value */
```

3. Now, it's time to create the PTY device with `posix_openpt()`. This will return a file descriptor, which we'll save in `master`. Then, we run `grantpt()`, which sets the owner of the device to the current user, the group to *tty*, and changes the mode of the device to `620`. We must also unlock it with `unlockpt()` before using it. To know where we should connect, we also print the path to the slave device, using `ptsname()`:

```
    master = posix_openpt(O_RDWR);
    grantpt(master);
    unlockpt(master);
    printf("Slave: %s\n", ptsname(master));
```

4. Next, we create the main loop of the program. In the loop, we read a character from the PTS and then write it back again to the PTS. Here, we also print the character to the master so that we'll see that it's a master/slave pair. Since a terminal device is rather primitive, we must manually check for a **carriage return** character (the *Enter* key) and instead print a **newline** and a carriage return to make a new line:

```
    while(1) /* main loop */
    {
        /* read from the master file descriptor */
        c = read(master, rxbuf, 1);
        if (c == 1)
        {
            /* convert carriage return to '\n\r' */
            if (rxbuf[0] == '\r')
            {
                printf("\n\r"); /* on master */
                sprintf(txbuf, "\n\r"); /* on slave */
            }
            else
            {
                printf("%c", rxbuf[0]);
                sprintf(txbuf, "%c", rxbuf[0]);
            }
            fflush(stdout);
            write(master, txbuf, strlen(txbuf));
        }
```

5. If no characters are received, the device connected to the slave has disconnected. If that is the case, we return, and hence exit from the program:

```
        else /* if c is not 1, it has disconnected */
        {
            printf("Disconnected\n\r");
            return 0;
        }
    }
    return 0;
}
```

6. Now, it's time to compile the program so that we can run it:

```
$> make my-pty
gcc -Wall -Wextra -pedantic -std=c99    my-pty.c    -o
my-pty
```

7. Now, run the program in your current terminal and make a note of the slave path:

```
$> ./my-pty
Slave: /dev/pts/31
```

8. Before we move on to connect to it, let's examine the device. Here, we'll see that my user owns it, and it's indeed a *character special* device, common for terminals:

```
$> ls -l /dev/pts/31
crw--w---- 1 jake tty 136, 31 jan  3 20:32 /dev/pts/31
$> file /dev/pts/31
/dev/pts/31: character special (136/31)
```

9. Now, open a new terminal and connect to the slave path you got from the master. In my case, it's `/dev/pts/31`. To connect to it, we'll use `screen`:

```
$> screen /dev/pts/31
```

10. Now, we can type away, and all the characters will be printed back to us. They will also appear on the master. To disconnect and quit `screen`, first hit *Ctrl* + *A* and then type a single *K*, as in kill. A question will then present to you (*Really kill this window [y/n]*); type *Y* here. You'll now see *Disconnected* in the terminal where you started `my-pty`, and the program will exit.

How it works...

We open a new PTY by using the `posix_openpt()` function. We set to both read and write using `O_RDWR`. By opening a new PTY, a new character device is created in `/dev/pts/`. It is that character device we later connected to using `screen`.

Since `posix_openpt()` returns a file descriptor, we can use all the regular system calls for file descriptors to read and write data, such as `read` and `write`.

A terminal device, such as the one we created here, is rather primitive. If we press *Enter*, the cursor will return to the start of the line. No new line will be created first. That's actually how the *Enter* key used to work. To solve this in our program, we check if the character read is a carriage return (that's what the *Enter* key sends), and if it is, we instead first print a newline character and then a carriage return.

If we only printed the newline character we would only get a new line, right under our current cursor. This behavior is a leftover from the old-school teletype devices with paper. After we have printed the current character (or newline and carriage return), we **flush** with `fflush()`. The reason is that the character printed on the master end (where the `my-pty` program is running) isn't followed by a new line. Stdout is line-buffered, meaning it only flushes on a line break. But since we want to see each character as it's typed we must flush it on every character, using `fflush()`.

See also

There's a lot of useful information in the manual pages. I particularly recommend you read the following manual pages: `man 3 posix_openpt`, `man 3 grantpt`, `man 3 unlockpt`, `man 4 pts`, and `man 4 tty`.

Disabling echo for password prompts

To protect users' passwords from shoulder surfing, it's always best to hide what they type. The way to hide a password from being displayed is to disable **echoing**. In this recipe, we'll write a simple password program with echoing disabled.

Knowing how to disable echoing is key when writing programs that take some form of secret input, such as a password or a key.

Getting ready

For this recipe, you'll need the GCC compiler, the Make tool, and the generic Makefile.

How to do it...

In this recipe, we'll build a small program with a password prompt

1. Since the code in this recipe will be rather long and some parts a bit arcane, I have split up the code into several steps. Note, however, that all code should go into a single file. Name the file `passprompt.c`. Let's start with the `include` lines, the `main()` function, and the variables we'll need. The struct named `term` of type `termios` is a special structure that holds the attributes for the terminal:

```
#include <stdio.h>
#include <string.h>
#include <unistd.h>
#include <termios.h>
int main(void)
```

```
{
    char mypass[] = "super-secret";
    char buffer[80];
    struct termios term;
```

2. Next, we'll start by disabling echoing, but first, we need to get all the current settings of the terminal by using `tcgetattr()`. Once we have all the settings, we modify them to disable echoing. The way we do it is to **bitwise AND** the current settings with the **negated value** of `ECHO`. The ~ sign negates a value. More on this in the *How it works...* section later:

```
    /* get the current settings */
    tcgetattr(STDIN_FILENO, &term);
    /* disable echoing */
    term.c_lflag = term.c_lflag & ~ECHO;
    tcsetattr(STDIN_FILENO, TCSAFLUSH, &term);
```

3. Then, we write the code for the password prompt; nothing new here that we don't already know:

```
    printf("Enter password: ");
    scanf("%s", buffer);
    if ( (strcmp(mypass, buffer) == 0) )
    {
        printf("\nCorrect password, welcome!\n");
    }
    else
    {
        printf("\nIncorrect password, go away!\n");
    }
```

4. Then, before we exit the program, we must turn on echoing again; otherwise, it will remain off even after the program has exited. The way to do that is to **bitwise OR** the current settings with `ECHO`. This will reverse what we previously did:

```
    /* re-enable echoing */
    term.c_lflag = term.c_lflag | ECHO;
    tcsetattr(STDIN_FILENO, TCSAFLUSH, &term);
    return 0;
}
```

5. Now, let's compile the program:

```
$> make passprompt
gcc -Wall -Wextra -pedantic -std=c99    passprompt.c   -o
passprompt
```

6. Now, we can try the program, and we'll notice that we don't see what we type:

```
$> ./passprompt
Enter password: test+Enter
Incorrect password, go away!
$> ./passprompt
Enter password: super-secret+Enter
Correct password, welcome!
```

How it works...

The way to make changes to the terminal with `tcsetattr()` is to get the current attributes with `tcgetattr()` and then modify them, and then finally apply those changed attributes to the terminal.

The first argument to both `tcgetattr()` and `tcsetattr()` is the file descriptor we want to change. In our case, it's stdin.

The second argument to `tcgetattr()` is the struct where the attributes will be saved.

The second argument to `tcsetattr()` determines when the changes will have an effect. Here, we use `TCSAFLUSH`, which means that changes occur after all output is written, and all input received but not read will be discarded.

The third argument to `tcsetattr()` is the struct that contains the attributes.

To save and set attributes, we need a structure called `termios` (the same name as the header file we use). That structure contains five members, four of which are the modes. These are input modes (`c_iflag`), output modes (`c_oflag`), control mode (`c_cflag`), and local mode (`c_lflag`). What we change here is the local mode.

First, we have the current attributes in the `c_lflag` member, which is an unsigned integer that's built up from a bunch of bits. Those bits are the attributes.

Then, to turn off a setting—for example, echoing in our case—we negate the `ECHO` macro ("inverting" it) and then add it back to `c_lflag` with bitwise AND (the `&` sign).

The `ECHO` macro is `010` (octal 10), or 8 in decimal, which is `00001000` in binary (with 8 bits). Negated, it is `11110111`. A bitwise AND operation is then carried out on those bits with the other bits from the original settings.

The result of the bitwise AND operation is then applied to the terminal with `tcsetattr()`, which turns off echoing.

Before we end the program, we reverse the process by a bitwise OR operation on the new value with the `ECHO` value. Then, we apply that value with `tcsetattr()`, turning on echoing again.

There's more...

There are lots and lots of attributes we can set this way—for example, it's possible to disable flushing on interrupt and quit signals, and so on. The `man 3 tcsetattr()` manual page has complete lists of macros to use for each of the modes.

Reading the terminal size

In this recipe, we'll continue digging around our terminal. Here, we write a funny little program that reports the size of the terminal live. As you resize your terminal window (assuming you are using an X console application), you'll instantly see the new size being reported.

To make this work, we'll make use of both a special **escape sequence** and the `ioctl()` function.

Knowing how to use these two tools, escape sequences, and `ioctl()` will enable you to do some amusing things with the terminal.

Getting ready

To make the most of this recipe, it's best to use an **X-Window** console, such as `xterm`, `rxvt`, *Konsole*, *Gnome Terminal*, and so on.

You'll also need the GCC compiler, the Make tool, and the generic Makefile.

How to do it...

Here, we will write a program that first clears the screen using a special escape sequence, then fetches the terminal's size and prints to the screen:

1. Write the following code in a file and save it as `terminal-size.c`. The program uses an endless loop, so to quit the program, we must use *Ctrl* + *C*. On each iteration of the loop, we first clear the screen by printing a special *escape sequence*. Then, we get the terminal size with `ioctl()` and print the size on the screen:

```
#include <stdio.h>
#include <unistd.h>
#include <termios.h>
#include <sys/ioctl.h>

int main(void)
{
   struct winsize termsize;
   while(1)
   {
      printf("\033[1;1H\033[2J");
      ioctl(STDOUT_FILENO, TIOCGWINSZ, &termsize);
      printf("Height: %d rows\n",
         termsize.ws_row);
      printf("Width: %d columns\n",
         termsize.ws_col);
      sleep(0.1);
   }
   return 0;
}
```

2. Compile the program:

```
$> make terminal-size
gcc -Wall -Wextra -pedantic -std=c99    terminal-size.c
-o terminal-size
```

3. Now, run the program in a terminal window. As the program is running, resize the window. You'll notice that the size is instantly updated. Quit the program with *Ctrl* + *C*:

```
$> ./terminal-size
Height: 20 rows
Width: 97 columns
Ctrl+C
```

How it works...

First, we define a structure name `termsize`, with the `winsize` type. We will save the terminal size in this structure later. The structure has two members (actually four, but only two are used). The members are `ws_row` for the number of rows and `wc_col` for the number of columns.

Then, to clear the screen, we use `printf()` to print a special escape sequence, `\033[1;1H\033[2J`. The `\033` sequence is the escape code. After the escape code, we have a `[` character, then we have the actual code telling the terminal what to do. The first one, `1;1H`, moves the cursor to position 1,1 (the first row and first column). Then, we use the `\033` escape code again so that we can use another code. First, we have the `[` character, just as before. Then, we have the `[2J` code, which means to erase the entire display.

Once we have cleared the screen and moved the cursor, we use `ioctl()` to get the terminal size. The first argument is the file descriptor; here, we use stdout. The second argument is the command to send; here, it's `TIOCGWINSZ` to get the terminal size. These macros/commands can be found in the `man 2 ioctl_tty` manual page. The third argument is the `winsize` structure.

Once we have the sizes in the `winsize` structure, we print the values using `printf()`.

To avoid draining the system resources, we sleep for 0.1 seconds before the next iteration.

There's more...

In the `man 4 console_codes` manual page, there are lots and lots of other codes you can use. You can do everything from using colors to bold fonts, to moving the cursor, to ringing the terminal bell, and so on.

For example, to print *Hello* in blinking magenta and then reset to the default values, you can use this:

```
printf("\033[35;5mHello!\033[0m\n");
```

Note, though, that not all terminals can blink.

See also

For more information about `ioctl()`, see both the `man 2 ioctl` and `man 2 ioctl_tty` manual pages. The latter contains information about the `winsize` struct and the macros/commands.

10 Using Different Kinds of IPC

In this chapter, we will learn about the various ways we can communicate between processes via so-called **inter-process communication** (**IPC**). We will write various programs that use different kinds of IPC, from signals and pipes to FIFOs, message queues, shared memory, and sockets.

Processes sometimes need to exchange information—for example, in the case of a client and a server program running on the same computer. It could also be a process that has forked into two processes, and they need to communicate somehow.

There are multiple ways in which this IPC can happen. In this chapter, we'll learn about some of the most common ones.

Knowing about IPC is essential if you want to write more than the most basic of programs. Sooner or later, you'll have a program consisting of multiple pieces or multiple programs that needs to share information.

In this chapter, we will cover the following recipes:

- Using signals for IPC—building a client for the daemon
- Communicating with a pipe
- FIFO—using it in the shell

- FIFO—building the sender
- FIFO—building the receiver
- Message queues—creating the sender
- Message queues—creating the receiver
- Communicating between child and parent with shared memory
- Using shared memory between unrelated processes
- Unix socket—creating the server
- Unix socket—creating the client

Let's get started!

Technical requirements

For this chapter, you'll need the GCC compiler, the Make tool, and the generic Makefile from *Chapter 3, Diving Deep into C in Linux*. If you haven't installed these tools yet, please see *Chapter 1, Getting the Necessary Tools and Writing Our First Linux Programs*, for installation instructions.

All the code samples—and the generic Makefile—for this chapter can be downloaded from GitHub at `https://github.com/PacktPublishing/Linux-System-Programming-Techniques/tree/master/ch10`.

Check out the following link to see the Code in Action video: `https://bit.ly/2TVecQs`

Using signals for IPC - building a client for the daemon

We have already used signals several times in this book. However, when we did, we always used the `kill` command to send the **signal** to the program. This time, we'll write a small client that controls the daemon, `my-daemon-v2`, from *Chapter 6, Spawning Processes and Using Job Control.*

This is a typical example of when signals are used for **IPC**. The daemon has a small "client program" that controls it, so that it can stop it, restart it, reload its configuration file, and so on.

Knowing how to use signals for IPC is a solid start in writing programs that can communicate between them.

Getting ready

For this recipe, you'll need the GCC compiler, the Make tool, and the generic Makefile. You will also need the `my-daemon-v2.c` file from *Chapter 6, Spawning Processes and Using Job Control*. There is a copy of that file in this chapter's GitHub directory at `https://github.com/PacktPublishing/Linux-System-Programming-Techniques/tree/master/ch10`.

How to do it...

In this recipe, we'll add a small client program to the daemon from *Chapter 6, Spawning Processes and Using Job Control*. This program will send signals to the daemon, just like the `kill` command does. However, this program will only send signals to the daemon, no other process:

1. Write the following code in a file and save it as `my-daemon-ctl.c`. This program is a bit longer, so it's split up into several steps. All the code goes into the same file, though. We'll start with the include lines, the prototype for the usage function, and all the variables we'll need:

```
#define _XOPEN_SOURCE 500
#include <stdio.h>
#include <sys/types.h>
#include <signal.h>
#include <getopt.h>
#include <string.h>
#include <linux/limits.h>
void printUsage(char progname[], FILE *fp);
int main(int argc, char *argv[])
{
   FILE *fp;
   FILE *procfp;
   int pid, opt;
   int killit = 0;
   char procpath[PATH_MAX] = { 0 };
   char cmdline[PATH_MAX] = { 0 };
   const char pidfile[] = "/var/run/my-daemon.pid";
   const char daemonPath[] =
      "/usr/local/sbin/my-daemon-v2";
```

2. Then, we want to be able to parse command-line options. We'll only need two options; that is, `-h` for help and `-k` to kill the daemon. The default is to show the status of the daemon:

```
/* Parse command-line options */
while ((opt = getopt(argc, argv, "kh")) != -1)
{
    switch (opt)
    {
        case 'k': /* kill the daemon */
            killit = 1;
            break;
        case 'h': /* help */
            printUsage(argv[0], stdout);
            return 0;
        default: /* in case of invalid options */
            printUsage(argv[0], stderr);
            return 1;
    }
}
```

3. Now, let's open the **PID** file and read it. Once we've done that, we need to assemble the complete path to the process's `cmdline` file in `/proc`. Then, we must open that file and read the complete command-line path from it:

```
if ( (fp = fopen(pidfile, "r")) == NULL )
{
    perror("Can't open PID-file (daemon isn't "
        "running?)");
}
/* read the pid (and check if we could read an
 * integer) */
if ( (fscanf(fp, "%d", &pid)) != 1 )
{
    fprintf(stderr, "Can't read PID from %s\n",
        pidfile);
    return 1;
}
/* build the /proc path */
sprintf(procpath, "/proc/%d/cmdline", pid);
/* open the /proc path */
if ( (procfp = fopen(procpath, "r")) == NULL )
```

```
{
    perror("Can't open /proc path"
        " (no /proc or wrong PID?)");
    return 1;
}
/* read the cmd line path from proc */
fscanf(procfp, "%s", cmdline);
```

4. Now that we have both the PID and the full command line, we can double-check that the PID belongs to `/usr/local/sbin/my-daemon-v2` and not some other process:

```
/* check that the PID matches the cmdline */
if ( (strncmp(cmdline, daemonPath, PATH_MAX))
    != 0 )
{
    fprintf(stderr, "PID %d doesn't belong "
        "to %s\n", pid, daemonPath);
    return 1;
}
```

5. If we give the `-k` option to the program, we must set the `killit` variable to 1. So, at this point, we must kill the process. Otherwise, we just print a message stating that the daemon is running:

```
if ( killit == 1 )
{
    if ( (kill(pid, SIGTERM)) == 0 )
    {
        printf("Successfully terminated "
            "my-daemon-v2\n");
    }
    else
    {
        perror("Couldn't terminate my-daemon-v2");
        return 1;
    }
}
else
{
    printf("The daemon is running with PID %d\n",
        pid);
}
```

```
    return 0;
}
```

6. Finally, we create the function for the `printUsage()` function:

```
void printUsage(char progname[], FILE *fp)
{
    fprintf(fp, "Usage: %s [-k] [-h]\n", progname);
    fprintf(fp, "If no options are given, a status "
        "message is displayed.\n"
        "-k will terminate the daemon.\n"
        "-h will display this usage help.\n");
}
```

7. Now, we can compile the program:

```
$> make my-daemon-ctl
gcc -Wall -Wextra -pedantic -std=c99    my-daemon ctl.c
-o my-daemon-ctl
```

8. Before we go any further, make sure you have disabled and stopped the `systemd` service for the daemon from *Chapter 7, Using systemd to Handle Your Daemons*:

```
$> sudo systemctl disable my-daemon
$> sudo systemctl stop my-daemon
```

9. Now, compile the daemon (`my-daemon-v2.c`) if you haven't done so already:

```
$> make my-daemon-v2
gcc -Wall -Wextra -pedantic -std=c99    my-daemon-v2.c
-o my-daemon-v2
```

10. Then, start the daemon manually (no `systemd` service this time):

```
$> sudo ./my-daemon-v2
```

11. Now, we can try out our new program to control the daemon. Notice that we can't kill the daemon as a regular user:

```
$> ./my-daemon-ctl
The daemon is running with PID 17802 and cmdline ./
my-daemon-v2
$> ./my-daemon-ctl -k
Couldn't terminate daemon: Operation not permitted
$> sudo ./my-daemon-ctl -k
Successfully terminated daemon
```

12. If we rerun the program once the daemon has been killed, it will tell us that there's no PID file and that the daemon is therefore not running:

```
$> ./my-daemon-ctl
Can't open PID-file (daemon isn't running?): No such file
or directory
```

How it works...

Since the daemon creates a PID file, we can use that file to get the PID of the running daemon. The daemon removes the PID file when it is terminated, so we can assume that the daemon isn't running if there's no PID file.

If the PID file does exist, first, we read the PID from the file. Then, we use the PID to assemble the path to that PID's `cmdline` file in the `/proc` filesystem. Each process on a Linux system has a directory in the `/proc` filesystem. Inside each process's directory, there is a file called `cmdline`. That file contains the complete command line of the process. For example, if the daemon was started from the current directory, it contains `./my-daemon-v2`, while if it was started from `/usr/local/sbin/my-daemon-v2`, it contains that complete path.

For example, if the PID of the daemon is `12345`, the complete path to `cmdline` is `/proc/12345/cmdline`. That is what we assemble with `sprintf()`.

Then, we read the content of `cmdline`. Later, we use that file's content to verify that the PID does match a process with the name `my-daemon-v2`. This is a safety measure so that we don't kill the wrong process by mistake. If the daemon is killed with the `KILL` signal, it has no chance to remove the PID file. If another process gets the same PID in the future, we run the risk of killing that process instead. PID numbers will eventually be reused.

When we have the PID of the daemon and have verified that it does belong to the correct process, we will either get its status or kill it, depending on whatever we specified with the `-k` option.

This is how many control programs work that are used to control complex daemons.

See also

For more information about the `kill()` system call, see the `man 2 kill` manual page.

Communicating with a pipe

In this recipe, we'll create a program that forks and then communicates between two processes using a **pipe**. Sometimes, when we **fork** a process, the **parent** and the **child** need a way to communicate. A pipe is often a simple way to do just that.

Knowing how to communicate and interchange data between a parent and a child process is important when you're writing more complex programs.

Getting ready

For this recipe, we'll only need the GCC compiler, the Make tool, and the generic Makefile.

How to do it...

Let's write a simple program that forks:

1. Write the following code in a file and name it `pipe-example.c`. We'll go through the code step by step. Remember that all the code goes in the same file.

   We'll start with the include lines and the `main()` function. Then, we'll create an integer array of size 2. The pipe will use that array later. The first integer in the array (0) is the file descriptor for the read end of the pipe. The second integer (1) is for the write end of the pipe:

```
#define _POSIX_C_SOURCE  200809L
#include <stdio.h>
#include <unistd.h>
#include <fcntl.h>
#include <errno.h>
#define MAX 128
int main(void)
{
   int pipefd[2] = { 0 };
   pid_t pid;
   char line[MAX];
```

2. Now, we will create the pipe using the `pipe()` system call. We'll give it the integer array as an argument. After that, we'll fork using the `fork()` system call:

```
   if ( (pipe(pipefd)) == -1 )
   {
      perror("Can't create pipe");
      return 1;
```

```
    }
    if ( (pid = fork()) == -1 )
    {
        perror("Can't fork");
        return 1;
    }
```

3. If we are inside the parent process, we close the read end (since we only want to write from the parent). Then, we write a message to the pipe's file descriptor (the write end) using `dprintf()`:

```
    if (pid > 0)
    {
        /* inside the parent */
        close(pipefd[0]); /* close the read end */
        dprintf(pipefd[1], "Hello from parent");
    }
```

4. Inside the child, we do the opposite; that is, we close the write end of the pipe. Then, we read the data in the pipe using the `read()` system call. Finally, we print the message using `printf()`:

```
    else
    {
        /* inside the child */
        close(pipefd[1]); /* close the write end */
        read(pipefd[0], line, MAX-1);
        printf("%s\n", line); /* print message from
                                * the parent */
    }
    return 0;
}
```

5. Now, compile the program so that we can run it:

```
$> make pipe-example
gcc -Wall -Wextra -pedantic -std=c99    pipe-example.c
-o pipe-example
```

6. Let's run the program. The parent sends the message `Hello from parent` to the child using a pipe. Then, it's the child that prints that message on the screen:

```
$> ./pipe-example
Hello from parent
```

How it works...

The `pipe()` system call returns two file descriptors to the integer array. The first one, `pipefd[0]`, is the read end of the pipe, while the other, `pipefd[1]`, is the write end of the pipe. In the parent, we write a message to the *write end* of the pipe. Then, in the child process, we read that data from the *read end* of the pipe. But before we do any reading or writing, we close the end of the pipe that we're not using in the respective process.

Pipes are one of the more common IPC techniques around. But they do have a drawback in that they can only be used between related processes; that is, processes with a common parent (or a parent and a child).

There's another form of pipe that overcomes this limitation: the so-called *named pipe*. Another name for a named pipe is FIFO. That's what we will cover in the next recipe.

See also

More information about the `pipe()` system call can be found in the `man 2 pipe` manual page.

FIFO - using it in the shell

In the previous recipe, I mentioned that there's a disadvantage to the `pipe()` system call—it can only be used between related processes. But there's another type of pipe we can use, called a **named pipe**. Another name for it is **First In, First Out** (**FIFO**). Named pipes can be used between any processes, related or not.

A named pipe, or a FIFO, is actually a special kind of file. The `mkfifo()` function creates that file on the filesystem, just like any other file. Then, we use that file to read and write data between processes.

There's also a command named `mkfifo`, which we can use directly from the shell to create named pipes. We can use this to pipe data between unrelated commands.

In this introduction to named pipes, we'll cover the `mkfifo` command. In the next two recipes, we'll write a C program using the `mkfifo()` function and then another program to read the pipe's data.

Knowing how to use named pipes will give you much more flexibility as a user, a system administrator, and a developer. You are no longer bound to only using pipes between related processes. You'll be free to pipe data between any processes or commands on the system—even between different users.

Getting ready

In this recipe, we won't write any programs, so there are no special requirements.

How to do it...

In this recipe, we'll explore the `mkfifo` command and learn how to use it to pipe data between unrelated processes:

1. We'll start by creating a named pipe—a FIFO file. We'll create it in the `/tmp` directory, which is commonplace for temporary files like this. You can, however, create it wherever you like:

   ```
   $> mkfifo /tmp/my-fifo
   ```

2. Let's confirm that's it indeed a FIFO by using the `file` and `ls` commands. Note the current permission mode of my FIFO. It can be read by everyone. This can differ on your system, though, depending on your `umask`. But we should be vigilant of this in case we are going to pipe sensitive data. In that case, we can change it using the `chmod` command:

   ```
   $> file /tmp/my-fifo
   /tmp/my-fifo: fifo (named pipe)
   $> ls -l /tmp/my-fifo
   prw-r--r-- 1 jake jake 0 jan 10 20:03 /tmp/my-fifo
   ```

3. Now, we can try sending data to the pipe. Since the pipe is a file, we will use redirections here instead of the pipe symbol. In other words, we redirect data to the pipe. Here, we'll redirect the output of the `uptime` command to the pipe. Once we've redirected the data to the pipe, the process will hang, which is normal since there's no one on the other end receiving the data. It doesn't actually hang; it *blocks*:

   ```
   $> uptime -p > /tmp/my-fifo
   ```

4. Open up a new terminal and type in the following command to receive the data from the pipe. Note that the process in the first terminal will now finish:

   ```
   $> cat < /tmp/my-fifo
   up 5 weeks, 6 days, 2 hours, 11 minutes
   ```

5. We can also do the reverse; that is, we can open the receiving end first and then send data to the pipe. This will **block** the receiving process until it gets some data. Run the following command to set up the receiving end, and leave it running:

```
$> cat < /tmp/my-fifo
```

6. Now, we send data to the pipe using the same `uptime` command. Notice that once the data is received, the first process will end:

```
$> uptime -p > /tmp/my-fifo
```

7. It's also possible to send data to a FIFO from multiple processes. Open up three new terminals. In each terminal, type the following command but replace 1 with 2 for the second terminal and 3 for the third:

```
$> echo "Hello from terminal 1" > /tmp/my-fifo
```

8. Now, open up another terminal and type in the following command. This will receive all the messages:

```
$> cat < /tmp/my-fifo
Hello from terminal 3
Hello from terminal 1
Hello from terminal 2
```

How it works…

A FIFO is simply a file on the filesystem, albeit a special file. Once we redirect data to a FIFO, that process will **block** (or "hang") until the data is received on the other end.

Likewise, if we start the receiving process first, that process will block until it gets the pipe's data. The reason for this behavior is that a FIFO isn't a regular file that we can save data in. We can only redirect data with it; that is, it's just a *pipe*. So, if we send data to it, but there's nothing on the other end, the process will just wait there until someone receives it on the other end. The data has nowhere to go in the pipe until someone connects to the receiving end.

There's more...

If you have multiple users on the system, you can try sending messages to them using FIFOs. Doing so provides us with an easy way to copy and paste data between users. Note that the permission mode of the FIFO must allow other users to read it (and write to it, if you like). It's possible to set the desired permission mode directly while creating the FIFO using the `-m` option. For example, `mkfifo /tmp/shared-fifo -m 666` will allow any user to read and write to the FIFO.

See also

There's a bit more information about the `mkfifo` command in the `man 1 mkfifo` manual page. For a more in-depth explanation about FIFOs in general, see the `man 7 fifo` manual page.

FIFO – building the sender

Now that we know what a FIFO is, we'll move on and write a program that can create and use a FIFO. In this recipe, we'll write a program that creates a FIFO and then sends a message to it. In the next recipe, we'll write a program that receives that message.

Knowing how to use FIFOs programmatically will enable you to write programs that can communicate between themselves using a FIFO directly, without needing to redirect the data via the shell.

Getting ready

We'll need the usual tools; that is, the GCC compiler, the Make tool, and the generic Makefile.

How to do it...

In this recipe, we'll write a program that creates a FIFO and sends a message to it:

1. Write the following code in a file and save it as `fifo-sender.c`. This code is a bit longer, so we'll cover it step by step here. Remember that all the code goes in the same file. Let's start with the `#include` lines, the prototype for the signal handler, and some global variables:

```
#define _XOPEN_SOURCE 700
#include <stdio.h>
#include <unistd.h>
```

```
#include <sys/types.h>
#include <sys/stat.h>
#include <unistd.h>
#include <fcntl.h>
#include <signal.h>
#include <stdlib.h>
#include <errno.h>

void cleanUp(int signum);
int fd; /* the FIFO file descriptor */
const char fifoname[] = "/tmp/my-2nd-fifo";
```

2. Now, we can start writing the `main()` function. First, we will create the struct for the `sigaction()` function. Then, we will check if the user provided a message as an argument:

```
int main(int argc, char *argv[])
{
   struct sigaction action; /* for sigaction */
   if ( argc != 2 )
   {
      fprintf(stderr, "Usage: %s 'the message'\n",
         argv[0]);
      return 1;
   }
```

3. Now, we must register the signal handler for all the signals we want to catch. We are doing this so that we can remove the FIFO when the program exits. Notice here that we are also registering the `SIGPIPE` signal—more on this in the *How it works…* section:

```
   /* prepare for sigaction and register signals
    * (for cleanup when we exit) */
   action.sa_handler = cleanUp;
   sigfillset(&action.sa_mask);
   action.sa_flags = SA_RESTART;
   sigaction(SIGTERM, &action, NULL);
   sigaction(SIGINT, &action, NULL);
   sigaction(SIGQUIT, &action, NULL);
   sigaction(SIGABRT, &action, NULL);
   sigaction(SIGPIPE, &action, NULL);
```

4. Now, let's create the FIFO with mode `644`. Since mode `644` is octal, we need to write it as `0644` in the C code; otherwise, it will be interpreted as 644 decimal (any number that starts with a 0 in C is an octal number). After that, we must open the FIFO using the `open()` system call—the same system call we use to open regular files:

```
    if ( (mkfifo(fifoname, 0644)) != 0 )
    {
        perror("Can't create FIFO");
        return 1;
    }
    if ( (fd = open(fifoname, O_WRONLY)) == -1)
    {
        perror("Can't open FIFO");
        return 1;
    }
```

5. Now, we must create an endless loop. Inside this loop, we will print the user-provided message once every second. After the loop, we will close the file descriptor and remove the FIFO file. We shouldn't reach this under normal circumstances, though:

```
    while(1)
    {
        dprintf(fd, "%s\n", argv[1]);
        sleep(1);
    }
    /* just in case, but we shouldn't reach this */
    close(fd);
    unlink(fifoname);
    return 0;
}
```

6. Finally, we must create the `cleanUp()` function, which we registered as the signal handler. We use this function to clean up before the program exits. We must then close the file descriptor and remove the FIFO file:

```
void cleanUp(int signum)
{
    if (signum == SIGPIPE)
        printf("The receiver stopped receiving\n");
    else
        printf("Aborting...\n");
    if ( (close(fd)) == -1 )
        perror("Can't close file descriptor");
```

```
    if ( (unlink(fifoname)) == -1)
    {
       perror("Can't remove FIFO");
       exit(1);
    }
    exit(0);
}
```

7. Let's compile the program:

```
$> make fifo-sender
gcc -Wall -Wextra -pedantic -std=c99    fifo-sender.c
-o fifo-sender
```

8. Let's run the program:

```
$> ./fifo-sender 'Hello everyone, how are you?'
```

9. Now, start another terminal so that we can receive the message using `cat`. The filename we used in the program is `/tmp/my-2nd-fifo`. The message will repeat each second. After a couple of seconds, hit *Ctrl* + *C* to exit from `cat`:

```
$> cat < /tmp/my-2nd-fifo
Hello everyone, how are you?
Hello everyone, how are you?
Hello everyone, how are you?
Ctrl+P
```

10. Now, go back to the first terminal. You'll notice that it says *The receiver stopped receiving.*
11. Start the `fifo-sender` program again in this first terminal.
12. Go to the second terminal again and restart the `cat` program in order to receive the messages. Leave the `cat` program running:

```
$> cat < /tmp/my-2nd-fifo
```

13. While the cat program is running on the second terminal, go back to the first one and abort the `fifo-sender` program by hitting *Ctrl* + *C*. Notice that this time, it says *Aborting* instead:

```
Ctrl+C
^CAborting...
```

The `cat` program in the second terminal has now exited.

How it works...

In this program, we register an extra signal that we haven't seen before: the `SIGPIPE` signal. When the other end terminates—in our case, the `cat` program—our program will receive a `SIGPIPE` signal. If we hadn't caught that signal, our program would have exited with signal 141, and no clean-up would have occurred. From this exit code, we can figure out that it was due to a `SIGPIPE` signal since 141-128 = 13; and signal 13 is `SIGPIPE`. See *Figure 2.2* in *Chapter 2, Making Your Programs Easy to Script*, for an explanation of reserved return values.

In the `cleanUp()` function, we use that signal number (`SIGPIPE`, which is a macro for 13) to print a special message when the receiver has stopped receiving data.

If we instead abort the `fifo-sender` program by hitting *Ctrl* + *C*, we get another message; that is, *Aborted*.

The `mkfifo()` function creates a FIFO file for us with the specified mode. Here, we specified the mode as an octal number. Any number in C that has a leading 0 is an octal number.

Since we opened the FIFO using the `open()` system call, we got a **file descriptor** in return. We use that file descriptor with `dprintf()` to print the user's message to the pipe. The first argument to the program—`argv[1]`—is the user's message.

As long as the FIFO stays open in the program, `cat` will also continue to listen. That's why we can repeat the message every second in the loop.

See also

See `man 3 mkfifo` for an in-depth explanation of the `mkfifo()` function.

For a list of the possible signals, see `kill -L`.

To learn more about `dprintf()`, see the `man 3 dprintf` manual page.

FIFO – building the receiver

In the previous recipe, we wrote a program that creates a FIFO and writes a message to it. We also tested it using `cat` to receive the messages. In this recipe, we'll write a C program that reads from the FIFO.

Reading from a FIFO isn't any different than reading from a regular file, or let's say, stdin.

Getting ready

Before you start this recipe, it's best if you complete the previous recipe first. We'll use the program from the previous recipe to write data to the FIFO that we'll receive in this recipe.

You'll also need the usual tools; that is, the GCC compiler, the Make tool, and the generic Makefile.

How to do it...

In this recipe, we'll write a receiving program for the sender we wrote in the previous recipe. Let's get started:

1. Write the following code in a file and save it as `fifo-receiver.c`. We will open the FIFO with a file stream and then read it character by character in a loop until we get an **End Of File** (**EOF**):

```
#include <stdio.h>
int main(void)
{
    FILE *fp;
    signed char c;
    const char fifoname[] = "/tmp/my-2nd-fifo";
    if ( (fp = fopen(fifoname, "r")) == NULL )
    {
        perror("Can't open FIFO");
        return 1;
    }
    while ( (c = getc(fp)) != EOF )
        putchar(c);
    fclose(fp);
    return 0;
}
```

2. Compile the program:

```
$> make fifo-receiver
gcc -Wall -Wextra -pedantic -std=c99    fifo-receiver.c
-o fifo-receiver
```

3. Start `fifo-sender` from the previous recipe and leave it running:

```
$> ./fifo-sender 'Hello from the sender'
```

4. Open up a second terminal and run `fifo-receiver`, which we just compiled. Abort it after a couple of seconds by hitting *Ctrl* + *C*:

```
$> ./fifo-receiver
Hello from the sender
Hello from the sender
Hello from the sender
Ctrl+C
```

`fifo-sender` will also abort, just like when we used the `cat` command to receive the data.

How it works...

Since the FIFO is a file on the filesystem, we can receive data from it using the usual functions in C, such as file streams, `getc()`, `putchar()`, and so on.

This program is similar to the `stream-read.c` program from *Chapter 5, Working with File I/O and Filesystem Operations*, except that we read character by character here instead of line by line.

See also

For more information about `getc()` and `putchar()`, see the `man 3 getc` and `man 3 putchar` manual pages, respectively.

Message queues - creating the sender

Another popular IPC technique is **message queues**. It's pretty much what the name suggests. A process leaves messages in a queue, and another process reads them.

There are two types of message queues available on Linux: **System V** and **POSIX**. In this recipe, we'll cover POSIX message queues since these are a bit more modern and simpler to handle. POSIX message queues are all about using the `mq_` functions, such as `mq_open()`, `mq_send()`, and so on.

Knowing how to use message queues enables you to choose from among a variety of IPC techniques.

Getting ready

For this recipe, we'll only need the GCC compiler and the Make tool.

How to do it...

In this recipe, we'll create the sender program. It's this program that will create a new message queue and some messages to it. In the next recipe, we'll receive those messages:

1. Write the following code in a file and save it as `msg-sender.c`. Since there are some new things in the code, I have broken it up into several steps. All the code goes into a single file, though, called `msg-sender.c`.

   Let's start with the header files that are required. We also define a macro for the maximum message size. Then, we will create a struct of the `mq_attr` type called `msgattr`. We will then set its members; that is, we'll set `mq_maxmsg` to 10 and `mq_msgsize` to `MAX_MSG_SIZE`. The first, `mq_maxmsg`, specifies the total number of messages in the queue. The second one, `mq_msgsize`, specifies the maximum size of a message:

```
#include <stdio.h>
#include <mqueue.h>
#include <fcntl.h>
#include <sys/stat.h>
#include <sys/types.h>
#include <string.h>
#define MAX_MSG_SIZE 2048
int main(int argc, char *argv[])
{
   int md; /* msg queue descriptor */
   /* attributes for the message queue */
   struct mq_attr msgattr;
   msgattr.mq_maxmsg = 10;
   msgattr.mq_msgsize = MAX_MSG_SIZE;
```

2. We'll take the first argument to the program as the message. So, here, we'll do a check to see if the user typed in an argument or not:

```
   if ( argc != 2)
   {
      fprintf(stderr, "Usage: %s 'my message'\n",
         argv[0]);
      return 1;
   }
```

3. Now, it's time to open and create the message queue with `mq_open()`. The first argument is the name of the queue; here, it's `/my_queue`. The second argument is the flags, which in our case are `O_CREATE` and `O_RDWR`. These are the same flags that we have seen previously, for example, with `open()`. The third argument is the permission mode; once again, this is the same as for files. The fourth and last argument is the struct we created earlier. The `mq_open()` function then returns a message queue descriptor to the `md` variable.

   Then, finally, we send the message to the queue using `mq_send()`. Here, first, we give it the `md` descriptor. Then, we have the message we want to send, which in this case is the first argument to the program. Then, as the third argument, we must specify the size of the message. Finally, we must set a priority for the message; in this case, we will just go with 1. It can be any positive number (an `unsigned int`).

   The last thing we will do before exiting the program is close the message queue descriptor with `mq_close()`:

```
    md = mq_open("/my_queue", O_CREAT|O_RDWR, 0644,
       &msgattr);
    if ( md == -1 )
    {
       perror("Creating message queue");
       return 1;
    }
    if ( (mq_send(md, argv[1], strlen(argv[1]), 1))
       == -1 )
    {
       perror("Message queue send");
       return 1;
    }
    mq_close(md);
    return 0;
}
```

4. Compile the program. Notice that we must link against the `rt` library, which stands for **Realtime Extensions library**:

```
$> gcc -Wall -Wextra -pedantic -std=c99 \
> msg-sender.c -o msg-sender -lrt
```

5. Now, run the program and send three or four messages to the queue:

```
$> ./msg-sender "The first message to the queue"
$> ./msg-sender "The second message"
$> ./msg-sender "And another message"
```

How it works...

In this recipe, we used the POSIX message queue functions to create a new queue and then sent messages to it. When we created the queue, we specified that this queue can contain a maximum of 10 messages using the `mq_maxmsg` member of `msgattr`.

We also set the maximum length of each message to 2,048 characters using the `mq_msgsize` member.

We named the queue `/my_queue` when we called `mq_open()`. A message queue must start with a forward slash.

Once the queue was created, we sent messages to it using `mq_send()`.

At the end of this recipe, we sent three messages to the queue. These messages are now queued, waiting to be received. In the next recipe, we'll learn how to write a program that receives these messages and prints them on the screen.

See also

There's a great overview of the POSIX message queue functionality in Linux in the `man 7 mq_overview` manual page.

Message queues – creating the receiver

In the previous recipe, we built a program that created a message queue named `/my_queue`, and then sent three messages to it. In this recipe, we'll create a program that receives the messages from that queue.

Getting ready

Before you start this recipe, you need to have completed the previous recipe. Otherwise, there will be no messages for us to receive.

You'll also need the GCC compiler and the Make tool for this recipe.

How to do it...

In this recipe, we'll receive the messages we sent in the previous recipe:

1. Write the following code in a file and save it as `msg-receiver.c`. This code is a bit longer than the code for the sending program, so it's been broken up into several steps, each one explaining a bit of the code. Remember, though, that all the code goes into the same file. We'll start with the header files, the variables, the struct, and a character pointer named `buffer`. We'll use this later to allocate memory:

```
#include <stdio.h>
#include <mqueue.h>
#include <fcntl.h>
#include <sys/stat.h>
#include <sys/types.h>
#include <stdlib.h>
#include <string.h>

int main(void)
{
   int md; /* msg queue descriptor */
   char *buffer;
   struct mq_attr msgattr;
```

2. The next step is to open the message queue using `mq_open()`. This time, we only need to provide two arguments; the name of the queue and the flags. In this case, we only want to read from the queue:

```
   md = mq_open("/my_queue", O_RDONLY);
   if (md == -1 )
   {
      perror("Open message queue");
      return 1;
   }
```

3. Now, we also want to get the attributes of the message queue using `mq_getattr()`. Once we have the attributes of the queue, we can use its `mq_msgsize` member to allocate memory for a message of that size using `calloc()`. We haven't seen `calloc()` before in this book. The first argument is the number of elements we want to allocate memory for, while the second argument is the size of each element. The `calloc()` function then returns a pointer to that memory (in our case, that's `buffer`):

```
    if ( (mq_getattr(md, &msgattr)) == -1 )
    {
        perror("Get message attribute");
        return 1;
    }
    buffer = calloc(msgattr.mq_msgsize,
        sizeof(char));
    if (buffer == NULL)
    {
        fprintf(stderr, "Couldn't allocate memory");
        return 1;
    }
```

4. Next, we will use another member of the `mq_attr` struct called `mq_curmsgs`, which contains the number of messages currently in the queue. First, we will print the number of messages. Then, we will loop over all the messages using a `for` loop. Inside the loop, first, we receive a message using `mq_receive`. Then, we print the message using `printf()`. Finally, before iterating over the next message, we reset the entire memory to NULL characters using `memset()`.

   The first argument to `mq_receive` is the descriptor, the second argument is the buffer where the message goes, the third argument is the size of the message, and the fourth argument is the priority of the message, which in this case is NULL, meaning we receive all messages with the highest priority first:

```
    printf("%ld messages in queue\n",
        msgattr.mq_curmsgs);
    for (int i = 0; i<msgattr.mq_curmsgs; i++)
    {
        if ( (mq_receive(md, buffer,
        msgattr.mq_msgsize, NULL)) == -1 )
        {
            perror("Message receive");
            return 1;
```

```
        }
        printf("%s\n", buffer);
        memset(buffer, '\0', msgattr.mq_msgsize);
    }
```

5. Finally, we have some cleanup to do. First of all, we must `free()` the memory being pointed to by the buffer. Then, we must close the `md` queue descriptor, before removing the queue from the system using `mq_unlink()`:

```
    free(buffer);
    mq_close(md);
    mq_unlink("/my_queue");
    return 0;
}
```

6. Now, it's time to compile the program:

```
$> gcc -Wall -Wextra -pedantic -std=c99 \
> msg-reveiver.c -o msg-reveiver -lrt
```

7. Finally, let's receive the messages using our new program:

```
$> ./msg-reveiver
3 messages in queue
The first message to the queue
The second message
And another message
```

8. If we try to rerun the program now, it will simply state that no such file or directory exists. This is because we removed the message queue with `mq_unlink()`:

```
$> ./msg-reveiver
Open message queue: No such file or directory
```

How it works...

In the previous recipe, we sent three messages to `/my_queue`. With the program we created in this recipe, we received those messages.

To open the queue, we used the same function we used when we created it; that is, `mq_open()`. But this time—since we're opening an already existing queue—we only needed to provide two arguments; that is, the queue's name and the flags.

Each call to an `mq_` function is error checked. If an error occurs, we print the error message with `perror()` and return to the shell with 1.

Before reading the actual messages from the queue, we get the queue's attribute with `mq_getattr()`. With this function call, we populate the `mq_attr` struct. The two most important members for reading the messages are `mq_msgsize`, which is the maximum size of each message in the queue, and `mq_curmsgs`, which is the number of messages currently in the queue.

We use the maximum message size from `mq_msgsize` to allocate memory for a message buffer using `calloc()`. The `calloc()` function returns "zeroed" memory, which its counterpart, `malloc()`, doesn't.

To allocate memory, we need to create a pointer to the type we want. This is what we did at the beginning of the program with `char *buffer`. The `calloc()` function takes two arguments: the number of elements to allocate and the size of each such element. Here, we want to number of elements to be the same as what the `mq_msgsize` value contains. And each element is a `char`, so the size of each element should be `sizeof(char)`. The function then returns a pointer to the memory, which in our case is saved to the `char` pointer's `buffer`.

Then, when we receive the queue messages, we save them in this buffer on each iteration of the loop.

The loop iterates through all the messages. We got the number of messages from the `mq_curmsgs` member.

Finally, once we finished reading all the messages, we closed and deleted the queue.

See also

For more information about the `mq_attr` struct, I suggest that you read the `man 3 mq_open` manual page.

Each of the functions we have covered in this and the previous recipe has its own manual page; for example, `man 3 mq_send`, `man 3 mq_recevie`, `man 3 mq_getattr`, and so on.

If you're unfamiliar with the `calloc()` and `malloc()` functions, I suggest that you read `man 3 calloc`. This manual page covers `malloc()`, `calloc()`, `free()`, and some other related functions.

The `memset()` function also has its own manual page; that is, `man 3 memset`.

Communicating between child and parent with shared memory

In this recipe, we'll learn how to use **shared memory** between two related processes—a parent and a child. Shared memory exists in various forms and can be used in different ways. In this book, we'll focus on the POSIX shared memory functions.

Shared memory in Linux can be used between related processes, as we are about to explore in this recipe, but also between unrelated processes using **file descriptors** to shared memory. When we use shared memory in this way, the memory is backed by a file in the `/dev/shm` directory. We'll look at this in the next recipe.

In this recipe, we'll be using *anonymous* shared memory—memory not backed by a file.

Shared memory is just what it sounds like—a piece of memory that is shared between processes.

Knowing how to use shared memory will enable you to write more advanced programs.

Getting ready

For this recipe, you'll only need the GCC compiler and the Make tool.

How to do it...

In this recipe, we'll write a program that uses shared memory. First, before forking, the process will write a message to the shared memory. Then, after forking, the child will replace the message in the shared memory. And then, finally, the parent process will replace the content of the shared memory once again. Let's get started:

1. Write the following code in a file and name it `shm-parent-child.c`. As usual, I'll break up the code into several smaller steps. All the code goes into the same file, though. First, we'll write all of the header files. There are quite a few of them here. We will also define a macro for the size of our memory. We will then write our three messages as character array constants:

```
#include <stdio.h>
#include <sys/mman.h>
#include <sys/types.h>
#include <sys/stat.h>
#include <sys/wait.h>
#include <fcntl.h>
#include <unistd.h>
#include <string.h>
```

```
#define DATASIZE 128

int main(void)
{
    char *addr;
    int status;
    pid_t pid;
    const char startmsg[] = "Hello, we are running";
    const char childmsg[] = "Hello from child";
    const char parentmsg[] = "New msg from parent";
```

2. Now comes the exciting part—mapping the shared memory space. There's a total of six arguments we need to provide to the memory mapping function; that is, `mmap()`.

   The first argument is the memory address, which we'll set to NULL—meaning the kernel will take care of it for us.

   The second argument is the size of the memory area.

   The third argument is the protection the memory should have. Here, we will set it to write and read.

   The fourth argument is our flags, which we set to shared and anonymous—meaning it can be shared among processes and won't be backed by a file.

   The fifth argument is a file descriptor. But in our case, we're using anonymous, which means that this memory won't be backed by a file. Due to this, we will set it to -1 for compatibility reasons.

   The last argument is the offset, which we will set to 0:

```
    addr = mmap(NULL, DATASIZE,
        PROT_WRITE | PROT_READ,
        MAP_SHARED | MAP_ANONYMOUS, -1, 0);
    if (addr == MAP_FAILED)
    {
        perror("Memory mapping failed");
        return 1;
    }
```

3. Now that the memory is ready for us, we will copy our first message to it using `memcpy()`. The first argument to `memcpy()` is a pointer to the memory, which in our case is the `addr` character pointer. The second argument is the data or message we want to copy from, which in our case is `startmsg`. The last argument is the size of the data we want to copy, which in this case is the length of the string in `startmsg` + 1. The `strlen()` function doesn't include the terminating null character; that's why we need to add 1.

   Then, we print the PID of the process and the message in the shared memory. After that, we fork:

```
    memcpy(addr, startmsg, strlen(startmsg) + 1);
    printf("Parent PID is %d\n", getpid());
    printf("Original message: %s\n", addr);
    if ( (pid = fork()) == -1 )
    {
        perror("Can't fork");
        return 1;
    }
```

4. If we are in the child process, we copy the child's message to the shared memory. If we are in the parent process, we'll wait for the child. Then, we can copy the parent message to the memory and also print both messages. Finally, we will clean up by unmapping the shared memory. This isn't strictly required, though:

```
    if (pid == 0)
    {
        /* child */
        memcpy(addr, childmsg, strlen(childmsg) + 1);
    }
    else if(pid > 0)
    {
        /* parent */
        waitpid(pid, &status, 0);
        printf("Child executed with PID %d\n", pid);
        printf("Message from child: %s\n", addr);
        memcpy(addr, parentmsg,
            strlen(parentmsg) + 1);
        printf("Parent message: %s\n", addr);
    }
    munmap(addr, DATASIZE);
    return 0;
}
```

5. Compile the program so that we can take it for a spin. Notice that we are using another C standard here—**GNU11**. We're doing this because the **C99** standard doesn't include the `MAP_ANONYMOUS` macro, but **GNU11** does. **GNU11** is the **C11** standard with some extra GNU extensions. Also, note that we link against the *Real-Time Extensions* library:

```
$> gcc -Wall -Wextra -std=gnu11 \
> shm-parent-child.c -o shm-parent-child -lrt
```

6. Now, we can test the program:

```
$> ./shm-parent-child
Parent PID is 9683
Original message: Hello, we are running
Child executed with PID 9684
Message from child: Hello from child
Parent message: New msg from parent
```

How it works...

Shared memory is a common IPC technique between unrelated processes, related processes, and threads. In this recipe, we saw how we could use shared memory between a parent and a child.

The memory area is mapped using `mmap()`. This function returns the address to the mapped memory. If an error occurs, it returns the `MAP_FAILED` macro. Once we mapped the memory, we checked the pointer variable for `MAP_FAILED` and aborted it in case there was an error.

Once we've mapped the memory and got a pointer to it, we used `memcpy()` to copy data to it.

Finally, we unmapped the memory with `munmap()`. This isn't strictly necessary since it will be unmapped anyway when the last process exists. However, it's a bad practice not to do so. You should always clean up after yourself and free up any allocated memory.

See also

For a more detailed explanation of `mmap()` and `munmap()`, see the `man 2 mmap` manual page. For a detailed explanation of `memcpy()`, see the `man 3 memcpy` manual page.

For a more in-depth explanation of the various C standards and what the GNU extensions are, see `https://gcc.gnu.org/onlinedocs/gcc/Standards.html`.

Using shared memory between unrelated processes

In the previous recipe, we used shared memory between a child and a parent. In this recipe, we'll learn how to use a file descriptor to mapped memory to share that memory between two unrelated processes. Using shared memory in this way automatically creates an underlying file for the memory in the `/dev/shm` directory, where **shm** stands for **shared memory**.

Knowing how to use shared memory between unrelated processes widens your use of this IPC technique.

Getting ready

For this recipe, you'll only need the GCC compiler and the Make tool.

How to do it...

First, we'll write a program that opens and creates a file descriptor for shared memory and also maps the memory. Then, we'll write another program that reads the memory area. Instead of just a message, as we did in the previous recipe, we'll write and retrieve an **array** of three floating-point numbers here.

Creating the writer

Let's create the writer first:

1. The first step is to create a program that will create a shared memory and write some data to it. Write the following code in a file and save it as `write-memory.c`. As usual, the code will be broken up into several steps, but all the code goes into a single file.

   Just as in the previous recipe, we'll have a bunch of header files. Then, we'll create all the variables we'll need. Here, we'll need a variable for a file descriptor. Note that even if I call it a file descriptor here, it's a descriptor to a memory area. `memid` contains the name of the memory-mapped descriptor. Then, we must use `shm_open()` to open and create the "file descriptor":

   ```
   #include <stdio.h>
   #include <sys/mman.h>
   #include <sys/types.h>
   #include <sys/stat.h>
   #include <fcntl.h>
   ```

```
#include <unistd.h>
#include <string.h>
#define DATASIZE 128

int main(void)
{
    int fd;
    float *addr;
    const char memid[] = "/my_memory";
    const float numbers[3] = { 3.14, 2.718, 1.202};
    /* create shared memory file descriptor */
    if ( (fd = shm_open(memid,
        O_RDWR | O_CREAT, 0600)) == -1)
    {
        perror("Can't open memory fd");
        return 1;
    }
```

2. The file-backed memory is 0 bytes in size initially. To extend it to our 128 bytes, we must truncate it with `ftruncate()`:

```
    /* truncate memory to DATASIZE */
    if ( (ftruncate(fd, DATASIZE)) == -1 )
    {
        perror("Can't truncate memory");
        return 1;
    }
```

3. Now, we must map the memory, just as we did in the previous recipe. But this time, we will give it the `fd` file descriptor instead of -1. We have also left out the `MAP_ANONYMOUS` part, thus making this memory backed by a file. Then, we must copy our array of floats to memory using `memcpy()`. To let the reading program have a chance to read the memory, we must pause the program and wait for an *Enter* key with `getchar()`. Then, it's just a matter of cleaning up by unmapping the memory and deleting the file descriptor and the underlying file with `shm_unlink()`:

```
    /* map memory using our file descriptor */
    addr = mmap(NULL, DATASIZE, PROT_WRITE,
        MAP_SHARED, fd, 0);
    if (addr == MAP_FAILED)
    {
```

```
        perror("Memory mapping failed");
        return 1;
    }

    /* copy data to memory */
    memcpy(addr, numbers, sizeof(numbers));

    /* wait for enter */
    printf("Hit enter when finished ");
    getchar();
    /* clean up */
    munmap(addr, DATASIZE);
    shm_unlink(memid);
    return 0;
}
```

4. Now, let's compile the program:

```
$> gcc -Wall -Wextra -std=gnu11 write-memory.c \
> -o write-memory -lrt
```

Creating the reader

Now, let's create the reader:

1. Now, we'll write the program that will read the memory area and print the numbers for the array. Write the following program and save it as `read-memory.c`. This program is similar to `write-memory.c`, but instead of writing to memory, we are reading from it:

```
#include <stdio.h>
#include <sys/mman.h>
#include <sys/types.h>
#include <sys/stat.h>
#include <fcntl.h>
#include <unistd.h>
#include <string.h>
#define DATASIZE 128

int main(void)
{
    int fd;
    float *addr;
```

```
    const char memid[] = "/my_memory";
    float numbers[3];

    /* open memory file descriptor */
    fd = shm_open(memid, O_RDONLY, 0600);
    if (fd == -1)
    {
        perror("Can't open file descriptor");
        return 1;
    }

    /* map shared memory */
    addr = mmap(NULL, DATASIZE, PROT_READ,
        MAP_SHARED, fd, 0);
    if (addr == MAP_FAILED)
    {
        perror("Memory mapping failed");
        return 1;
    }

    /* read the memory and print the numbers */
    memcpy(numbers, addr, sizeof(numbers));
    for (int i = 0; i<3; i++)
    {
        printf("Number %d: %.3f\n", i, numbers[i]);
    }
    return 0;
}
```

2. Now, compile this program:

```
$> gcc -Wall -Wextra -std=gnu11 read-memory.c \
> -o read-memory -lrt
```

Testing everything

Follow these steps:

1. Now, it's time to try it all out. Open up a terminal and run the `write-memory` program that we compiled. Leave the program running:

```
$> ./write-memory
Hit enter when finished
```

2. Open up another terminal and check out the file in /dev/shm:

```
$> ls -l /dev/shm/my_memory
-rw------- 1 jake jake 128 jan 18 19:19 /dev/shm/my_
memory
```

3. Now, run the read-memory program we just compiled. This will retrieve the three numbers from the shared memory and print them on the screen:

```
$> ./read-memory
Number 0: 3.140
Number 1: 2.718
Number 2: 1.202
```

4. Go back to the terminal where the `write-memory` program is running and hit *Enter*. Doing so will clean up and delete the file. Once you have done this, let's see if the file is still in /dev/shm:

```
./write-memory
Hit enter when finished Enter

$> ls -l /dev/shm/my_memory
ls: cannot access '/dev/shm/my_memory': No such file or
directory
```

How it works...

Using non-anonymous shared memory is similar to what we did in the previous recipe. The only exception is that we first open a special file descriptor using `shm_open()`. As you might have noticed, the flags are similar to those of the regular `open()` call; that is, `O_RDWR` for reading and writing and `O_CREATE` for creating the file if it doesn't exist. Using `shm_open()` in this fashion creates a file in the /dev/shm directory with the name specified as the first argument. Even the permission mode is set the same way as regular files—in our case, `0600` for reading and writing for the user, and no permissions for anyone else.

The file descriptor we get from `shm_open()` is then passed to the `mmap()` call. We also left out the `MAP_ANONYMOUS` macro to the `mmap()` call, as we saw in the previous recipe. Skipping `MAP_ANONYMOUS` means that the memory will no longer be anonymous, meaning it will be backed by a file. We inspected this file using `ls -l` and saw that it did indeed have the name we gave it and the correct permissions.

The next program we wrote opened the same shared memory file descriptor using `shm_open()`. After `mmap()`, we looped over the floating-point numbers in the memory area.

Finally, once we hit *Enter* in the `write-memory` program, the file in `/dev/shm` was removed using `shm_unlink()`.

See also

There's a lot more information about `shm_open()` and `shm_unlink()` in the `man 3 shm_open` manual page.

Unix socket – creating the server

Unix sockets are similar to **TCP/IP** sockets, but they are only local and are represented by a socket file on the filesystem. But the overall functions that are used with Unix sockets are more or less the same as for TCP/IP sockets. The complete name for Unix sockets is *Unix domain sockets.*

Unix sockets are a common way for programs to communicate locally on a machine.

Knowing how to use Unix sockets will make it easier to write programs that need to communicate between them.

Getting ready

In this recipe, you'll only need the GCC compiler, the Make tool, and the generic Makefile.

How to do it...

In this recipe, we'll write a program that will act as a server. It will receive messages from a client and respond with "*Message received*" every time a message is received. It will also clean up after itself when either the server or the client exits. Let's get started:

1. Write the following code in a file and save it as `unix-server.c`. This code is a bit longer than most of our previous examples, so it's been broken up into several steps. All the code goes in the same file, though.

There are quite a few header files here. We'll also define a macro for the maximum message length that we will accept. We will then write the prototype for the `cleanUp()` function, which will be used to clean up the file. This function will also be used as a signal handler. Then, we'll declare some global variables (so that they can be reached from `cleanUp()`):

```
#define _XOPEN_SOURCE 700
#include <stdio.h>
#include <sys/types.h>
#include <sys/socket.h>
#include <sys/un.h>
#include <string.h>
#include <unistd.h>
#include <signal.h>
#include <stdlib.h>
#include <errno.h>
#define MAXLEN 128

void cleanUp(int signum);
const char sockname[] = "/tmp/my_1st_socket";
int connfd;
int datafd;
```

2. Now, it's time to start writing the `main()` function and declaring some variables. Most of this should be familiar to you by now. We will also register the signal handler here for all the signals. What's new is the `sockaddr_un` struct. This will contain the socket type and file path:

```
int main(void)
{
   int ret;
   struct sockaddr_un addr;
   char buffer[MAXLEN];
   struct sigaction action;
   /* prepare for sigaction */
   action.sa_handler = cleanUp;
   sigfillset(&action.sa_mask);
   action.sa_flags = SA_RESTART;
   /* register the signals we want to handle */
   sigaction(SIGTERM, &action, NULL);
   sigaction(SIGINT, &action, NULL);
   sigaction(SIGQUIT, &action, NULL);
```

```
    sigaction(SIGABRT, &action, NULL);
    sigaction(SIGPIPE, &action, NULL);
```

3. Now that we have all the signal handlers, variables, and structures in place, we can create a socket file descriptor using the `socket()` function. Once that has been taken care of, we will set the type of connection (of the *family* type) and the path to the socket file. Then, we will call `bind()`, which will bind the socket for us so that we can use it:

```
    /* create socket file descriptor */
    connfd = socket(AF_UNIX, SOCK_SEQPACKET, 0);
    if ( connfd == -1 )
    {
       perror("Create socket failed");
       return 1;
    }
    /* set address family and socket path */
    addr.sun_family = AF_UNIX;
    strcpy(addr.sun_path, sockname);
    /* bind the socket (we must cast our sockaddr_un
     * to sockaddr) */
    if ( (bind(connfd, (const struct sockaddr*)&addr,
       sizeof(struct sockaddr_un))) == -1 )
    {
       perror("Binding socket failed");
       return 1;
    }
```

4. Now, we will prepare the socket file descriptor for connections by calling `listen()`. The first argument is the socket file descriptor, while the second argument is the buffer size we want for the backlog. Once we've done that, we will accept a connection using `accept()`. This will give us a new socket **file descriptor** (which we will call `datafd`), which we will use when we send and receive data. Once a connection has been accepted, we can print *Client connected* to the local terminal:

```
    /* prepare for accepting connections */
    if ( (listen(connfd, 20)) == -1 )
    {
       perror("Listen error");
       return 1;
    }
    /* accept connection and create new file desc */
```

```
    datafd = accept(connfd, NULL, NULL);
    if (datafd == -1 )
    {
       perror("Accept error");
       return 1;
    }
    printf("Client connected\n");
```

5. Now, we will start the main loop of the program. In the outer loop, we'll just write a confirmation message when we received a message. In the inner loop, we'll read data from the new socket file descriptor, save it in `buffer`, and then print it on our terminal. If `read()` returns -1, then something has gone wrong, and we must break out of the inner loop to read the next line. If `read()` returns 0, then the client has disconnected, and we must run `cleanUp()` and quit:

```
    while(1) /* main loop */
    {
       while(1) /* receive message, line by line */
       {
          ret = read(datafd, buffer, MAXLEN);
          if ( ret == -1 )
          {
             perror("Error reading line");
             cleanUp(1);
          }
          else if ( ret == 0 )
          {
             printf("Client disconnected\n");
             cleanUp(1);
          }
          else
          {
             printf("Message: %s\n", buffer);
             break;
          }
       }
    /* write a confirmation message */
    write(datafd, "Message received\n", 18);
    }
    return 0;
}
```

6. Finally, we must create the body for the `cleanUp()` function:

```
void cleanUp(int signum)
{
    printf("Quitting and cleaning up\n");
    close(connfd);
    close(datafd);
    unlink(sockname);
    exit(0);
}
```

7. Now, compile the program. This time, we'll get a warning from GCC about an unused variable, `signum`, in the `cleanUp()` function. This is because we never used the `signum` variable inside `cleanUp()`, so we can safely ignore this warning:

```
$> make unix-server
gcc -Wall -Wextra -pedantic -std=c99    unix-server.c
-o unix-server
unix-server.c: In function 'cleanUp':
unix-server.c:94:18: warning: unused parameter 'signum'
[-Wunused-parameter]
 void cleanUp(int signum)
             ~~~~^~~~~~
```

8. Run the program. Since we don't have a client, it won't say or do anything just yet. However it does create the socket file. Leave the program as-is:

```
$> ./unix-server
```

9. Open a new terminal and check out the socket file. Here, we can see that it's a socket file:

```
$> ls -l /tmp/my_1st_socket
srwxr-xr-x 1 jake jake 0 jan 19 18:35 /tmp/my_1st_socket
$> file /tmp/my_1st_socket
/tmp/my_1st_socket: socket
```

10. For now, go back to the terminal with the server program running and abort it with *Ctrl* + *C*. Then, see if the file is still there (it shouldn't be):

```
./unix-server
Ctrl+C
Quitting and cleaning up
$> file /tmp/my_1st_socket
```

```
/tmp/my_1st_socket: cannot open `/tmp/my_1st_socket' (No
such file or directory)
```

How it works...

The `sockaddr_un` struct is a special structure for Unix domain sockets. There's another one called `sockaddr_in` for TCP/IP sockets. The `_un` ending stands for Unix sockets, while `_in` stands for internet family sockets.

The `socket()` function that we used to create a socket file descriptor takes three arguments: the address family (`AF_UNIX`), the type (`SOCK_SEQPACKET`, which provides a two-way communication), and the protocol. We specified the protocol as 0 since there aren't any to choose from with a socket.

There's also a general structure called `sockaddr`. When we pass our `sockaddr_un` structure as an argument for `bind()`, we need to typecast it to a `sockaddr`, the general type, since that's what the function expects—more precisely, a `sockaddr` pointer. The last argument that we supply for `bind()` is the size of the structure; that is, `sockaddr_un`.

Once we created the socket and bounded it with `bind()`, we prepared it for incoming connections with `listen()`.

Finally, we accepted incoming connections with `accept()`. This gave us a new socket file descriptor, which we then used to send and receive messages.

See also

There's some deeper information in the manual pages for the functions we used in this recipe. I suggest that you check them all out:

- `man 2 socket`
- `man 2 bind`
- `man 2 listen`
- `man 2 accept`

Unix socket – creating the client

In the previous recipe, we created a Unix domain socket server. In this recipe, we'll create a client for that socket and then communicate between the client and the server.

In this recipe, we'll see how we can use the socket to communicate between a server and a client. Knowing how to communicate over a socket is essential to using sockets.

Getting ready

Before doing this recipe, you should have finished the previous recipe; otherwise, you won't have a server to talk to.

You'll also need the GCC compiler, the Make tool, and the generic Makefile for this recipe.

How to do it...

In this recipe, we'll write a client for the server that we wrote in the previous recipe. Once they are connected, the client can send messages to the server, and the server will respond with *Message received*. Let's get started:

1. Write the following code in a file and save it as `unix-client.c`. Since this code is also a bit longer, it's been split up into several steps. All the code goes in the `unix-client.c` file, though. The first half of this program is similar to that of the server, except we have two buffers instead of one and no signal handling:

```
#define _XOPEN_SOURCE 700
#include <stdio.h>
#include <sys/types.h>
#include <sys/socket.h>
#include <sys/un.h>
#include <string.h>
#include <unistd.h>
#include <signal.h>
#include <stdlib.h>
#include <errno.h>
#define MAXLEN 128

int main(void)
{
   const char sockname[] = "/tmp/my_1st_socket";
   int fd;
   struct sockaddr_un addr;
   char sendbuffer[MAXLEN];
   char recvbuffer[MAXLEN];

   /* create socket file descriptor */
   fd = socket(AF_UNIX, SOCK_SEQPACKET, 0);
   if ( fd == -1 )
   {
      perror("Create socket failed");
```

```
        return 1;
    }
    /* set address family and socket path */
    addr.sun_family = AF_UNIX;
    strcpy(addr.sun_path, sockname);
```

2. Now, instead of using `bind()`, `listen()`, and `accept()`, we will use `connect()` to initiate a connection to the server. The `connect()` function takes the same arguments as `bind()`:

```
    /* connect to the server */
    if ( (connect(fd, (const struct sockaddr*) &addr,
        sizeof(struct sockaddr_un))) == -1 )
    {
        perror("Can't connect");
        fprintf(stderr, "The server is down?\n");
        return 1;
    }
```

3. Now that we have connected to the server, we can use `write()` to send messages over the socket file descriptor. Here, we will use `fgets()` to read the messages from the user to a buffer, convert a **newline character** into a **null character**, and then write the buffer to a file descriptor:

```
    while(1) /* main loop */
    {
        /* send message to server */
        printf("Message to send: ");
        fgets(sendbuffer, sizeof(sendbuffer), stdin);
        sendbuffer[strcspn(sendbuffer, "\n")] = '\0';
        if ( (write(fd, sendbuffer,
            strlen(sendbuffer) + 1)) == -1 )
        {
            perror("Couldn't write");
            break;
        }

        /* read response from server */
        if ( (read(fd, recvbuffer, MAXLEN)) == -1 )
        {
            perror("Can't read");
            return 1;
        }
```

```
        printf("Server said: %s\n", recvbuffer);
    }
    return 0;
}
```

4. Compile the program:

```
$> make unix-client
gcc -Wall -Wextra -pedantic -std=c99    unix-client.c
-o unix-client
```

5. Let's try to run the program now. It won't work since the server hasn't started yet:

```
$> ./unix-client
Can't connect: No such file or directory
The server is down?
```

6. Start the server in a separate terminal and leave it running:

```
$> ./unix-server
```

7. Go back to the terminal with the client and rerun it:

```
$> ./unix-client
Message to send:
```

You should now see a message in the server saying *Client connected.*

8. Write some messages in the client program. You should see them appear in the server at the same time you hit *Enter*. After a couple of messages, hit *Ctrl* + *C*:

```
$> ./unix-client
Message to send: Hello, how are you?
Server said: Message received

Message to send: Testing 123
Server said: Message received

Message to send: Ctrl+C
```

9. Switch over to the terminal with the server. You should see something similar to this:

```
Client connected
Message: Hello, how are you?
Message: Testing 123
Client disconnected
Quitting and cleaning up
```

How it works...

In the previous recipe, we wrote a socket server. In this recipe, we wrote a client that connects to that server using the `connect()` system call. This system call takes the same argument as `bind()`. Once the connection has been established, both the server and the client can write and read from the socket file descriptor (two-way communication) using `write()` and `read()`.

So, in essence, once the connection has been established, it's not that different than reading and writing to a file using a file descriptor.

See also

For more information about the `connect()` system call, see the `man 2 connect` manual page.

11
Using Threads in Your Programs

In this chapter, we will learn what threads are and how to use them in Linux. We will write several programs using **POSIX threads**, otherwise known as **pthreads**. We will also learn what race conditions are and how to prevent them by using mutexes. Then, we'll learn how to make a mutex program more efficient. Lastly, we'll learn what condition variables are.

Knowing how to write threaded programs will make them faster and more efficient.

In this chapter, we will cover the following recipes:

- Writing your first threaded program
- Reading return values from threads
- Causing a race condition
- Avoiding race conditions with mutexes
- Making the mutex program more efficient
- Using condition variables

Let's get started!

Technical requirements

For this chapter, you'll need the GCC compiler, the Make tool, and the generic Makefile. If you haven't installed these tools yet, please refer to *Chapter 1, Getting the Necessary Tools and Writing Our First Linux Programs*, for installation instructions.

You'll also need a program called `htop` to view the CPU load. You install it with your distribution's package manager. The program is called `htop` on all distributions.

All of the code samples for this chapter can be downloaded from GitHub at the following URL: `https://github.com/PacktPublishing/Linux-System-Programming-Techniques/tree/master/ch11`.

Check out the following link to see the Code in Action video: `https://bit.ly/3gkAP9O`

Writing your first threaded program

In this first recipe, we'll write a small program that checks whether two numbers are prime numbers—in parallel. While those two numbers are checked, each in their own **thread**, another thread will write dots in the terminal to indicate that the program is still running. A total of three threads will run in this program. Each thread will print its own result, so there's no need to save and return the values in this program.

Knowing the basics of threading will give the foundation to move along to more advanced programs.

Getting ready

For this recipe, you'll need the `htop` program so you can see the **CPU** load go up for two CPU cores. Of course, other similar programs work as well, such as KSysGuard for **K Desktop Environment** (**KDE**). It's also best if your computer has more than one CPU **core**. Most computers today have more than one core, even Raspberry Pis and similar small computers, so this shouldn't be a problem. The program still works, even if you only have a single-core CPU, but it's harder to visualize the threads.

You also require the GCC compiler and the Make tool.

How to do it...

In this chapter, we are going to use **pthreads** a lot (short for **POSIX threads**). To use pthreads, we need to link to the pthread library. Therefore, we'll start by writing a new Makefile for this entire chapter. Create a new directory for this chapter and write the following code in a file (inside that directory). Save it as `Makefile`. Notice the added `-lpthread`, something we didn't have in the generic Makefile:

```
CC=gcc
CFLAGS=-Wall -Wextra -pedantic -std=c99
LDFLAGS=-lpthread
%: %.c
	$(CC) $< $(CFLAGS) -o $@ $(LDFLAGS)
```

Now, let's move on and write the program. The code is a bit long, so it's broken up into several steps. All the code goes into a single file, though. Save the code as `first-threaded.c`:

1. Let's start with the header files, some function prototypes, the `main()` function, and some necessary variables. Notice the new header file, `pthread.h`. We have a new type here also, called `pthread_t`. This type is used for thread IDs. There's also a `pthread_attr_t` type, which is used for the attributes of the threads. We also perform a check to see whether the user entered two arguments (the numbers that will be checked to establish whether they are prime numbers). Then, we'll convert the first and second arguments to `long long` integers with `atoll()`:

```
#include <stdio.h>
#include <stdlib.h>
#include <unistd.h>
#include <pthread.h>

void *isprime(void *arg);
void *progress(void *arg);

int main(int argc, char *argv[])
{
    long long number1;
    long long number2;
    pthread_t tid_prime1;
    pthread_t tid_prime2;
    pthread_t tid_progress;
    pthread_attr_t threadattr;
    if ( argc != 3 )
```

```
    {
        fprintf(stderr, "Please supply two numbers.\n"
            "Example: %s 9 7\n", argv[0]);
        return 1;
    }
    number1 = atoll(argv[1]);
    number2 = atoll(argv[2]);
```

2. Next, we'll initialize the threads attribute structure, `threadattr`, with some default settings using `pthread_attr_init()`.

   Then, we will create the three threads using `pthread_create()`. The `pthread_create()` function takes four arguments. The first argument is the thread ID variable; the second argument is the attributes for the thread; the third argument is the function that will execute in the thread; the fourth argument is the argument for that function. We will also mark the thread for the "progress bar" as detached using `pthread_detach()`. This makes the thread's resources release automatically when it terminates:

```
    pthread_attr_init(&threadattr);
    pthread_create(&tid_progress, &threadattr,
        progress, NULL);
    pthread_detach(tid_progress);
    pthread_create(&tid_prime1, &threadattr,
        isprime, &number1);
    pthread_create(&tid_prime2, &threadattr,
        isprime, &number2);
```

3. To make the program wait for all the threads to finish, we must use `pthread_join()` for each thread. Notice that we don't wait for the progress thread, but we did mark it as detached. Here, we will cancel the progress thread before we exit the program using `pthread_cancel()`:

```
    pthread_join(tid_prime1, NULL);
    pthread_join(tid_prime2, NULL);
    pthread_attr_destroy(&threadattr);
    if ( pthread_cancel(tid_progress) != 0 )
        fprintf(stderr,
            "Couldn't cancel progress thread\n");
    printf("Done!\n");
    return 0;
}
```

4. Now it's time to write the body for the function that will calculate whether the given number is a prime number. Notice that the return type of the function is a void pointer. The argument is also a void pointer. This is the requirement in order for `pthread_create()` to work. Since the argument is a void pointer, and we want it as a `long long int`, we must first convert it. We do this by casting the void pointer to a `long long int` and save what it's pointing to in a new variable (refer to the *See also* section for a more verbose option). Notice that we return `NULL` in this function. This is because we have to return *something*, so `NULL` will do just fine here:

```
void *isprime(void *arg)
{
    long long int number = *((long long*)arg);
    long long int j;
    int prime = 1;

    /* Test if the number is divisible, starting
     * from 2 */
    for(j=2; j<number; j++)
    {
        /* Use the modulo operator to test if the
         * number is evenly divisible, i.e., a
         * prime number */
        if(number%j == 0)
        {
            prime = 0;
        }
    }
    if(prime == 1)
    {
        printf("\n%lld is a prime number\n",
            number);
        return NULL;
    }
    else
    {
        printf("\n%lld is not a prime number\n",
            number);
        return NULL;
    }
}
```

5. Finally, we write the function for the progress meter. It isn't really a progress meter; it just prints a dot every second to show the user that the program is still running. We must use `fflush()` after the call to `printf()` since we aren't printing any newline characters (remember that stdout is line-buffered):

```
void *progress(void *arg)
{
    while(1)
    {
        sleep(1);
        printf(".");
        fflush(stdout);
    }
    return NULL;
}
```

6. Now it's time to compile the program using our new Makefile. Note that we receive a warning regarding an unused variable here. This is the `arg` variable for the progress function. We can safely ignore this warning since we know we aren't using it:

```
$> make first-threaded
gcc first-threaded.c -Wall -Wextra -pedantic -std=c99 -o
first-threaded -lpthread
first-threaded.c: In function 'progress':
first-threaded.c:75:22: warning: unused parameter 'arg'
[-Wunused-parameter]
 void *progress(void *arg)
```

7. Now, before we run the program, start a new terminal and start `htop` in it. Place it somewhere where you can see it.

8. Now we run the program in the first terminal. Choose two numbers that aren't so small that the program will finish immediately but not so large that it will run forever. For me, the following numbers are sufficiently large to make the program run for about a minute and a half. This will vary depending on the CPU. While you run the program, check the `htop` program. You'll notice that two cores will use 100% until the first number is computed, and then it will only use one core at 100%:

```
$> ./first-threaded 990233331 9902343047
.........
990233331 is not a prime number
...........................................................
......................
```

```
9902343047 is a prime number
Done!
```

How it works...

The two numbers are checked individually, each in their own thread. This speeds up the process when compared to a non-threaded program. A non-threaded program would check each number after the other. That is, the second number would have to wait until the first number was completed. But with a threaded program, like the one we made here, check both numbers simultaneously.

The `isprime()` function is where the calculations are performed. The same function is used for both threads. We also use the same default attributes for both threads.

We execute the functions in threads by calling `pthread_create()` for each number. Notice that we don't put any parentheses after the `isprime()` function in the `pthread_create()` argument. Putting parentheses after the function name executes the function. However, we want the `pthread_create()` function to execute the function instead.

Since we won't be **joining** with the progress thread—it will simply run until `pthread_cancel()` is called—we mark it as detached so that its resources will be released when the thread terminates. We mark it as detached with `pthread_detach()`.

By default, a thread has its **cancelability state** enabled, meaning that the thread can be canceled. However, by default, its **cancelability type** is *deferred*, meaning that the cancellation will be delayed until the thread calls the next function that is a **cancellation point**. `sleep()` is one such function; therefore, the progress thread will cancel once it executes `sleep()`. The *cancelability type* can be changed to asynchronous, meaning it can cancel at any time.

At the end of the `main()` function, we called `pthread_join()` on both of the thread IDs (that are executing `isprime()`). This is necessary to make the process wait until the threads are finished; otherwise, it would end right away. The first argument for `pthread_join()` is the thread ID. The second argument is a variable wherein the thread's return value can be saved. But since we aren't interested in the return value here—it just returns `NULL`—we set it to `NULL`, which ignores it.

There's more...

To change the *cancelability state* of a thread, you use `pthread_setcancelstate()`. See `man 3 pthread_setcancelstate` for more information.

To change the *cancelability type* of a thread, you use `pthread_setcanceltype()`. See `man 3 pthread_setcanceltype` for more information.

To see a list of which functions are **cancellation points**, see `man 7 pthreads` and search for *cancelation points* in that manual page.

The conversion from a void pointer to a `long long int` can seem a bit cryptic. Instead of doing it all in one line, as we did here:

```
long long int number = *((long long*)arg);
```

We could have written it in two steps, which is a bit more verbose, like so:

```
long long int *number_ptr = (long long*)arg;
long long int number = *number_ptr;
```

See also

There's a lot of useful information in the manual pages for `pthread_create()` and `pthread_join()`. You can read them with `man 3 pthread_create` and `man 3 pthread_join`.

For more information regarding `pthread_detach()`, see `man 3 pthread_detach`.

For information regarding `pthread_cancel()`, see `man 3 pthread_cancel`.

Reading return values from threads

In this recipe, we'll continue from the previous recipe. Here, we'll fetch the answers as **return values** from the threads instead of letting them print the result themselves. This is like the return values from functions.

Knowing how to fetch the return values from threads enables you to do much more complicated things with threads.

Getting ready

In order for this recipe to make sense, it's advised that you complete the previous recipe first.

You'll also need the Makefile that we wrote in the previous recipe.

How to do it...

This program is similar to that of the previous recipe, but instead of each thread printing its own result, they return it to `main()`. This is similar to how functions return a value to `main()`, only here we need to do some **casting** back and forth. The downside of this approach is that we won't see the result until both threads are finished unless we intentionally give the first thread the smallest number. If the first thread has the largest number, we won't get the result of the second thread until the second thread is finished, even if it has been completed. However, even if we don't see the results printed right away, they are still being processed in two separate threads, just as before:

1. The code is long, so it's split up into several steps. Write the code in a single file called `second-threaded.c`. As usual, we start with the headers file, the function prototypes, and the beginning of the `main()` function. Notice that we have an extra header file here, called `stdint.h`. This is for the `uintptr_t` type, which we'll cast the returned value to. This is safer than casting to an `int`, since this is guaranteed to be of the same size as the pointer we're casting from. We also create two void pointers (`prime1Return` and `prime2Return`) that we'll save the return values in. Apart from these changes, the rest of the code is the same:

```
#include <stdio.h>
#include <stdlib.h>
#include <unistd.h>
#include <pthread.h>
#include <stdint.h>

void *isprime(void *arg);
void *progress(void *arg);

int main(int argc, char *argv[])
{
   long long number1;
   long long number2;
   pthread_t tid_prime1;
   pthread_t tid_prime2;
   pthread_t tid_progress;
   pthread_attr_t threadattr;
   void *prime1Return;
   void *prime2Return;
   if ( argc != 3 )
   {
      fprintf(stderr, "Please supply two numbers.\n"
```

```
            "Example: %s 9 7\n", argv[0]);
        return 1;
    }
    number1 = atoll(argv[1]);
    number2 = atoll(argv[2]);
    pthread_attr_init(&threadattr);
    pthread_create(&tid_progress, &threadattr,
        progress, NULL);
    pthread_detach(tid_progress);
    pthread_create(&tid_prime1, &threadattr,
        isprime, &number1);
    pthread_create(&tid_prime2, &threadattr,
        isprime, &number2);
```

2. In the next part, we add the void pointers we created earlier as the second argument to `pthread_join()`, or actually the address of those variables. This will save the thread's return value in these variables. Then, we check those return values to see whether the numbers were a prime number. But since the variable is a void pointer, we must first cast it to a `unitptr_t` type:

```
    pthread_join(tid_prime1, &prime1Return);
    if (  (uintptr_t)prime1Return == 1 )
        printf("\n%lld is a prime number\n",
            number1);
    else
        printf("\n%lld is not a prime number\n",
            number1);

    pthread_join(tid_prime2, &prime2Return);
    if ( (uintptr_t)prime2Return == 1 )
        printf("\n%lld is a prime number\n",
            number2);
    else
        printf("\n%lld is not a prime number\n",
            number2);

    pthread_attr_destroy(&threadattr);
    if ( pthread_cancel(tid_progress) != 0 )
        fprintf(stderr,
            "Couldn't cancel progress thread\n");
```

```
    return 0;
}
```

3. Then we have the functions as before. But this time, we return 0 or 1 cast to a void pointer (since that is what the function is declared to do, we cannot violate that):

```
void *isprime(void *arg)
{
    long long int number = *((long long*)arg);
    long long int j;
    int prime = 1;

    /* Test if the number is divisible, starting
     * from 2 */
    for(j=2; j<number; j++)
    {
        /* Use the modulo operator to test if the
         * number is evenly divisible, i.e., a
         * prime number */
        if(number%j == 0)
            prime = 0;
    }
    if(prime == 1)
        return (void*)1;
    else
        return (void*)0;
}

void *progress(void *arg)
{
    while(1)
    {
        sleep(1);
        printf(".");
        fflush(stdout);
    }
    return NULL;
}
```

4. Now, let's compile the program. We still get the same warning regarding an unused variable, but this is safe to ignore. We know we aren't using it for anything:

```
$> make second-threaded
gcc second-threaded.c -Wall -Wextra -pedantic -std=c99 -o
second-threaded -lpthread
second-threaded.c: In function 'progress':
second-threaded.c:83:22: warning: unused parameter 'arg'
[-Wunused-parameter]
 void *progress(void *arg)
                ~~~~~~^~~
```

5. Let's now try the program, first with the bigger number as the first argument, and then with the smaller number as the first argument:

```
$> ./second-threaded 9902343047 99023117
.........................................................
.............................
9902343047 is a prime number
99023117 is not a prime number
$> ./second-threaded 99023117 9902343047
.
99023117 is not a prime number
.........................................................
.............................
9902343047 is a prime number
```

How it works...

The overall basics of this program are the same as in the previous recipe. The difference here is that we return the result of the calculations from the threads to `main()`, just like a function. But since the return value of our `isprime()` function is a void pointer, we must also return this type. To save the return values, we pass the address of a variable as the second argument to `pthread_join()`.

Since each call to `pthread_join()` will *block* until its thread has finished, we won't get the result until both threads are completed (unless we give it the smallest number first).

The new type we used in this recipe, `uintptr_t`, is a special type that matches the size of an unsigned integer pointer. Using a regular `int` will probably work as well, but it's not guaranteed.

Causing a race condition

A **race condition** is when more than one thread (or process) tries to write to the same variable simultaneously. Since we don't know which thread will access the variable first, we can't safely predict what will happen. Both threads will try to access it first; they will *race* to access the variable.

Knowing what's causing a race condition will help you avoid them, making your programs safer.

Getting ready

For this recipe, you'll only need the Makefile we wrote in the first recipe of this chapter, along with the GCC compiler and the Make tool.

How to do it...

In this recipe, we'll write a program that causes a race condition. If the program were to work properly, it should add 1 to the `i` variable on every run, ending up at 5,000,000,000. There are five threads, and each thread adds 1 up to 1,000,000,000. But since all the threads access the `i` variable simultaneously—more or less—it never reaches 5,000,000,000. Each time a thread accesses it, it takes the current value and adds 1. But during that time, another thread might also read the current value and add 1, which then overwrites the added 1 from the other thread. In other words, the threads are overwriting each other's work:

1. The code is broken up into several steps. Note that all code goes into a single file. Name the file `race.c`. We'll start with the header files, a **function prototype**, and a global variable `i` of the type `long long int`. Then we write the `main()` function, which is pretty self-explanatory. It creates five threads with `pthread_create()` and then waits for them to finish with `pthread_join()`. Finally, it prints the resulting `i` variable:

```
#include <stdio.h>
#include <pthread.h>

void *add(void *arg);
long long int i = 0;

int main(void)
{
   pthread_attr_t threadattr;
   pthread_attr_init(&threadattr);
```

```
    pthread_t tid_add1, tid_add2, tid_add3,
      tid_add4, tid_add5;

    pthread_create(&tid_add1, &threadattr,
       add, NULL);
    pthread_create(&tid_add2, &threadattr,
       add, NULL);
    pthread_create(&tid_add3, &threadattr,
       add, NULL);
    pthread_create(&tid_add4, &threadattr,
       add, NULL);
    pthread_create(&tid_add5, &threadattr,
       add, NULL);

    pthread_join(tid_add1, NULL);
    pthread_join(tid_add2, NULL);
    pthread_join(tid_add3, NULL);
    pthread_join(tid_add4, NULL);
    pthread_join(tid_add5, NULL);

    printf("Sum is %lld\n", i);
    return 0;
}
```

2. Now we write the `add()` function that will run inside the threads:

```
void *add(void *arg)
{
    for (long long int j = 1; j <= 1000000000; j++)
    {
        i = i + 1;
    }
    return NULL;
}
```

3. Let's compile the program. Once again, it's safe to ignore the warning:

```
$> make race
gcc race.c -Wall -Wextra -pedantic -std=c99 -o race
-lpthread
race.c: In function 'add':
race.c:35:17: warning: unused parameter 'arg' [-Wunused-
parameter]
 void *add(void *arg)
           ~~~~~~^~~
```

4. Now, let's try out the program. We'll run it several times. Notice that each time we run it, we get a different value. That's because the timing of the threads can't be predicted. But most likely, it will never reach 5,000,000,000, which should be the correct value. Note that the program will take several seconds to complete:

```
$> ./race
Sum is 1207835374
$> ./race
Sum is 1132939275
$> ./race
Sum is 1204521570
```

5. This program is rather inefficient at the moment. We'll time the program before we move on using the `time` command. The time it takes to complete will be different on different computers. In a later recipe, *Making the mutex program more efficient*, we'll make the program much more efficient:

```
$> time ./race
Sum is 1188433970

real    0m20,195s
user    1m31,989s
sys     0m0,020s
```

How it works...

Since all the threads read and write to the same variable at the same time, they all undo each other's work. If they all ran in succession, like a non-threaded program, the result would be 5,000,000,000, which is what we want.

To better understand what's happening here, let's take it step by step. Note that this is just a rough estimation; the exact values and thread differ from one time to the next.

The first thread reads the value of `i`; let's say it's 1. The second thread also reads `i`, which is still 1, since the first thread hasn't incremented the value yet. Now the first thread increments the value to 2 and saves it to `i`. The second thread does the same; it also increments the value to 2 (1+1=2). Now, the third thread starts and reads the variable `i` as 2 and increments it to 3 (2+1=3). The result is now 3, instead of 4. This continues throughout the program's execution, and there's no telling what the result will be. Each time the program runs, the **timing** of the threads will be slightly different. The following diagram contains a simplified example of the problems that can arise:

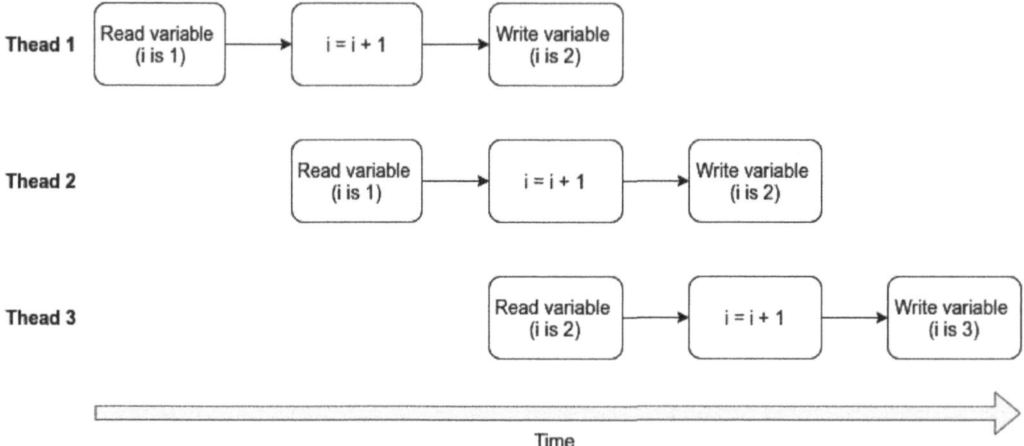

Figure 11.1 – Example of a race condition

Avoiding race conditions with mutexes

A **mutex** is a **locking mechanism** that prevents access to a **shared variable** so that no more than one thread can access it simultaneously. This prevents race conditions. With a mutex, we only lock the critical part of the code, for example, the updating of a shared variable. This will make sure that all other parts of the program run in parallel (if this is possible with the locking mechanism).

However, if we are not careful when we write our programs, a mutex can slow down the program a lot, which we'll see in this recipe. In the next recipe, we'll fix this problem.

Knowing how to use mutexes will help you overcome many of the problems associated with race conditions, making your programs safer and better.

Getting ready

In order for this recipe to make sense, it's advised that you complete the previous recipe first. You'll also need the Makefile that we wrote in the first recipe of this chapter, the GCC compiler, and the Make tool.

How to do it...

This program builds upon the previous recipe, but the complete code is shown here. The code is broken up into several steps. However, remember that all the code goes into the same file. Name the file `locking.c`:

1. We'll start at the top as usual. The added code is highlighted. First, we create a new variable called `mutex` of the `pthread_mutex_t` type. This is the variable that is used for locking. We place this variable in the global area so that it can be reached from both `main()` and `add()`. The second added bit is the initialization of the mutex variable, using `pthread_mutex_init()`. `NULL` as the second argument means that we want the default attributes for the mutex:

```
#include <stdio.h>
#include <pthread.h>

void *add(void *arg);
long long int i = 0;
pthread_mutex_t i_mutex;

int main(void)
{
   pthread_attr_t threadattr;
   pthread_attr_init(&threadattr);
   pthread_t tid_add1, tid_add2, tid_add3,
     tid_add4, tid_add5;

   if ( (pthread_mutex_init(&i_mutex, NULL)) != 0 )
   {
      fprintf(stderr,
         "Couldn't initialize mutex\n");
      return 1;
   }
   pthread_create(&tid_add1, &threadattr,
      add, NULL);
   pthread_create(&tid_add2, &threadattr,
      add, NULL);
```

```
    pthread_create(&tid_add3, &threadattr,
       add, NULL);
    pthread_create(&tid_add4, &threadattr,
       add, NULL);
    pthread_create(&tid_add5, &threadattr,
       add, NULL);

    pthread_join(tid_add1, NULL);
    pthread_join(tid_add2, NULL);
    pthread_join(tid_add3, NULL);
    pthread_join(tid_add4, NULL);
    pthread_join(tid_add5, NULL);
```

2. After we are done with the calculations, we destroy the `mutex` variable with `pthread_mutex_destroy()`:

```
    printf("Sum is %lld\n", i);
    if ( (pthread_mutex_destroy(&i_mutex)) != 0 )
    {
       fprintf(stderr, "Couldn't destroy mutex\n");
       return 1;
    }
    return 0;
}
```

3. And finally, we use the locking and unlocking mechanisms in the `add()` function. We lock the part where the `i` variable is updated and unlock it once the update is complete. That way, the variable is locked while the update is in progress so that no other threads can access it until the update is complete:

```
void *add(void *arg)
{
    for (long long int j = 1; j <= 1000000000; j++)
    {
       pthread_mutex_lock(&i_mutex);
       i = i + 1;
       pthread_mutex_unlock(&i_mutex);
    }
    return NULL;
}
```

4. Now, let's compile the program. As usual, we can ignore the warning regarding an unused variable:

```
$> make locking
gcc locking.c -Wall -Wextra -pedantic -std=c99 -o locking
-lpthread
locking.c: In function 'add':
locking.c:47:17: warning: unused parameter 'arg'
[-Wunused-parameter]
 void *add(void *arg)
           ~~~~~~^~~
```

5. Now it's time to run the program. Just as in the previous recipe, we'll time the execution using the `time` command. This time, the calculation will be correct; it will end up at 5,000,000,000. However, the program will take a long time to finish. On my computer, it takes well over 5 minutes to complete:

```
$> time ./locking
Sum is 5000000000

real    5m23,647s
user    8m24,596s
sys     16m11,407s
```

6. Let's compare this result to a simple, non-threaded program that accomplishes the same result with the same basic algorithm. Let's name this program `non-threaded.c`:

```
#include <stdio.h>

int main(void)
{
   long long int i = 0;
   for (int x = 1; x <= 5; x++)
   {
      for (long long int j = 1; j <= 1000000000; j++)
      {
         i = i + 1;
      }
   }
   printf("Sum is %lld\n", i);
   return 0;
}
```

7. Let's compile this program and time it. Note how much faster this program executes while, at the same time, attaining the same result:

```
$> make non-threaded
gcc non-threaded.c -Wall -Wextra -pedantic -std=c99 -o
non-threaded -lpthread
$> time ./non-threaded
Sum is 5000000000

real    0m10,345s
user    0m10,341s
sys     0m0,000s
```

How it works...

Threaded programs aren't automatically going to be faster than non-threaded programs. The non-threaded program that we ran in *step 7* was even faster than the threaded program from the previous recipe, even though that program didn't even use any mutexes.

So why is this, then?

The threaded program we've written has several inefficiencies. We'll start by discussing the issues with the `race.c` program from the previous recipe. The reason why that program is slower than the non-threaded version is because of numerous small things. For example, it takes some time to start each thread (a small amount of time, but still). Then there's the inefficiency of updating the global `i` variable by only one step each time. All the threads are also accessing the same global variable at the same time. We have five threads, and each thread increments its local `j` variable by one. And each time that happens, the thread updates the global `i` variable. And since all of this happens 5,000,000,000 times, it takes a bit longer than it would have taken to run it sequentially in a single thread.

Then, in the `locking.c` program in this recipe, we added a mutex to lock the `i = i + 1` part. Since this ensures that only one thread can access the `i` variable simultaneously, it makes the entire program sequential again. Instead of all the threads running side by side, the following happens:

1. Run a thread.
2. Lock the `i = i + 1` part.
3. Run `i = i + 1` to update `i`.
4. Unlock `i = i + 1`.

5. Run the next thread.
6. Lock the `i = i + 1` part.
7. Run `i = i + 1` to update `i`.
8. Unlock `i = i + 1`.

These steps will repeat over and over again 5,000,000,000 times in a row. Each time a thread starts takes time. Then it takes additional time to lock and unlock the mutex, and it also takes time to increment the `i` variable. It also takes time to switch to another thread and start the whole locking/unlocking process all over again.

In the next recipe, we'll address these issues and make the program run much faster.

See also

For more information about mutexes, see the manual pages `man 3 pthread_mutex_init`, `man 3 phtread_mutex_lock`, `man 3 phthread_mutex_unlock`, and `man 3 pthread_mutex_destroy`.

Making the mutex program more efficient

In the previous recipe, we saw that a threaded program isn't necessarily any faster than a non-threaded program. We also saw that when we introduced mutexes, the program got horribly slow. Much of this slowness is due to switching back and forth and locking and unlocking billions of times.

The solution to all of this locking and unlocking and switching back and forth is to lock and unlock as few times as possible. And also, to update the `i` variable as few times as possible and do as much work as possible in each thread.

In this recipe, we'll make our threaded program much faster and much more efficient.

Knowing how to write efficient threaded programs will help you stay away from many of the pitfalls when it comes to threading.

Getting ready

In order for this recipe to make sense, it's advised that you complete the two previous recipes in this chapter. Other than that, the same requirements apply here; we need the Makefile, the GCC compiler, and the Make tool.

How to do it...

This program builds on the previous `locking.c` program from the previous recipe. The only difference is the `add()` function. Therefore, only the `add()` function is shown here; the rest is the same as `locking.c`. The complete program can be downloaded from this chapter's GitHub directory. The name of the file is `efficient.c`:

1. Make a copy of `locking.c` and name the new file `efficient.c`.
2. Rewrite the `add()` function so that it looks like this code instead. Notice that we have removed the `for` loop. Instead, we increment a local `j` variable in a `while` loop until it reaches 1,000,000,000. Then, we add the local `j` variable to the global `i` variable. This reduces the number of times we have to lock and unlock the mutex (from 5,000,000,000 times to only 5 times):

```
void *add(void *arg)
{
    long long int j = 1;
    while(j < 1000000000)
    {
        j = j + 1;
    }

    pthread_mutex_lock(&i_mutex);
    i = i + j;
    pthread_mutex_unlock(&i_mutex);
    return NULL;
}
```

3. Compile the program:

```
$> make efficient
gcc efficient.c -Wall -Wextra -pedantic -std=c99 -o
efficient -lpthread
efficient.c: In function 'add':
efficient.c:47:17: warning: unused parameter 'arg'
[-Wunused-parameter]
 void *add(void *arg)
             ~~~~~~^~~
```

4. Now, let's run the program and time it using the `time` command. Notice how much faster this program is:

```
$ time ./efficient
Sum is 5000000000

real    0m1,954s
user    0m8,858s
sys     0m0,004s
```

How it works…

This program is much faster than both the non-threaded version and the first locking version. As a reminder of the execution times, the non-threaded version took around 10 seconds to complete; the first threaded version (`race.c`) took around 20 seconds to complete; the first mutex version (`locking.c`) took well over 5 minutes to complete. The final version (`efficient.c`) took just under 2 seconds to complete—a huge improvement.

There are two main reasons why this program is so much faster. First, this program only locks and unlocks the mutex 5 times (compared to 5,000,000,000 times in the previous recipe). Secondly, each thread can now complete its work (the `while` loop) fully before writing anything to the global variable.

Simply put, each thread can now do its work without any interruptions, making it truly threaded. Only when the threads have completed their work will they write their result to the global variable.

Using condition variables

With **condition variables**, we can **signal** a thread when another thread has finished its work or when some other event occurs. For example, with condition variables, we can rewrite the prime number program from the *Reading return values from threads* recipe to join with the thread that finishes first. That way, the program isn't compelled to join with thread 1 first and then thread 2. Instead, the thread that finishes first signals to `main()` using a condition variable that it has finished and then joins with that thread.

Knowing how to use condition variables will help you make your threaded programs more flexible.

Getting ready

In order for this recipe to make sense, it's advised that you have completed the *Reading return values from threads* recipe first. You'll also need the GCC compiler, the Makefile we wrote in the *Writing your first threaded program* recipe, and the Make tool.

How to do it...

In this recipe, we'll rewrite the prime number program from the *Reading return values from threads* recipe to use condition variables. The complete program will be shown here, but we will only discuss the added parts for this recipe.

Since the code is long, it has been broken up into several steps. Save the code in a file called `cond-var.c`:

1. We'll start at the top as usual. Here we have added three new variables, a mutex that we name `lock`, a condition variable that we name `ready`, and a thread ID for the prime thread, which we name `primeid`. The `primeid` variable will be used to send the thread ID from the thread that has finished:

```
#include <stdio.h>
#include <stdlib.h>
#include <unistd.h>
#include <pthread.h>
#include <stdint.h>

void *isprime(void *arg);
void *progress(void *arg);
pthread_mutex_t lock;
pthread_cond_t ready;
pthread_t primeid = 0;

int main(int argc, char *argv[])
{
   long long number1;
   long long number2;
   pthread_t tid_prime1;
   pthread_t tid_prime2;
   pthread_t tid_progress;
   pthread_attr_t threadattr;
   void *prime1Return;
   void *prime2Return;
```

2. Then we must initialize both the **mutex** and the **condition variable**:

```
if ( (pthread_mutex_init(&lock, NULL)) != 0 )
{
   fprintf(stderr,
      "Couldn't initialize mutex\n");
   return 1;
}

if ( (pthread_cond_init(&ready, NULL)) != 0 )
{
   fprintf(stderr,
     "Couldn't initialize condition variable\n");
   return 1;
}
```

3. After that, we check the number of arguments, just as before. If the argument count is correct, we start the threads with `pthread_create()`, also as before:

```
if ( argc != 3 )
{
   fprintf(stderr, "Please supply two numbers.\n"
      "Example: %s 9 7\n", argv[0]);
   return 1;
}
number1 = atoll(argv[1]);
number2 = atoll(argv[2]);
pthread_attr_init(&threadattr);
pthread_create(&tid_progress, &threadattr,
   progress, NULL);
pthread_detach(tid_progress);
pthread_create(&tid_prime1, &threadattr,
   isprime, &number1);
pthread_create(&tid_prime2, &threadattr,
   isprime, &number2);
```

4. Now comes the interesting stuff. We'll start by locking the mutex so that the `primeid` variable is protected. Then, we wait for the signal from the condition variable using `pthread_cond_wait()`. This will release the mutex so that the threads can write to `primeid`. Note that we also loop the `pthread_cond_wait()` call in a `while` loop. We do this because we only want to wait for the signal if `primeid` is still 0. Since `pthread_cond_wait()` will block, it won't use any CPU cycles. When we get the signal, we move down to the `if` statement. This checks which thread it was that finished and joins it. Then we go back and start again using the `for` loop. Each time an `if` or `else` statement has completed—when a thread has joined—the `primeid` variable is reset to 0. This will make the next iteration wait again with `pthread_cond_wait()`:

```
pthread_mutex_lock(&lock);
for (int i = 0; i < 2; i++)
{
    while (primeid == 0)
        pthread_cond_wait(&ready, &lock);
    if (primeid == tid_prime1)
    {
        pthread_join(tid_prime1, &prime1Return);
        if (  (uintptr_t)prime1Return == 1 )
            printf("\n%lld is a prime number\n",
                number1);
        else
            printf("\n%lld is not a prime number\n",
                number1);
        primeid = 0;
    }
    else
    {
        pthread_join(tid_prime2, &prime2Return);
        if ( (uintptr_t)prime2Return == 1 )
            printf("\n%lld is a prime number\n",
                number2);
        else
            printf("\n%lld is not a prime number\n",
                number2);
        primeid = 0;
    }
}
pthread_mutex_unlock(&lock);
```

```
    pthread_attr_destroy(&threadattr);
    if ( pthread_cancel(tid_progress) != 0 )
        fprintf(stderr,
            "Couldn't cancel progress thread\n");

    return 0;
}
```

5. Next up, we have the `isprime()` function. Here we have some new lines. Once the function is done calculating the number, we lock the mutex to protect the `primeid` variable. Then we set the `primeid` variable to the thread's ID. Then, we signal the condition variable (`ready`) and release the mutex lock. This will wake up the `main()` function since it's now waiting with `pthread_cond_wait()`:

```
void *isprime(void *arg)
{
    long long int number = *((long long*)arg);
    long long int j;
    int prime = 1;

    for(j=2; j<number; j++)
    {
        if(number%j == 0)
            prime = 0;
    }
    pthread_mutex_lock(&lock);
    primeid = pthread_self();
    pthread_cond_signal(&ready);
    pthread_mutex_unlock(&lock);
    if(prime == 1)
        return (void*)1;
    else
        return (void*)0;
}
```

6. And finally, we have the `progress()` function. Nothing has changed here:

```
void *progress(void *arg)
{
    while(1)
    {
        sleep(1);
        printf(".");
        fflush(stdout);
    }
    return NULL;
}
```

7. Now, let's compile the program:

```
$> make cond-var
gcc cond-var.c -Wall -Wextra -pedantic -std=c99 -o cond-var -lpthread
cond-var.c: In function 'progress':
cond-var.c:114:22: warning: unused parameter 'arg' [-Wunused-parameter]
 void *progress(void *arg)
```

8. Let's now try out the program. We'll test it with both the smaller number as the first argument and then as the second argument. Either way, the fastest number to compute will be displayed instantly, without having to wait for the other thread to join:

```
$> ./cond-var 990231117 9902343047
........
990231117 is not a prime number
.........................................................................................
9902343047 is a prime number
$> ./cond-var 9902343047 990231117
........
990231117 is not a prime number
........................................................................................
9902343047 is a prime number
```

How it works...

When we waited in the `while` loop with `pthread_cond_wait()`, we called it with both the condition variable (`ready`) and the mutex (`lock`). That way, it knows which mutex to release and which signal to wait for. It's when we wait that the mutex is released.

During the waiting, the other threads can write to the `primeid` variable. The other threads will first lock the variable with the mutex before writing to it. Once they have written to the variable, they signal the condition variable and release the mutex. This wakes up the `main()` function, which is currently waiting with `pthread_cond_wait()`. The `main()` function then checks which thread it was that finished and joins it with `pthread_join()`. Then, the `main()` function will reset the `primeid` variable to 0 and go back to waiting with `pthread_cond_wait()` until the next thread signals that it's finished. There are two threads we are waiting for, so the `for` loop in `main()` will run the loop two times.

Each thread gets its own thread ID using `pthread_self()`.

See also

Refer to the following manual pages for more information regarding condition variables:

- `man 3 pthread_cond_init()`
- `man 3 pthread_cond_wait()`
- `man 3 pthread_cond_signal()`

12 Debugging Your Programs

No program is perfect on the first try. In this chapter, we'll learn how to debug our programs using **GDB** and **Valgrind**. With the latter tool, Valgrind, we can find **memory leaks** in our programs.

We'll also take a look at what memory leaks are, what they can cause, and how to prevent them. Debugging programs and looking at memory is an important step to understanding system programming fully.

In this chapter, we will cover the following recipes:

- Starting GDB
- Stepping inside functions with GDB
- Investigating memory with GDB
- Modifying variables during runtime
- Using GDB on a program that forks
- Debugging programs with multiple threads
- Finding a simple memory leak with Valgrind
- Finding buffer overflows with Valgrind

Technical requirements

For this chapter, you'll need the GBD tool, Valgrind, the GCC compiler, a generic Makefile, and the Make tool.

If you haven't installed GDB and Valgrind yet, you can do so now. Follow these instructions depending on your distributions. If you don't have `sudo` installed or don't have `sudo` privileges, you can switch to root using `su` instead (and leave out the `sudo` part).

For Debian and Ubuntu systems, run the following command:

```
$> sudo apt-get install gdb valgrind
```

For CentOS, Fedora, and Red Hat systems, run the following command:

```
$> sudo dnf install gdb valgrind
```

All the code samples for this chapter can be found on GitHub at `https://github.com/PacktPublishing/Linux-System-Programming-Techniques/tree/master/ch12`.

Check out the following link to see the Code in Action videos: `https://bit.ly/2TTiIPp`

Starting GDB

In this recipe, we'll learn the basics of **GDB**, the **GNU debugger**. We'll learn how to start GDB, how to set a breakpoint, and how to step forward in a program, one step at a time. We'll also learn what **debugging symbols** are and how we enable them.

GDB is the most popular debugger for Linux and other Unix-like systems. It allows you to examine—and change—variables on the fly, step through instructions one at a time, view the code as the program is running, read return values, and much more.

Knowing how to use a debugger can save you many hours of frustration. Instead of guessing what the problem is with your program, you can follow the execution with GDB and spot the error. This can save you a lot of time.

Getting ready

For this recipe, you'll need the GCC compiler, the Make tool, and the GDB tool. For installation instructions for GDB, see the *Technical requirements* section of this chapter.

How to do it...

In this recipe, we'll use GDB on a working program. There are no bugs here. Instead, we want to focus on how to do some basic things in GDB:

1. Write the following small program in a file and save it as `loop.c`. Later, we will examine the program using GDB:

```
#include <stdio.h>
int main(void)
{
    int x;
    int y = 5;
    char text[20] = "Hello, world";
    for (x = 1; y < 100; x++)
    {
        y = (y*3)-x;
    }
    printf("%s\n", text);
    printf("y = %d\n", y);
    return 0;
}
```

2. Before we can use GDB to its fullest, we need to enable **debugging symbols** when compiling the program. Therefore, write the following new Makefile and save it as `Makefile` in the same directory as the `loop.c` program. Notice we added the `-g` option to `CFLAGS`. These debugging symbols make it possible to see the code as we execute it in GDB:

```
CC=gcc
CFLAGS=-g -Wall -Wextra -pedantic -std=c99
```

3. Now, it's time to compile the program using our new Makefile:

```
$> make loop
gcc -g -Wall -Wextra -pedantic -std=c99    loop.c   -o
loop
```

4. Let's try the program before we move on:

```
$> ./loop
Hello, world
y = 117
```

5. From the same directory as `loop` and `loop.c`, start GDB with the loop program by typing the following (the source code, `loop.c`, is needed to display the code within GBD):

```
$> gdb ./loop
```

6. You are now presented with some copyright text and version information. Down at the bottom, there's a prompt saying `(gdb)`. This is where we type our commands. Let's run the program and see what happens. We run the program by simply typing `run` and hitting *Enter*:

```
(gdb) run
Starting program: /home/jack/ch12/code/loop
Hello, world
y = 117
[Inferior 1 (process 10467) exited normally]
```

7. That didn't really tell us much; we could have just run the program directly from the terminal. So, this time we set a **breakpoint** at line 1. The breakpoint won't actually be at line 1 since that is just an `include` line. Instead, GDB automatically sets it on the first logical place where there is actual code. A breakpoint is where the execution should stop in the code so that we'll have a chance to investigate it:

```
(gdb) break 1
Breakpoint 1 at 0x55555555514d: file loop.c, line 6.
```

8. Now we can rerun the program. This time the execution will stop at line 6 (the breakpoint):

```
$> (gdb) run
Starting program: /home/jack/ch12/code/loop

Breakpoint 1, main () at loop.c:6
6           int y = 5;
```

9. We can start watching over the `y` variable using the `watch` command. GDB will then tell us every time `y` is updated:

```
$> (gdb) watch y
Hardware watchpoint 2: y
```

10. Now we can execute the next statement in the code by using the `next` command. To avoid having to type `next` every time we want to move forward in the code, we can just hit *Enter*. Doing so will make GDB execute the last command. Notice the updated `y` variable. Also, notice that we see the code we are executing for every step we take:

```
(gdb) next

Hardware watchpoint 2: y

Old value = 0
New value = 5
main () at loop.c:7
7           char text[20] = "Hello, world";
(gdb) next
8           for (x = 1; y < 100; x++)
(gdb) next
10              y = (y*3)-x;
```

11. The line of code being displayed is the next statement that is to be executed. So, from the previous step, we see that the next line to execute is line 10, which is `y = (y*3)-x`. So let's hit *Enter* here, and that will update the `y` variable, and the **watchpoint** will tell us about it:

```
(gdb) next

Hardware watchpoint 2: y

Old value = 5
New value = 14
main () at loop.c:8
8           for (x = 1; y < 100; x++)
(gdb) next
10              y = (y*3)-x;
(gdb) next

Hardware watchpoint 2: y

Old value = 14
New value = 40
main () at loop.c:8
8           for (x = 1; y < 100; x++)
```

```
(gdb) next
10          y = (y*3)-x;
(gdb) next

Hardware watchpoint 2: y

Old value = 40
New value = 117
8           for (x = 1; y < 100; x++)
```

12. Before we go any further, let's examine the content of the `text` character array and the x variable. We print the content of variables and arrays with the `print` command. Here we see that the `text` array is filled with **null characters** after the actual text:

```
(gdb) print text
$1 = "Hello, world\000\000\000\000\000\000\000"
(gdb) print x
$2 = 3
```

13. Let's continue the execution. After the process has exited in the last step, we can exit GDB with `quit`:

```
(gdb) next
12          printf("%s\n", text);
(gdb) next
Hello, world
13          printf("y = %d\n", y);
(gdb) next
y = 117
14          return 0;
(gdb) next
15      }
(gdb) next

Watchpoint 2 deleted because the program has left the
block in which its expression is valid.
__libc_start_main (main=0x555555555145 <main>, argc=1,
argv=0x7fffffffdbe8,
    init=<optimized out>, fini=<optimized out>, rtld_
fini=<optimized out>,
    stack_end=0x7fffffffdbd8) at ../csu/libc-start.c:342
342     ../csu/libc-start.c: No such file or directory.
```

```
(gdb) next
[Inferior 1 (process 14779) exited normally]
(gdb) quit
```

How it works...

We've just learned all the basics of GDB. With these commands, we can do a lot of debugging. There are a few more things to learn, but we've already come a long way.

We started the GDB program with the `loop` program. To prevent GDB from running through the entire program without investigating things, we set a breakpoint using the `break` command. In our example, we set the break on a line, using `break 1`. It's also possible to set a breakpoint on a specific function, such as `main()`. We can do this with the `break main` command.

Once the breakpoint was in place, we could run the program with `run`. We then watched over the `y` variable with `watch`. We executed one statement at a time, using the `next` command. We also learned how to print variables and arrays using the `print` command.

For all of this to be possible, we had to compile the program with the `-g` option to GCC. That enables debugging symbols. But, to see the actual code in GDB, we also need the source code file.

There's more...

GDB has some nice built-in help. Start GDB without a program. Then type `help` at the `(gdb)` prompt. This will give you a list of different classes of commands. If we want to read more about breakpoints, we type `help breakpoints`. This gives you a long list of breakpoint commands, for example, `break`. To read more about the `break` command, type `help break`.

Stepping inside a function with GDB

When we use the `next` command in a program with a function, it will simply execute the function and move on. However, there's another command called `step` that will enter the function, step through it, and then return to `main()` again. In this recipe, we'll examine the difference between `next` and `step`.

Knowing how to step into a function with GDB will help you debug an entire program, including its functions.

Getting ready

For this recipe, you'll need the GDB tool, the GCC compiler, the Makefile we wrote in the *Starting GDB* recipe in this chapter, and the Make tool.

How to do it...

In this recipe, we'll write a small program that has a function. Then, we'll step into that function with GDB, using the `step` command:

1. Write the following code in a file and save it as `area-of-circle.c`. The program takes the radius of a circle as an argument and prints its area:

```
#include <stdio.h>
#include <stdlib.h>
float area(float radius);

int main(int argc, char *argv[])
{
    float number;
    float answer;
    if (argc != 2)
    {
        fprintf(stderr, "Type the radius of a "
            "circle\n");
        return 1;
    }
    number = atof(argv[1]);
    answer = area(number);
    printf("The area of a circle with a radius of "
        "%.2f is %.2f\n", number, answer);
    return 0;
}

float area(float radius)
{
    static float pi = 3.14159;
    return pi*radius*radius;
}
```

2. Compile the program using the Makefile from the *Starting GDB* recipe:

```
$> make area-of-circle
gcc -g -Wall -Wextra -pedantic -std=c99    area-of-
circle.c   -o area-of-circle
```

3. Let's try it out before stepping through it with GDB:

```
$> ./area-of-circle 9
The area of a circle with a radius of 9.00 is 254.47
```

4. Now it's time to step through the program with GDB. Start GDB with the `area-of-circle` program:

```
$> gdb ./area-of-circle
```

5. We start by setting a breakpoint at the `main()` function:

```
(gdb) break main
Breakpoint 1 at 0x1164: file area-of-circle.c, line 9.
```

6. Now we run the program. To specify an argument to a program while inside GDB, we set the argument at the `run` command:

```
(gdb) run 9
Starting program: /home/jack/ch12/code/area-of-circle 9

Breakpoint 1, main (argc=2, argv=0x7fffffffdbd8) at area-
of-circle.c:9
9           if (argc != 2)
```

7. Let's move ahead one step with the `next` command:

```
(gdb) next
15          number = atof(argv[1]);
```

8. As we can see from the previous step, the next statement to execute will be the `atof()` function. This is a standard library function, so we don't have any debugging symbols or source code for it. Therefore, we can't see anything inside the function. However, we can still step inside it. Once we are inside the function, we can let it execute and finish using the `finish` command. This will tell us the function's **return value**, which can be very handy:

```
(gdb) step
atof (nptr=0x7fffffffdfed "9") at atof.c:27
27      atof.c: No such file or directory.
```

```
(gdb) finish
Run till exit from #0  atof (nptr=0x7fffffffdfed "9") at
atof.c:27
main (argc=2, argv=0x7fffffffdbd8) at area-of-circle.c:15
15          number = atof(argv[1]);
Value returned is $1 = 9
```

9. Now we do another `next`, which will take us to our `area` function. We want to step inside the `area` function, so we use `step` here. This will tell us that the value it was called with is 9. Since there isn't much left to do inside the area function but to return, we can type `finish` to get its return value:

```
(gdb) next
16          answer = area(number);
(gdb) step
area (radius=9) at area-of-circle.c:25
25          return pi*radius*radius;
(gdb) finish
Run till exit from #0  area (radius=9) at area-of-
circle.c:25
0x00005555555551b7 in main (argc=2, argv=0x7fffffffdbd8)
at area-of-circle.c:16
16          answer = area(number);
Value returned is $2 = 254.468796
```

10. And now, we can walk through the rest of the program with `next`:

```
(gdb) next
17          printf("The area of a circle with a radius of
"
(gdb) next
The area of a circle with a radius of 9.00 is 254.47
19          return 0;
(gdb) next
20      }
(gdb) next
__libc_start_main (main=0x555555555155 <main>, argc=2,
argv=0x7fffffffdbd8,
    init=<optimized out>, fini=<optimized out>, rtld_
fini=<optimized out>,
    stack_end=0x7fffffffdbc8) at ../csu/libc-start.c:342
342     ../csu/libc-start.c: No such file or directory.
(gdb) next
```

```
[Inferior 1 (process 2034) exited normally]
(gdb) quit
```

How it works...

With the `step` command, we step inside a function. However, functions from the standard library don't have any debugging symbols or source code available; therefore, we can't see what's happening inside them. If we wanted to, we could get the source code and compile it with debugging symbols; Linux is, after all, open source.

But even when we don't see what's happening inside a function, it can still be valuable to step inside them since we can get their return value with `finish`.

Investigating memory with GDB

With GDB, we can learn more about how things work under the hood, for example, strings. A **string** is an array of characters terminated by a null character. In this recipe, we'll investigate a character array with GDB and see how the null character ends a string.

Knowing how to examine the memory using GDB can be really handy if you encounter weird **bugs**. Instead of guessing or looping over each character in C, we can directly examine them in GDB.

Getting ready

For this recipe, you'll need the Makefile we wrote in the *Starting GDB* recipe. You'll also need the GCC compiler and the Make tool.

How to do it...

In this recipe, we'll write a simple program that fills a character array with the character *x*. Then we'll copy a new, shorter string on top of that and finally print the string. It's only the newly copied string that is printed, even if all the *x* characters are still there. With GDB, we can confirm this fact:

1. Write the following code in a file and save it as `memtest.c`:

```
#include <stdio.h>
#include <string.h>
int main(void)
{
    char text[20];
    memset(text, 'x', 20);
```

```
    strcpy(text, "Hello");
    printf("%s\n", text);
    return 0;
}
```

2. Compile the program using the Makefile from the *Starting GDB* recipe:

```
$> make memtest
gcc -g -Wall -Wextra -pedantic -std=c99    memtest.c    -o
memtest
```

3. Let's run it as we would with any other program:

```
$> ./memtest
Hello
```

4. Let's start GDB with our `memtest` program:

```
$> gdb ./memtest
```

5. Now, let's examine what's really inside the `text` array using GDB. First, we set a breakpoint on `main()`, then we run the program and step forward in the program with `next` until after the `strcpy()` function has been executed. Then, we examine the **memory** using the x command in GDB (x for eXamine). We must also tell GDB to examine 20 bytes and print the content using decimal notation. The x command will therefore be `x/20bd text`. To interpret the decimals to characters, see the ASCII table we talked about in *Chapter 2, Making Your Programs Easy to Script,* at `https://github.com/PacktPublishing/B13043-Linux-System-Programming-Cookbook/blob/master/ch2/ascii-table.md`:

```
(gdb) break main
Breakpoint 1 at 0x114d: file memtest.c, line 6.
(gdb) run
Starting program: /mnt/localnas_disk2/linux-sys/ch12/
code/memtest

Breakpoint 1, main () at memtest.c:6
warning: Source file is more recent than executable.
6           memset(text, 'x', 20);
(gdb) next
7           strcpy(text, "Hello");
(gdb) next
8           printf("%s\n", text);
(gdb) x/20bd text
```

```
0x7fffffffdae0: 72   101  108  108  111  0    120  120
0x7fffffffdae8: 120  120  120  120  120  120  120  120
0x7fffffffdaf0: 120  120  120  120
```

How it works...

To examine the memory using GDB, we used the `x` command. `20bd` says the size we want to read is 20, and we want to present it in groups of bytes (the `b`) and print the content using decimal notation (the `d`). With this command, we get a nice-looking table that shows us every character in the array printed as a decimal number.

The content of the memory—when translated to characters—is `Hello\0xxxxxxxxxxxxxx`. The null character separates the *Hello* string from all the *x* characters. There's a lot to learn by using GDB and examining the memory during runtime.

There's more...

Instead of just printing the content as decimal notation, it's also possible to print as regular characters (`c`), hexadecimal notation (`x`), floating points (`f`), and so on. These letters are the same as for `printf()`.

See also

You can learn more about how to use the `x` command by typing `help x` while inside GDB.

Modifying variables during runtime

With GDB it's even possible to modify variables during runtime. This can be very handy for experimentation. Instead of changing the source code and recompiling the program, you can change the variable with GDB and see what happens.

Knowing how to change variables and arrays during runtime can speed up your debugging and experimentation phase.

Getting ready

For this recipe, you'll need the `memtest.c` program from the previous recipe. You'll also need the Makefile from the *Starting GDB* recipe in this chapter, the Make tool, and the GCC compiler.

How to do it...

In this recipe, we'll continue using the program from the previous recipe. Here, we'll replace the **null character** in the sixth place with another character and the last character with a null character:

1. If you haven't yet compiled the `memtest` program from the previous recipe, do so now:

```
$> make memtest
gcc -g -Wall -Wextra -pedantic -std=c99    memtest.c   -o
memtest
```

2. Start GDB with the `memtest` program you just compiled:

```
$> gdb ./memtest
```

3. Start by setting a breakpoint at `main()` and run the program. Step forward to just after the `strcpy()` function using `next`:

```
(gdb) break main
Breakpoint 1 at 0x114d: file memtest.c, line 6.
(gdb) run
Starting program: /home/jack/ch12/code/memtest

Breakpoint 1, main () at memtest.c:6
6           memset(text, 'x', 20);
(gdb) next
7           strcpy(text, "Hello");
(gdb) next
8           printf("%s\n", text);
```

4. Before changing the array, let's print it first using the `x` command like in the previous recipe:

```
(gdb) x/20bd text
0x7fffffffdae0: 72   101  108  108  111  0    120  120
0x7fffffffdae8: 120  120  120  120  120  120  120  120
0x7fffffffdaf0: 120  120  120  120
```

5. Now that we know what the content looks like, we can replace the null character at the sixth position—the fifth actually, we start counting from 0—with a `y`. We also replace the last position with a null character. Setting **variables** and array positions in GDB is done using the `set` command:

```
(gdb) set text[5] = 'y'
(gdb) set text[19] = '\0'
(gdb) x/20bd text
0x7fffffffdae0: 72    101   108   108   111   121   120   120
0x7fffffffdae8: 120   120   120   120   120   120   120   120
0x7fffffffdaf0: 120   120   120   0
```

6. Let's continue running the rest of the program. Instead of stepping forward with the `next` command one step at a time, we can use the `continue` command to let the program run until the end. Notice that the `printf()` function will now print the string `Helloyxxxxxxxxxxxxxx`:

```
(gdb) continue
Continuing.
Helloyxxxxxxxxxxxxxx
[Inferior 1 (process 4967) exited normally]
(gdb) quit
```

How it works...

Using the `set` command in GDB, we managed to change the content of the `text` array during runtime. With the `set` command, we removed the first null character and inserted a new one at the end, making it a long valid string. Since we had removed the null character after *Hello*, `printf()` then printed the entire string.

Using GDB on a program that forks

Using GDB to debug a program that **forks** will automatically follow the **parent process**, just like a regular non-forking program. But it's possible to follow the **child process** instead, which is what we will learn in this recipe.

Being able to follow the child process is important in debugging since many programs spawn child processes. We don't want to limit ourselves to only non-forking programs.

Getting ready

For this recipe, you'll need the Makefile from the *Starting GDB* recipe in this chapter, the Make tool, and the GCC compiler.

How to do it...

In this recipe, we'll write a small program that forks. We'll put a `for` loop inside the child to confirm whether we are inside the child or the parent. On the first run in GDB, we'll run through the program like we usually would. This will make GDB follow the parent process. Then, in the next run, we'll follow the child process instead:

1. Write the following code in a file and save it as `forking.c`. The code is similar to the `forkdemo.c` program we wrote in *Chapter 6*, *Spawning Processes and Using Job Control*:

```
#include <sys/types.h>
#include <unistd.h>
#include <sys/wait.h>

int main(void)
{
   pid_t pid;
   printf("My PID is %d\n", getpid());
   /* fork, save the PID, and check for errors */
   if ( (pid = fork()) == -1 )
   {
      perror("Can't fork");
      return 1;
   }
   if (pid == 0)
   {
      /* if pid is 0 we are in the child process */
      printf("Hello from the child process!\n");
      for(int i = 0; i<10; i++)
      {
          printf("Counter in child: %d\n", i);
      }
   }
   else if(pid > 0)
   {
      /* parent process */
      printf("My child has PID %d\n", pid);
```

```
        wait(&pid);
    }
    return 0;
}
```

2. Compile the program:

```
$> make forking
gcc -g -Wall -Wextra -pedantic -std=c99    forking.c   -o
forking
```

3. Let's try the program before we run it in GDB:

```
$> ./forking
My PID is 9868
My child has PID 9869
Hello from the child process!
Counter in child: 0
Counter in child: 1
Counter in child: 2
Counter in child: 3
Counter in child: 4
Counter in child: 5
Counter in child: 6
Counter in child: 7
Counter in child: 8
Counter in child: 9
```

4. On the first run through GDB, we'll run it like we usually would. This will make GDB follow the parent process automatically. Begin with starting GDB with the `forking` program:

```
$> gdb ./forking
```

5. Set the breakpoint at `main()` as usual and run it. Then, we'll step forward with the next command until we see the *Counter in child* text. That will prove that we are indeed in the parent process since we never stepped through the `for` loop. Also, notice that GDB tells us that the program has forked and detached from the child process (meaning we are in the parent process). GDB also prints the PID of the child process:

```
(gdb) break main
Breakpoint 1 at 0x118d: file forking.c, line 9.
(gdb) run
```

```
Starting program: /home/jack/ch12/code/forking

Breakpoint 1, main () at forking.c:9
9           printf("My PID is %d\n", getpid());
(gdb) next
My PID is 10568
11          if ( (pid = fork()) == -1 )
(gdb) next
[Detaching after fork from child process 10577]
Hello from the child process!
Counter in child: 0
Counter in child: 1
Counter in child: 2
Counter in child: 3
Counter in child: 4
Counter in child: 5
Counter in child: 6
Counter in child: 7
Counter in child: 8
Counter in child: 9
16          if (pid == 0)
(gdb) continue
Continuing.
My child has PID 10577
[Inferior 1 (process 10568) exited normally]
(gdb) quit
```

6. Now, let's run through the program again. But this time, we will tell GDB to follow the child process instead. Start GDB with the `forking` program as before:

```
$> gdb ./forking
```

7. Set the breakpoint at `main()` as we did before. After that, we tell GDB to follow the child process using the `set` command as we've seen before. Only this time, we set something called `follow-fork-mode`. We set it to `child`. Then run the program as usual:

```
(gdb) break main
Breakpoint 1 at 0x118d: file forking.c, line 9.
(gdb) set follow-fork-mode child
(gdb) run
Starting program: /home/jack/ch12/code/forking
```

```
Breakpoint 1, main () at forking.c:9
9           printf("My PID is %d\n", getpid());
```

8. Now, move forward one step at a time with the `next` command twice. The program will now fork, and GDB will tell us that it's attaching to the child process and detaching from the parent process. This means that we are now inside the child process:

```
(gdb) next
My PID is 11561
11          if ( (pid = fork()) == -1 )
(gdb) next
[Attaching after process 11561 fork to child process
11689]
[New inferior 2 (process 11689)]
[Detaching after fork from parent process 11561]
[Inferior 1 (process 11561) detached]
My child has PID 11689
[Switching to process 11689]
main () at forking.c:11
11          if ( (pid = fork()) == -1 )
```

9. Let's move forward a bit again to see that we end up inside the `for` loop, which is inside the child process:

```
(gdb) next
16          if (pid == 0)
(gdb) next
19             printf("Hello from the child process!\n");
(gdb) next
Hello from the child process!
20             for(int i = 0; i<10; i++)
(gdb) next
22                 printf("Counter in child: %d\n", i);
(gdb) next
Counter in child: 0
20             for(int i = 0; i<10; i++)
(gdb) next
22                 printf("Counter in child: %d\n", i);
(gdb) next
Counter in child: 1
20             for(int i = 0; i<10; i++)
```

```
(gdb) next
22              printf("Counter in child: %d\n", i);
(gdb) continue
Continuing.
Counter in child: 2
Counter in child: 3
Counter in child: 4
Counter in child: 5
Counter in child: 6
Counter in child: 7
Counter in child: 8
Counter in child: 9
[Inferior 2 (process 11689) exited normally]
```

How it works...

With `set follow-fork-mode`, we can tell GDB which process to follow when the program forks. This is handy for debugging daemons that fork. You can set `follow-fork-mode` to either `parent` or `child`. The default is `parent`. The process that we don't follow will continue to run as usual.

There's more...

There's also `follow-exec-mode`, which tells GDB which process to follow if the program calls an `exec()` function.

For more information about `follow-exec-mode` and `follow-fork-mode`, you can use the `help set follow-exec-mode` and `help set follow-fork-mode` commands inside GDB.

Debugging programs with multiple threads

It's possible to view threads in a program using GBD and also to jump between **threads**. Knowing how to jump between the threads in a program will make threaded programs easier to debug. Writing threaded programs can be hard, but with GDB it's easier to make sure they are working correctly.

Getting ready

In this recipe, we'll use the `first-threaded.c` program from *Chapter 11, Using Threads in Your Programs*. There's a copy of the source code in this chapter's GitHub directory.

You'll also need the GCC compiler.

How to do it...

In this recipe, we'll look at the threads from the `first-threaded.c` program using GDB:

1. Let's start by compiling the program:

```
$> gcc -g -Wall -Wextra -pedantic -std=c99 \
> first-threaded.c -o first-threaded -lpthread
```

2. Before we run the program through the debugger, let's first run it to recap how the program works:

```
$> ./first-threaded 990233331 9902343047
........
990233331 is not a prime number
..............................................................
......................
9902343047 is a prime number
Done!
```

3. Now that we know how the programs works, let's start it up in GDB:

```
$> gdb ./first-threaded
```

4. Let's set a breakpoint at `main()` as we have done previously. Then we run it with the same two numbers:

```
(gdb) break main
Breakpoint 1 at 0x11e4: file first-threaded.c, line 17.
(gdb) run 990233331 9902343047
Starting program: /home/jack/ch12/code/first-threaded
990233331 9902343047
[Thread debugging using libthread_db enabled]
Using host libthread_db library "/lib/x86_64-linux-gnu/
libthread_db.so.1".

Breakpoint 1, main (argc=3, argv=0x7fffffffdbb8) at
first-threaded.c:17
17          if ( argc != 3 )
```

5. Now we move forward using the `next` command. Once a thread has started, GDB will notify us with the text *New thread*:

```
(gdb) next
23          number1 = atoll(argv[1]);
(gdb) next
24          number2 = atoll(argv[2]);
(gdb) next
25          pthread_attr_init(&threadattr);
(gdb) next
26          pthread_create(&tid_progress, &threadattr,
(gdb) next
[New Thread 0x7ffff7dad700 (LWP 19182)]
28          pthread_create(&tid_prime1, &threadattr,
(gdb) next
[New Thread 0x7ffff75ac700 (LWP 19183)]
30          pthread_create(&tid_prime2, &threadattr,
```

6. Now we can print information about the current threads using the `info threads` command. Notice that this will also tell us what function the threads are currently executing. The number before the word *Thread* on each line is GDB's thread ID:

```
(gdb) info threads
  Id   Target Id
Frame
* 1    Thread 0x7ffff7dae740 (LWP 19175) "first-threaded"
main (argc=3, argv=0x7fffffffdbb8)
    at first-threaded.c:30
  2    Thread 0x7ffff7dad700 (LWP 19182) "first-threaded"
0x00007ffff7e77720 in __GI___nanosleep
    (requested_time=requested_time@entry=0x7ffff7dacea0,
    remaining=remaining@entry=0x7ffff7dacea0) at ../
sysdeps/unix/sysv/linux/nanosleep.c:28
  3    Thread 0x7ffff75ac700 (LWP 19183) "first-threaded"
0x000055555555531b in isprime (
    arg=0x7fffffffdac8) at first-threaded.c:52
```

7. Now, let's switch over to thread number 3, which is currently executing the `isprime` function. We switch threads with the `thread` command:

```
(gdb) thread 3
[Switching to thread 3 (Thread 0x7ffff75ac700 (LWP 
19183))]
#0  0x000055555555531b in isprime (arg=0x7fffffffdac8) at 
first-threaded.c:52
52              if(number%j == 0)
```

8. While inside the thread, we can print the content of variables, move forward using the `next` command, and so on. Here we also see that the other thread is starting:

```
(gdb) print number
$1 = 990233331
(gdb) print j
$2 = 13046
(gdb) next
.[New Thread 0x7ffff6dab700 (LWP 19978)]
47            for(j=2; j<number; j++)
(gdb) next
.52              if(number%j == 0)
(gdb) next
.47            for(j=2; j<number; j++)
(gdb) continue
Continuing.
........
990233331 is not a prime number
[Thread 0x7ffff75ac700 (LWP 19183) exited]
...............................................................
......................
9902343047 is a prime number
Done!
[Thread 0x7ffff6dab700 (LWP 19978) exited]
[Thread 0x7ffff7dad700 (LWP 19182) exited]
[Inferior 1 (process 19175) exited normally]
```

How it works...

Just like we could follow a child process, we can follow a thread. It's a bit of a different approach with threads, but still. Once each thread started, GDB notified us about it. We could then print information about the currently running threads using the `info threads` command. That command gave us a thread ID for each thread, its address, and what frame or function it was currently on. We then jumped to thread 3 using the `thread` command. Once we were inside the thread, we could print the content of the `number` and `j` variables, move forward in the code, and so on.

There's more...

There are more things you could do with threads in GDB. To find more commands regarding threads, you can use the following commands inside GDB:

- `help thread`
- `help info threads`

See also

There's a lot of information about GDB at `https://www.gnu.org/software/gdb`, so check it out for more in-depth information.

Finding a simple memory leak with Valgrind

Valgrind is a neat program for finding **memory leaks** and other memory-related bugs. It can even tell you if you put too much data inside an allocated memory area. These can all be hard bugs to find without a tool like Valgrind. Even if a program leaks memory or puts too much data in a memory area, it can still run fine for a long time. That's what makes those bugs so hard to find. But with Valgrind, we can check the program for all sorts of memory-related problems.

Getting started

For this recipe, you'll need the Valgrind tool installed on your computer. If you haven't already installed it, you can follow the instructions listed in the *Technical requirements* section of this chapter.

You'll also need the Make tool, the GCC compiler, and the Makefile from the *Starting GDB* recipe.

How to do it...

In this recipe, we'll write a program that allocates memory using `calloc()` but never frees it with `free()`. We then run the program through Valgrind and see what it says about it:

1. Write the following program and save it as `leak.c`. First, we create a pointer to a character. Then we allocate 20 bytes of memory using `calloc()` and return its address to `c`. Then we copy a string into that memory and print the content using `printf()`. However, we never free the memory using `free()`, which we always should:

```
#include <stdio.h>
#include <stdlib.h>
#include <string.h>

int main(void)
{
    char *c;
    c = calloc(sizeof(char), 20);
    strcpy(c, "Hello!");
    printf("%s\n", c);
    return 0;
}
```

2. Compile the program:

```
$> make leak
gcc -g -Wall -Wextra -pedantic -std=c99    leak.c   -o
leak
```

3. First, we run the program as we normally would. Everything works just fine:

```
$> ./leak
Hello!
```

4. Now, we run the program through Valgrind. Under `HEAP SUMMARY`, it will tell us that there are 20 bytes still allocated when the program exits. Under `LEAK SUMMARY`, we also see that there are 20 bytes *definitely lost*. What this means is that we forgot to free the memory using `free()`:

```
$> valgrind ./leak
==9541== Memcheck, a memory error detector
==9541== Copyright (C) 2002-2017, and GNU GPL'd, by
Julian Seward et al.
```

```
==9541== Using Valgrind-3.14.0 and LibVEX; rerun with -h
for copyright info
==9541== Command: ./leak
==9541==
Hello!
==9541==
==9541== HEAP SUMMARY:
==9541==     in use at exit: 20 bytes in 1 blocks
==9541==   total heap usage: 2 allocs, 1 frees, 1,044
bytes allocated
==9541==
==9541== LEAK SUMMARY:
==9541==    definitely lost: 20 bytes in 1 blocks
==9541==    indirectly lost: 0 bytes in 0 blocks
==9541==      possibly lost: 0 bytes in 0 blocks
==9541==    still reachable: 0 bytes in 0 blocks
==9541==         suppressed: 0 bytes in 0 blocks
==9541== Rerun with --leak-check=full to see details of
leaked memory
==9541==
==9541== For counts of detected and suppressed errors,
rerun with: -v
==9541== ERROR SUMMARY: 0 errors from 0 contexts
(suppressed: 0 from 0)
```

5. Open up `leak.c` and add `free(c);` just before `return 0;`. Then, recompile the program.
6. Rerun the program in Valgrind. This time, there won't be any bytes lost or in use when the program exits. We also see that there have been two allocations, and they were both freed:

```
$>  valgrind ./leak
==10354== Memcheck, a memory error detector
==10354== Copyright (C) 2002-2017, and GNU GPL'd, by
Julian Seward et al.
==10354== Using Valgrind-3.14.0 and LibVEX; rerun with -h
for copyright info
==10354== Command: ./leak
==10354==
Hello!
==10354==
==10354== HEAP SUMMARY:
==10354==     in use at exit: 0 bytes in 0 blocks
```

```
==10354==   total heap usage: 2 allocs, 2 frees, 1,044
bytes allocated
==10354==
==10354== All heap blocks were freed -- no leaks are
possible
==10354==
==10354== For counts of detected and suppressed errors,
rerun with: -v
==10354== ERROR SUMMARY: 0 errors from 0 contexts
(suppressed: 0 from 0)
```

How it works...

The reason Valgrind said we had two allocations even though we only allocated one block of memory is that other functions in the program have allocated memory.

At the end of the output from Valgrind, we also saw the text *All heap blocks were freed*, meaning we have freed all memory using `free()`.

Valgrind doesn't strictly require debugging symbols; we can test just about any program for memory leaks. For example, we can run `valgrind cat leak.c`, and Valgrind will check `cat` for memory leaks.

See also

There's a lot more you can do with Valgrind. Check out its manual page with `man valgrind`. There's also a lot of useful information at `https://www.valgrind.org`.

Finding buffer overflows with Valgrind

Valgrind can also help us find **buffer overflows**. That is when we put more data in a buffer than it can hold. Buffer overflows are the cause of many security bugs and are hard to detect. But with Valgrind, it gets a little easier. It might not be 100% accurate at all times, but it's a really good help along the way.

Knowing how to find buffer overflows will make your program more secure.

Getting ready

For this recipe, you'll need the GCC compiler, the Make tool, and the Makefile from the *Starting GDB* recipe in this chapter.

How to do it...

In this recipe, we'll write a small program that copies too much data into a buffer. We'll then run the program through Valgrind and see how it points out the problem:

1. Write the following code in a file and save it as `overflow.c`. The program allocates 20 bytes with `calloc()`, then copies a string of 26 bytes into that buffer. It then frees up the memory using `free()`:

```
#include <stdio.h>
#include <string.h>
#include <stdlib.h>

int main(void)
{
    char *c;
    c = calloc(sizeof(char), 20);
    strcpy(c, "Hello, how are you doing?");
    printf("%s\n", c);
    free(c);
    return 0;
}
```

2. Compile the program:

```
$> make overflow
gcc -g -Wall -Wextra -pedantic -std=c99    overflow.c
-o overflow
```

3. First, we run the program like we normally would. Most likely, we won't see any problems with it. It will just work. That's why these kinds of bugs are so hard to find:

```
$> ./overflow
Hello, how are you doing
```

4. Now, let's run the program through Valgrind and see what it has to say about it:

```
$> valgrind ./overflow
```

Since the output of the preceding command is several pages long, it's been omitted from the book. Notice that at the end, Valgrind says *no leaks are possible*. This is because everything is freed as it should. But at the very end of the output, we see *14 errors from 4 contexts*. And a bit further up in the output, we find a lot of text blocks that look like this:

```
Invalid write of size 8
at 0x109199: main (overflow.c:9)
Address 0x4a43050 is 16 bytes inside a block of size 20
alloc'd
at 0x4837B65: calloc (vg_replace_malloc.c:752)
by 0x10916B: main (overflow.c:8)
Invalid write of size 2
at 0x10919D: main (overflow.c:9)
Address 0x4a43058 is 4 bytes after a block of size 20
alloc'd
at 0x4837B65: calloc (vg_replace_malloc.c:752)
by 0x10916B: main (overflow.c:8)
```

This a good indication that we overflowed the `c` buffer, especially the text *4 bytes after a block of size 20 alloc'd*. That means that we have written 4 bytes of data *after* the 20 bytes we allocated. There are more lines like these, and they all point us toward the overflow.

How it works...

Since the program writes data outside of the allocated memory, Valgrind will detect it as invalid writes and invalid reads. We can even follow how many bytes are written after the allocated memory and its addresses. This will make it even easier to find the problem in the code. We might have allocated several buffers, but here we clearly see that it's the buffer of 20 bytes that's overflowed.

There's more...

For a more detailed output, you can add `-v` to Valgrind, for example, `valgrind -v ./overflow`. This will output several pages of detailed output.

Packt.com

Subscribe to our online digital library for full access to over 7,000 books and videos, as well as industry leading tools to help you plan your personal development and advance your career. For more information, please visit our website.

Why subscribe?

- Spend less time learning and more time coding with practical eBooks and Videos from over 4,000 industry professionals
- Improve your learning with Skill Plans built especially for you
- Get a free eBook or video every month
- Fully searchable for easy access to vital information
- Copy and paste, print, and bookmark content

Did you know that Packt offers eBook versions of every book published, with PDF and ePub files available? You can upgrade to the eBook version at packt.com and as a print book customer, you are entitled to a discount on the eBook copy. Get in touch with us at customercare@packtpub.com for more details.

At www.packt.com, you can also read a collection of free technical articles, sign up for a range of free newsletters, and receive exclusive discounts and offers on Packt books and eBooks.

Other Books You May Enjoy

If you enjoyed this book, you may be interested in these other books by Packt:

Mastering Linux Device Driver Development

John Madieu

ISBN: 978-1-78934-204-8

- Explore and adopt Linux kernel helpers for locking, work deferral, and interrupt management
- Understand the Regmap subsystem to manage memory accesses and work with the IRQ subsystem
- Get to grips with the PCI subsystem and write reliable drivers for PCI devices
- Write full multimedia device drivers using ALSA SoC and the V4L2 framework

Linux Kernel Programming

Kaiwan N Billimoria

ISBN: 978-1-78995-343-5

- Write high-quality modular kernel code (LKM framework) for 5.x kernels
- Configure and build a kernel from source
- Explore the Linux kernel architecture
- Get to grips with key internals regarding memory management within the kernel
- Understand and work with various dynamic kernel memory alloc/dealloc APIs
- Discover key internals aspects regarding CPU scheduling within the kernel
- Gain an understanding of kernel concurrency issues

Packt is searching for authors like you

If you're interested in becoming an author for Packt, please visit `authors.packtpub.com` and apply today. We have worked with thousands of developers and tech professionals, just like you, to help them share their insight with the global tech community. You can make a general application, apply for a specific hot topic that we are recruiting an author for, or submit your own idea.

Leave a review - let other readers know what you think

Please share your thoughts on this book with others by leaving a review on the site that you bought it from. If you purchased the book from Amazon, please leave us an honest review on this book's Amazon page. This is vital so that other potential readers can see and use your unbiased opinion to make purchasing decisions, we can understand what our customers think about our products, and our authors can see your feedback on the title that they have worked with Packt to create. It will only take a few minutes of your time, but is valuable to other potential customers, our authors, and Packt. Thank you!

Index

A

B

C

D

E

F

G

H

I

J

K

L

M

N

O

S

T

U

V

W

X

Z

Made in the USA
Las Vegas, NV
01 July 2021